COLUMBIA UNIVERSITY STUDIES IN ENGLISH
AND COMPARATIVE LITERATURE
NUMBER 132

MEDIEVAL NUMBER SYMBOLISM

MEDIEVAL NUMBER SYMBOLISM

Its Sources, Meaning, and Influence on Thought and Expression

BY

VINCENT FOSTER HOPPER

*Assistant Professor of Literature, New York University
School of Commerce, Accounts and Finance*

COOPER SQUARE PUBLISHERS, INC.
NEW YORK
1969

Originally Published 1938
Published by Cooper Square Publishers, Inc.
59 Fourth Avenue, New York, N. Y. 10003
Standard Book Number 8154-0305-4
Library of Congress Catalog Card No. 70-85372

Printed in the United States of America

In Memory of
ABRAM WHITTAKER HOPPER
and to
ISABEL JAYNE HOPPER
with Gratitude and Affection

PREFACE

THE symbolic nature of medieval thought and expression has been subjected to a number of thoughtful scrutinies with much consequent illumination of dark places. An important result of these studies has been to reveal in the medieval mind a weblike structure of abstract ideas and concrete realities so closely interwoven and interdependent that no serious gap was felt to exist between them. In consequence, what appears to the modern mind as a conscious and often artificial and strained divagation from simplicity and sincerity was more often than not an entirely natural mode of expression. To put it another way, what the modern mind denominates with some impatience as "symbol" was often in the medieval mind the result of an inevitable association of ideas. Most of these symbols, moreover, being connected with Scripture, were believed to have been of God's own implanting. A reasonably extended acquaintance with medieval writings is all that is needed to put one in a frame of mind to accept this "symbolism," much as one accepts metaphor or simile or any kind of imagery, whether ancient or modern. Images change from generation to generation, but the impulse which produces them is universal and familiar.

The recognized value of figurative utterance lies in its ability to clarify or intensify ideas or emotions through appeal to sense experience. By symbolism, the abstract may be brought into the realm of the concrete, where it is immediately recognizable and meaningful. By symbolism, the abstract beauty and loving-kindness of the Deity were humanly realized in the person of the Virgin. The concept of the Virgin was, in turn, brought even closer to sense experience through the artistic media of sculpture and painting. Thus does image transmit idea. On a more elementary level, the light and glory and life-giving properties of the sun won for that planet almost universal veneration as an image of Godhead.

What, then, is to be said in explanation of the number symbol where the symbol, far from providing a concrete image, is itself very nearly the limit of abstraction? In all seriousness, does the author of the *Vita Nuova* expect to capture the reader's admiration and regard for Beatrice by describing her as a *nine*? The simple answer is "yes" — and the prominence of numbers in the sacred and the profane writings of the Middle Ages, in cathedral architecture, in the ritual of the mass, is sufficient indication of their contemporary effectiveness.

Commentators have been at some pains to explain isolated number symbols, with a considerable degree of success. But the explanations have tended to clarify the text without illuminating the soul of the author or warming the imagination of the reader. The lack of a frame of reference, together with a failure to comprehend the philosophic as well as the symbolic implications of number, has resulted in a general tendency to regard number symbols as a pleasant variety of anagrams. It is the purpose of this study to reveal how deeply rooted in medieval thought was the consciousness of numbers, not as mathematical tools, nor yet as the counters in a game, but as fundamental realities, alive with memories and eloquent with meaning. The fact that 3 disciples were present at the transfiguration was, in the Middle Ages, a circumstance not to be lightly passed over. For in the Sacred Text was known to be enshrined the mystery of Trinity, and the sanctity of the number 3 hovered like a halo about the figure of Christ and all Godly things. And the especial sanctity of this integer, which had been recognized by man from the earliest times,

endowed every repetition of the number 3 with a richness
of meaning which can be but dimly grasped by the modern
reader. As a result of the derivative and eclectic nature of medieval
science and philosophy, it is next to impossible to arrive at a
clear statement of either without considerable digging at the
individual roots from which these hybrid plants developed.
By the same token, medieval number philosophy, which often
appears as sheer nonsense or at best as the product of extraordinarily confused thinking, is explicable only by reference
to its origins. For apart from certain minor influences, medieval number philosophy may be said to be a combination of
three distinct modes of thought, and the number symbols
themselves supplied from three major sources. The first of
these, which I have labeled "elementary," is basic in all number symbolism, being derived from man's original struggles
to enumerate and his identification of certain immediately
observable and fixed natural groups with their corresponding
numbers; for instance, a *hand* is 5; 20 (10 fingers + 10 toes)
is a *man*. The second and most prolific source of significant
numbers, which is really an elaboration of the first, is the
ancient Babylonian science of astrology. Numbers derived
from constellations, planets, and stellar revolutions were held
in awe as being divinely ordained. Each number was given its
own sacred or baleful connotations. Most important, the
astrological axiom of the relationship of macrocosm and
microcosm was to provide for the relationship of all fixed
aggregates defined by the same number. Thus the 7 days
of the week were named from the 7 planets. The Middle
Ages inherited this theory by virtue of the stubborn vitality
of astrology itself, but the sanctity and incorruptibility of the
astrological numbers was made unquestionable by their presence in page after page of Holy Writ, there to be pondered
over and expounded by generations of Churchmen. The third

and best-known number theory is the Pythagorean, which fixed the relationship of the numbers to one another and, accordingly, the places of the astrological aggregates in the Cosmic Order.

My first three chapters, therefore, concern themselves with the fundamentals of each of these theories, without which no medieval number symbol is more than superficially comprehensible. In my fourth chapter I deal with the elaborate combination of these theories by the Gnostics, who, together with the Neo-Pythagoreans, were most influential in the formation of Christian number theory. In my fifth chapter I discuss the adoption and elaboration of number philosophy by the early Church Fathers (up to and including Augustine), with the intention of stating as clearly as possible the fundamentals of medieval Christian number symbolism. My sixth chapter is devoted to a résumé of the diversified appearances and usages of number symbols in the Middle Ages in the attempt to evoke, as clearly as I can, the medieval attitude toward number. Dante's use of number symbolism and the effect of number on Dante's philosophy are considered in my seventh chapter.

A great deal of scholarly work has already been done on the primitive, astrological, and Pythagorean symbolism to which my early chapters are devoted. Without pretending to make any contribution whatever to these fields, I have nevertheless deemed it necessary to summarize the results of these investigations, in order to explain the medieval complex made up of these factors. In doing this I have made use of recognized authorities (such as Farbridge, Cumont, Webster, Conant, Jastrow, Rogers, McLean, Thompson, Lenormant, Karpinski) who have integrated the results of many special studies with their own investigations and conclusions. Whenever possible, I have verified these conclusions by reference to the documents in which the original number symbols occurred.

My own efforts (with whatever originality I may claim) have been devoted to finding and explaining the relationship of these number theories to medieval number-symbolism. Even here, it would be possible to write an exhaustive work on a single number symbol. Instead, I have chosen to do what seemed to me more valuable and more immediately meaningful: to explain the basis, meaning, purpose, extent, and use of number symbolism in the Middle Ages — with the aim of providing a frame of reference for such isolated number symbols as might be encountered in medieval texts. Similarly, in the case of Dante, it is my desire to explain the basic numerical framework of the *Comedy*, the relationship of the parts to the whole, rather than to treat each individual number symbol as an isolated problem. It is my belief that such treatment of individual problems is bound to be ultimately unsatisfactory, because, however exhaustive, it misses the carefully articulated plan of the whole work.

Of general studies of a type most germane to this book should be mentioned Harold Bayley's *The Lost Language of Symbolism* (1922), which includes a partial review of number symbolism; and two very recent considerations of the ancient and modern variations of Pythagoreanism, *Number, The Language of Science* (1930) by Tobias Dantzig, and *Numerology* (1933) by E. T. Bell. The paucity of general studies in the medieval field is probably the result of the irritating failure of number symbolism to remain confined to any single field of investigation. To the mathematician, medieval number science is but an attenuated Pythagoreanism, corrupted by Christian theology, which goes beyond his province. To the student of medieval symbolism, the mathematical aspect is similarly remote. Belonging personally to the latter classification, I must confess that I should hardly have had the courage to enter upon this investigation without the aid of my wife, to whose mathematical guidance I am deeply indebted.

I should also like to acknowledge with gratitude the assistance of Professor Harry Morgan Ayres in offering criticism and advice, and of my friend, Professor Gerald Edwin Se-Boyar, in allowing me to peruse the results of his studies of medieval encyclopedias. I am also indebted to Professors Lynn Thorndike, Oscar James Campbell, Samuel Lee Wolff, Roger Sherman Loomis, John Strong Perry Tatlock, and Henry Willis Wells for particular suggestions and comments. For the use of the many books listed in my bibliography, my thanks are owed to the libraries of Columbia, Yale, Princeton, Vassar, and New York University, and particularly to Miss Fanny Borden, librarian of Vassar, who procured for me the use of many rare books from other libraries.

Of Professor Jefferson Butler Fletcher, who has given unsparingly of his time, energy, and knowledge, it need only be said that, from his first opening to me of the book of Dante to the last paragraph of this study, and in the words of his own translation of the *Divine Comedy*,

"He was for me a light."

VINCENT FOSTER HOPPER

New York
February 1, 1938

CONTENTS

I. ELEMENTARY NUMBER SYMBOLISM   .   3

II. THE ASTROLOGICAL NUMBERS   .   .   12

III. PYTHAGOREAN NUMBER THEORY.   .   33

IV. THE GNOSTICS   50

V. THE EARLY CHRISTIAN WRITERS.   .   69

VI. MEDIEVAL NUMBER PHILOSOPHY.   .   89

VII. THE BEAUTY OF ORDER — DANTE.   .   136

APPENDIX: NUMBER SYMBOLS OF
NORTHERN PAGANISM   203

BIBLIOGRAPHY   213

INDEX   233

MEDIEVAL NUMBER SYMBOLISM

ABBREVIATIONS

AN	Ante Nicene Christian Library
MLN	Modern Language Notes
MLR	Modern Language Review
MP	Modern Philology
NPN	Nicene and Post-Nicene Fathers
P.G.	Migne, J. P., Patrologiae cursus completus, Series graeca
P.L.	Migne, J. P., Patrologiae cursus completus, Series latina
PMLA	Publications of the Modern Language Association of America

I. ELEMENTARY NUMBER SYMBOLISM

NOTHING in the history of number symbolism is so striking as the unanimity of all ages and climates in regard to the meanings of a certain few number symbols. Inasmuch as these same number beliefs color the literature of the ancient world and recur in the superstitions of our own contemporary primitives, we are justified in classifying them as "elementary" and in isolating them, in order to define the nature of at least one fixed and universal type of number symbolism.

An examination of these earliest number symbols indicates that numbers originally carried concrete associations, as a result of man's early inability to comprehend abstraction. Such a hypothesis is in keeping with the recognizable trend of language from the concrete to the abstract, and is demonstrable in the commonplace method of teaching addition and subtraction by the aid of concrete illustration. These associations must originally have been more real than the number itself, 3 trees more real than the abstract 3, so that particularly prominent and fixed numerical groups might readily come to be thought of as attributes of the numbers themselves.

Presumably every early civilization once passed through a stage today duplicated in certain Brazilian tribes whose languages are almost completely barren of number words.[1] One tribe uses only the word *etama, alone,* to indicate a single object or one of a group. The first advance toward counting develops the use of words for *one* and *many,* the differentiation of the individual or the ego from the group.[2]

But man must soon have become conscious of the duals of

1. Conant, *The Number Concept,* p. 1.
2. *Ibid.,* pp. 1, 22, 24, 28; Tylor, *Primitive Culture,* I, 243.

nature: male and female, day and night, sun and moon, earth and sky, or earth and water. Doubtless Alcmaeon of Crotona was repeating a very common observation when he remarked that "most human things go in pairs." [3] It is probable, then, that the early mathematician chose some noteworthy duality of nature, such as *marriage*, as his word for 2. At any rate, the number 2 appears always to have carried with it the idea of mutual antithesis found in the duals of nature, whether in the great Manichean duad, or in the Christian God-man, or in the double head of the Egyptian Horus "whereof the one beareth right and truth and the other wickedness," [4] or in the opposed but related active and contemplative lives of the Middle Ages.

Having invented a term for "pair," man was in possession of three numerical terms, "1, 2, many," and there are tribes today who count in just such a fashion. [5] Through some process not clearly traceable, there came to be an identification of the word for *many* with the concept of 3, possibly because 3 is the first integer to which the idea of *many* may be applied, or because, given three terms, "1, 2, many," the *many* word became incorporated as the third integer in a more advanced number system. This stage is reflected in the distinction between the dual and the plural in the Egyptian, Arabian, Hebrew, Sanskrit, Greek, and Gothic languages, [6] or in the common use of positive, comparative, and superlative degrees: good of one, better of two, best of three or many.

The idea of 3 as implying the superlative, or the all, was never lost. It appears in such common phrases as *ter felix* and *trismegistus*, in the use of the trident and triple thunderbolt as symbols of greatness and power, in the Egyptian hiero-

3. Aristotle, *Metaphysica*, I, 5.
4. *Book of the Dead*, XCII, 28.
5. *Conant*, *op. cit.*, p. 22; D. E. Smith, *History of Mathematics*, I, 6, 9; Tylor, *op. cit.*, I, 243.
6. Tylor, *op. cit.*, I, 265.

glyphs, where a single bar marking the picture of an object indicates but 1, a double bar 2, but 3 lines indicate 3 or an indefinite number of objects.[7] As Aristotle put it, "Of two things, or men, we say 'both' but not 'all.' Three is the first number to which the term 'all' has been appropriated." [8]

This may be described as the "cumulative" or "statistical" 3, by which we are still affected in preliminary verification of scientific experiments and generally in inductive reasoning. A single occurrence is of no significance. A repetition is noticeable, but might easily be the result of coincidence. A third occurrence of the same nature gives the event the impress of law. In the Babylonian flood legend, Utnapishtim (the Babylonian Noah) simultaneously releases a dove, a raven, and a swallow. There is no need to release more to obtain the desired information, nor is it a sufficient test to send out fewer than 3. In the Atalanta legend, the dropping of 3 golden apples is sufficient to state comprehensively the idea, although the story might just as well have been prolonged by making it 4 or 7 apples.

The persistence of this half-instinctive mode of reasoning is one of the curiosities of human logic. Eratosthenes (c. 240 B.C.) observes that "the gods vouchsafe moral improvement to those who have thrice wiped themselves clean." [9] Legends, myths, folk tales of all nations abound in 3 wishes, 3 tries, 3 suitors — there is no necessity of prolonging the story when 3 is all. In the Old Testament we are told that "a threefold cord is not quickly broken." [10] The medieval theologian makes a point of the 3 days entombment of Christ, for "in three days is proved all deed and fait veritable." [11] Lewis Carroll was possibly hinting at the frailty of even modern scientific minds in accepting 3 examples as proof

7. *Ibid.*
8. *De caelo*, I, 1.
9. Conybeare, *Myth, Magic and Morals*, p. 318.
10. Eccles. 4: 12.
11. *Legenda aurea, Resurrection*, (Temple Classics), pp. 87-88.

when he has the Bellman gravely announce, "What I tell you three times is true." [12]

The importance of this same number 3 became greatly enhanced by its early application to the gods. Many numbers have been used to express divinity or godlike attributes, but either because of its antiquity or because of its numerous simple analogies in the physical and social world, the all-embracing 3 became the most universal number of deity.

The commonest social 3 is the triad of the family; male, female, and child; a simple distinction regardless of the number of children, or of wives for that matter. Since the idea of generation, as Zeller remarks,[13] is the most obvious reason for the existence of the world and the gods, it is a short step from the recognition of the family on earth to the hypothesis of the family in heaven. Osiris, Isis, and Horus form the best known of celestial families. In Egypt, the local gods had all been grouped in divine families before the beginning of the Pyramid period.[14] Extension of triadic grouping led to the Ennead, triple triad of Heliopolis, which was in turn expanded to include a second dynasty of 9 gods, then a third group, until 9, 18, and 27 gods are recognized as being essentially 3 in spirit and mystically in number. The Rigveda recognizes the same elaboration in the triple subdivision of its 3 principal deities.[15]

The physical world was also subject to a triple division. In the Rigveda, all deities are grouped in 3 classes: gods of the sky, of the atmosphere, and of earth.[16] Sumerian theology of the scholastic period (twenty-fifth to twenty-third century) established the oldest triad (as distinct from trinity) in Anu, Enlil, and Enki, gods of heaven, earth, and water.[17] With

12. *The Hunting of the Snark*, Fit I.
13. *History of Greek Philosophy*, I, 86.
14. Moret, *The Nile and Egyptian Civilization*, p. 356; Müller, *Mythology of All Races*, XII, 20.
15. Keith, *Mythology of All Races*, VI, 15.
16. *Ibid.*
17. Langdon, *Mythology of All Races*, V, 88-89.

the later theological invention of an underworld, the triad is somewhat altered. Anu remains the god of heaven, but the second member of the group is replaced by Bel or Baal as god of earth, and Hea (a variant of Enlil or Ea, water) becomes the custodian of the underworld.[18] Zeus, Hades, and Poseidon later duplicate this type of triad.

Sun worship is among the most primitive forms of religion and in his early devotions man apparently distinguished between the rising, the midday, and the setting sun. The Rigveda commemorates this division in the 3 strides of Vishnu.[19] The earliest division of the Indian year was also threefold; spring, summer, and winter being analogous to the 3 strides of Vishnu.[20] The Egyptians divided the god into 3 distinct personalities: Horus, morning; Ra, noonday; and Atun, setting sun.[21] The fact that this is a trinity rather than a triad would be more noteworthy were it not for the circumstance that the Christian Trinity had a predecessor in the ancient Gilgamish Epic (before 2000 B.C.): "Two-thirds of him is god, one-third of him is man."[22]

The triplicity of rising, midday, and setting sun provides another instance where 3 is all: beginning, middle, and end. It is strikingly presented in the above-mentioned 3 seasons of India where autumn and winter are indistinguishable. In the human cycle, to go no further in search of analogies, birth, life, and death represent the triple division which is common to all mundane affairs. This conception of life is recognized in the Greek fates (Klotho is the spinner, Lachesis assigns the lot, Atropos cuts the thread), and in the Norns (Urd, past; Verdandi, present; Skuld, future). In Indian theology, Brahma, Vishnu, and Siva are similarly disposed. In a fragment

---

18. Conway, *Demonology and Devil-Lore*, p. 109.
19. Keith, *op. cit.*, p. 29.
20. *Ibid.*, p. 58.
21. Müller, *op. cit.*, p. 27.
22. *Op. cit.*, I, 51.

of the Orphic theogony, Zeus is described as the beginning, middle, and end of all things.[23] The precise degree of relationship of any of these triads to the statistical 3 is not of great importance to our present study. It is enough to take cognizance of the fact that at the dawn of history the number 3 had already robed itself in manifold meanings, and bore a ruling and godly aspect from whose dominion man was not soon to escape.

Somewhere during the gradual formulation of arithmetic, man became conscious of the 4 directions: toward the sunrise, East; toward the sunset, West; and the two verticals to the course of the sun, North and South.[24] The majority of the semi-primitive tribes of North America, South America, and Asia bow to the cult of 4 and recognize as its symbol the Greek or equal-armed cross, the swastika, and other cruciform emblems.[25] The invention of 4 winds is a simple enough addition.[26] So is the creation of a 4-eyed, 4-eared supervising God,[27] "and the eyes beheld all things." [28] In Egypt the number assumed unusual importance. Egyptian cosmogony pictures the heavenly roof as supported by 4 pillars, mountains, or women at the cardinal points.[29] When personified, it is graphically represented as a woman bending over the earth, or by a cow, the extremities in both representations stationed at the cardinal points.[30] The "fourness" of earth became an-

23. Zeller, op. cit., I, 64.
24. Tozer, A History of Ancient Geography, p. 100; Cary and Warmington, The Ancient Explorers, p. 6.
25. Buckland, "Four as a Sacred Number" (North America and Aryan); Rivers, Medicine, Magic and Religion (Phoenicia, Egypt, North America), pp. 88-89; McGee, "Primitive Numbers" (North America, South America, Africa, Asia), p. 834; Levy-Bruhl, Les Fonctions mentales dans les sociétés inférieures (North America), pp. 241-47; D. E. Smith, History of Mathematics (North America), p. 17.
26. Epic of Creation, IV, 42.
27. Ibid., I, 95-97.
28. Ibid., I, 98.
29. Müller, op. cit., p. 35.
30. Ibid., p. 37.

other almost universal commonplace as a result of this simple recognition of the cardinal points.

The discovery of the fingers and the toes as natural adding machines presided over the birth of actual arithmetic, and incidentally created additional number symbols. Among primitive tribes, 5 is referred to as a hand, 10 as two hands; 20 is a man.[31] The score became a convenient limit or round number by which a group of "about 20" might be loosely indicated. But the adoption of the decimal system itself was to have the most far-reaching consequences, with the integers of the decad later taking on the semblance of immortal essences, and the fact of the infinite repetition of digits providing infinite variations of fundamental number symbols. Accordingly, when we read that the weapons of Indra consisted of a stone 100-jointed, 1000-angled, and arrows 100-pointed and 1000-feathered,[32] we recognize that the basic 10 is implied. The 300 beaters of the Hellespont[33] are in the same numeral category as the 3 daughters of Atlas. The *Thousand Songs* of Thebes (*ca.* 1300 B.C.), although containing but 28 poems, is divided into chapters numbered 1 to 10, then 20, 30, and so on, to 100, then the hundreds to Chapter 1000, which is actually the twenty-eighth chapter. Each member of the decad is thereby repeated 3 times and the contents of Chapter 80, for example, will be found to refer to the sanctity of the number 8.[34] A similar mental operation is occasionally involved in the repetition of a digit, as in the inscription on a Cainite tablet, "If Cain is avenged 7-fold, then Lamech 70 and 7."[35] Centuries later, Thomas Aquinas in his solution of 666, the number of the beast in Revelations, discusses 6 in relation to unity, 6 in relation to the

31. Conant, *The Number Concept*, pp. 98-99; Tylor, *Primitive Culture*, I, 246-47; D. E. Smith, *History of Mathematics*, p. 12.
32. Keith, *op. cit.*, p. 32.
33. Herodotus, *Persian Wars*, VI, 97.
34. Erman, *The Literature of the Ancient Egyptians*, pp. 293-302.
35. H. P. Smith, *Old Testament History*, p. 24.

denarius, and 6 in relation to the hundred.[36] The meaning of the 6 itself does not change by reason of its decimal position. With the use of a decimal system, it follows naturally that 10, symbol of the entire method of numeration, becomes an important number. In its earliest appearances it is a number of finality or completeness, as in higher ranges are 100 and 1,000. In the Babylonian spring festival (3500-1900 B.C.) the tenth day was marked by a procession of *all* the gods.[37] In the flood legend of the same people, 10 kings, intimating 10 ages, are named as preceding the flood.[38] Sargon recognizes 10 gods as guardians of the city.[39] The Rigveda (1200-800 B.C.) is made up of 10 books of hymns celebrating the chief Vedic gods. Herodotus was struck by the 10 divisions of Athens, the tenth paid for ransom (the Hebrew tithe), and the chorus of 10 for each god in Aeginetan worship.[40] By extension of 10, the Egyptians, according to the same writer, gave 100 days as the time for the rising of the Nile.[41] It is also recorded that Croesus, upon sending to the oracle to learn if he might conquer Cyrus, instructed his messenger to keep count of the days, and on the hundredth day to consult the oracle.[42]

With the adoption of 10 as a complete cycle, the number 9 comes into prominence as "almost complete." Troy was besieged for 9 years and fell on the tenth. Odysseus wandered 9 years and arrived home on the tenth. The 9-10 relationship is very common in the *Iliad* and the *Odyssey*, which both indicate a much earlier stage of number symbolism than the most ancient of Babylonian tablets. The New Testament Gos-

36. *Expositio II in Apocalypsim*, xiv.
37. Langdon, *op. cit.*, p. 328.
38. Clay, *The Origin of Biblical Traditions*, p. 125; McLean, *Babylonian Astrology and Its Relations to the Old Testament*, p. 36.
39. Jastrow, *The Religion of Babylonia and Assyria*, p. 237.
40. Herodotus, *Persian Wars*, V, 83.
41. *Ibid.*, II, 19.
42. *Ibid.*, I, 47.

pel of Luke [43] recounts the parable of the 10 pieces of silver, one of which was lost, and certain of the medieval theologians interpreted the lost piece as the rebellious angels whose fall left only 9 orders in heaven until man should make the tenth.[44]

With the exception of the 5, all the numbers so far considered, though receiving additional connotations, seldom lose their fundamental elementary meanings. Two is diversity — antithetical pairs. Three is "all" (beginning, middle, end), 3 is best (superlative), 3 is holy (triads of gods). Four is the number of earth. Ten is completeness, finality, perfection; and 9 is all-but-complete or all-but-perfect.

43. Luke 15: 8.
44. Cf. Bonaventura, *Sentences*, II, dist. 9, qu. 7.

II. THE ASTROLOGICAL NUMBERS

THE earliest known development of an extensive number symbolism took place in ancient Babylon. There, as Cumont says,

a *number* was a very different thing from a *figure*. Just as in ancient times, and above all, in Egypt the *name* had a magic power, and ceremonial words formed an irresistible incantation, so here the number possesses an active force, the number is a symbol, and its properties are sacred attributes.[1]

The supreme secret which Ea taught to his son was always called "the number." [2] A couplet from Akkad testifies to the occult power thought to reside in number:

> The corn which stands upright
> Shall come to the end of its prosperous growth;
> The number [to produce that]
> We know it.
> The corn of abundance
> Shall come to the end of its prosperous growth;
> The number [to produce that]
> We know it.[3]

A goddess, Nisaba, is characterized as "she who knows the significance of numbers and carries the tablet of the stars." [4]

The relation of number and the stars was to establish the sanctity of numbers, written as they were in the heavenly tablet of the gods, as well as to provide new number symbols. In the opinion of Cumont,

the progress of mathematics must often have been the result of the progress of astronomy and the former participated in the sacred character of the latter. Certainly numerals were thus considered for astronomical reasons as endowed with an especial potency.[5]

1. *Astrology and Religion among the Greeks and Romans*, pp. 29-30.
2. Lenormant, *Chaldean Magic and Sorcery*, p. 41.
3. *Ibid.*
4. McLean, *Babylonian Astrology and Its Relation to the Old Testament*, p. 22.
5. *Op. cit.*, p. 111.

The first temporal observations of man probably centered about the lunations [6] and for some reason, possibly a recognition of the importance of 4, the lunar month was divided into 4 weeks of 7 days each. Although weeks of many lengths have been known to exist, only the decadic unit of the decimal system can approximate the 7-day week in prevalence.[7] The *Creation Epic*, written during the First Babylonian Dynasty (2225-1926),[8] describes the lunar divisions:

[And] caused the new moon to shine forth, entrusting to him the night.
He fixed him as a being of the night to determine the "days."
Monthly without ceasing he magnified him with a crown
At the beginning of the month [the time] of the shining forth over the land.
Thou shalt shine with horns to determine six days
And on the seventh with half a crown.
At the full moon verily art thou in opposition [to the sun], monthly,
When the sun on the foundation of heaven has overtaken thee.
The . . . keep and shine thou [in thy course] backward.
At the period of darkness approach to the way of the sun,
And on the twenty-ninth day verily thou standest in opposition to the sun a second time.[9]

The seventh days came to take on a baleful aspect, on which it was considered dangerous to perform any important act. In a Babylonian calendar possibly of the time of Hammurabi (2123-2081) these evil days are listed. They include not only the 7th, 14th, 21st, and 28th days but also the 19th; that is, the 49th (7 x 7) day from the first of the preceding month.[10] Possibly the Hebrew Jahveh was observing this tradition when he rested on the 7th day and "hallowed the Sabbath."

6. Webster, *Rest Days*, p. 173.
7. *Ibid.*, p. 187.
8. Langdon, *Epic of Creation*, p. 10.
9. *Op. cit.*, V, 12-23.
10. Webster, *op. cit.*, pp. 223, 232; Thompson, *Semitic Magic*, p. 138; Farbridge, *Studies in Biblical and Semitic Symbolism*, p. 135 (30-day month).

Apart from any special creations of number symbols, the overwhelming importance of the astrological concept to number symbolism lay in the belief that the stars imaged the will of the gods, and that in the sacred number groups might be found the impress of the divine hand. Consequently, having discovered 4 directions and 4 lunar phases, man diligently pursued the search for other examples of quaternity in the universe. He soon educed 4 winds, then 4 seasons, then 4 watches of the day and night, then 4 elements and 4 humours and 4 cardinal virtues. Seneca made a rather keen guess when he assigned the discovery of the 4 elements to the Egyptians,[11] since Egypt appears to have been more conscious of this number than any other nation.

The phases of the moon indicate to early man an important relationship between 4 and 7, and consequently in early Babylon the 4 winds required amplification into 7 winds. Nothing more clearly reveals the peculiar nature and force of number symbolism than the lines of the *Creation Epic*, wherein 4 becomes 7:

He caused the four winds to come under control that nothing of her
    might escape,
The south-wind, the north-wind, the east-wind, the west-wind.
At his side he brought near the net, the gift of his father Anu.
He created Imhullu, the evil wind, the Tempest, the Hurricane,
The Four-fold-wind, the Seven-fold-wind, the Devastating-wind,
    the Unrivalled-wind.
He caused to come forth the winds which he created — the seven
    of them.[12]

With 7 thus emphasized, the navigator, the explorer, sees 7 stars in the Pleiades and the Bear, the constellations by which he steers.[13] Blake believes that the Bear was the first recognized constellation,[14] as it is certainly the most obvious to the

11. *Naturales quaestiones*, III, 4.
12. *Op. cit.*, IV, 42-47.
13. Tozer, *op. cit.*, p. 100; Thompson, "Science and the Classics," p. 29.
14. *Astronomical Myths*, p. 7.

untutored eye. It is also the most prominent among the especially venerable "indestructible stars," visible during the entire year, "and alone hath no part in the baths of Ocean."[15] From a hint given in the *Brahmanas*,[16] it seems likely that these 7 stars provided the pattern for the 7 gods who precede the flood,[17] and the 7 wise ones saved after the flood who wrote down the secrets of divination, magic, and wisdom,[18] for the 7 Hathors of Egypt[19] and the 7 seers of Vedic ritual[20] or the 7 sages of Greece, whose names are variously given but whose number remains constant.[21] Seven becomes thus a number of wisdom and godliness.

From the 40-day disappearance of the Babylonian Pleiades, the significance of 40 was apparently derived.[22] This 40-day period coincided with the rainy season. It was a time of fearsome storms for the sailor, a time of flood and inundation for the land dweller, a time of trial, of danger, and of exile of the beneficent stars. The return of the Pleiades was the signal for the New Year Festival, in which a part of the ceremonial consisted of burning a bundle of 40 reeds,[23] perhaps symbolical of the destruction of 40 devils who had held the Pleiades in bondage for the 40 days during which the evil spirits raged.[24] The connotations of 40 live on in the 40 days of Lent, the 40 years of Hebrew wandering in the desert, the 40 days of the isolation period of the Roman port, to survive to our day in the word *quarantine*.

If the disappearance of the Pleiades gave an unfavorable

15. *Iliad*, XVIII, 489.
16. Müller, *Mythology of All Races*, XII, 59.
17. Langdon, *Mythology of All Races*, V, 167.
18. *Ibid.*, p. 139.
19. Müller, *op. cit.*, p. 40.
20. Keith, *Mythology of All Races*, VI, 65, 144-45.
21. Zeller, *History of Greek Philosophy*, I, 119.
22. Langdon, *Epic of Creation*, pp. 26-27; Hesiod, *Works and Days*, I, 17; Pliny, *Naturalis historia*, XVIII, 59.
23. Langdon, *ibid.*
24. Farbridge, *op. cit.*, p. 148.

aspect to the number 40, it also produced a 7 of evil to balance the 7 of good. Inconsistently enough, the Pleiades, welcomed at the New Year Festival, appear to have been blamed for their own disappearance. In a well-known Babylonian tablet they are castigated as malevolent demons:

> Seven are they! Seven are they!
> In the Ocean Deep, seven are they!
> Battening in heaven, seven are they
> Bred in the depths of ocean;
> Nor male nor female are they,
> But are as the roaring wind-blast,
> No wife have they, no son can they beget;
> Knowing neither mercy nor pity,
> They hearken not to prayer or supplication.
> They are as horses reared amid the hills,
> The Evil Ones of Ea;
> Throne-bearers of the gods are they,
> They stand in the highway to befoul the path;
> Evil are they, evil are they! [25]

Other tablets describe them uniformly as demons of evil, merciless and destructive, to combat whose power all the resources of Chaldean magic were enlisted.[26] Magic cords were knotted 7 times, 7-fold incantations were repeated, 7 loaves of corn were roasted. Naaman is told to bathe 7 times in the Jordan to cure his leprosy,[27] and the child whom Elisha raised from the dead sneezed 7 times,[28] thus presumably emitting successively the evil spirits. The 7 devils boast as great a recorded antiquity as the 7 gods.

Having discovered 7 days, 7 winds, 7 gods, and 7 devils, the astronomer proceeded to search for 7 planets and, what is remarkable, to find them! His quest was long and difficult.

25. Thompson, *op. cit.*, pp. 47-48; Lenormant, *op. cit.*, p. 18.
26. Originally the Pleiades must have been regarded as beneficient stars, whose "exile" was mourned and whose return signalized the advent of spring. But, through the perversity of human logic, the bane of their absence was apparently blamed on the stars themselves.
27. II Kings 5:10.
28. II Kings 4:35.

In early days, only Jupiter and Venus were recognized as planets.[29] But when he had found 7, his task was ended; he need seek no further.[30] The planets became the "fate-deciding gods," [31] and at a much later time were appointed to rule the days of the week, a notion which seems not to have gained general currency until the first century B.C. at Alexandria.[32] Meanwhile the Baylonian priest-geographer divides the earth into 7 zones,[33] the architect builds Gudea's temple, "the house of the 7 divisions of the world," of 7 steps.[34] The Zikkurats, towers of Babel, originally 3 or 4 stories in height but never 5 or 6, were dedicated to the 7 planets and came to consist of 7 steps, faced with glazed bricks of the 7 colors, their angles facing the 4 cardinal points.[35] These 7 steps symbolize the ascent to heaven, and a happy fate is promised the person who ascends to their summit.[36] The tree of life, with 7 branches, each bearing 7 leaves,[37] is perhaps the ancestor of the 7-branched candlestick of the Hebrews. Even the goddesses are called by 7 names and boast of them.[38]

We have already observed the twin sevens of gods and

---

29. Farbridge, *op. cit.*, p. 132.

30. This is sound astrological reasoning. Dr. J. B. Fletcher has called to my attention the argument of Francesco Sizzi, Florentine astronomer, against Galileo's discovery of satellites of Jupiter, making more than 7 planets: "There are 7 windows in the head, 2 nostrils, 2 eyes, 2 ears, and a mouth; so in the heavens there are 2 favorable stars, 2 unpropitious, 2 luminaries, and Mercury alone undecided and indifferent. From which and many other similar phenomena of nature, such as the 7 metals, etc., which it were tedious to enumerate, we gather that the number of planets is necessarily 7. . . . Besides, the Jews and other ancient nations as well as modern Europeans have adopted the division of the week into 7 days, and have named them from the 7 planets: now if we increase the number of the planets this whole system falls to the ground" (Sir Oliver Lodge, *Pioneers of Science*, Macmillan, 1913, p. 106).

31. McLean, *op. cit.*, p. 11.

32. Farbridge, *op. cit.*, p. 133; Webster, *op. cit.*, p. 215.

33. Jastrow, *The Religion of Babylonia and Assyria*, pp. 570, 620.

34. Farbridge, *op. cit.*, p. 133; Jastrow, *op. cit.*, p. 619. Gudea (*ca.* 2700 B.C.) — a Babylonian king of the Ur dynasty.

35. Jastrow, *op. cit.*, pp. 616-17; Fletcher, *History of Architecture*, p. 56.

36. McLean, *op. cit.*, p. 29.

37. Farbridge, *op. cit.*, p. 126.

38. Thompson, *op. cit.*, p. 41.

devils. The 7 gradations of the planets, or tower steps, added the 7 of ascent or descent, of heaven and hell. Ishtar, in her descent to Hades, presents herself at 7 gates where her garments are successively removed, until she is lost in the shadows.[39] Alarmed by her continuing absence, the people pray to the great god who commands:

Go Uddushu-naonir, to the gate of the land without return, turn thy fate;
The seven gates of the land will be opened before thee.[40]

Ishtar is led forth, pausing at each gate to reclaim the symbols of her majesty.

Though doubtless unknown to Dante, this ancient conception was the ultimate plan for the construction of the 7 ledges of the mount of Purgatory. The 7 steps mark successive stages of purification, to be rewarded by the vision of the Earthly Paradise at the summit, or eighth step. Here, as in most instances, the survival of the *idea* is more important than the survival of any particular legend. The conception of 7 steps to perfection was a common medieval notion, whether by the 7 arts or the 7 virtues or, more specifically, the 7 steps or stages of contemplation.

The early conception of the 7 steps received astrological amplification in the belief in the descent of the soul through the planetary spheres, acquiring its abilities and faults from the stars. After death it reascends, returning to each planet the passions and dispositions appropriate to it and reaching at last the eighth Heaven — the one beyond 7 — to enjoy eternal bliss.[41] This became sound enough astrology to justify Dante in allocating (symbolically), in a similar fashion, the souls of the blessed to the several planets in the *Paradiso*. The culminating vision of Church Triumphant (which actually includes all the others), appears in the *eighth* heaven, just as

39. Rogers, *Cuneiform Parallels to the Old Testament*, pp. 121-25.
40. Jastrow, *op. cit.*, p. 57.
41. Cumont, *Astrology and Religion*, pp. 197-98; *Oriental Religions*, p. 121.

the apotheosis of Church Militant was seen on the eighth step of Purgatory.

So we may multiply the 7's of Babylonian cosmogony and religion, and add to them their uncounted descendants in other lands and later times, for few other numbers were to be so universally venerated.

With the approximation of the year as 360 days, the attempt to enumerate its lunations gave rise to the 30-day month. The number is brought into prominence in the ideogram for month, which is "30," plus the ideogram for "day." Similarly the sign of the moon god, Sin, is made up of 30 and the symbol for "god." [42] Subsequently, a 30-year cycle was found in the journey of Saturn through the signs of the zodiac.[43] Probably the earliest year was that of 12 lunations with a thirteenth month later intercalated from time to time,[44] this carrying with it an inauspicious and baleful aspect.[45] The 12 signs of the zodiac were discovered as the appointed rulers of the months.[46]

The duodecad became the symbol for a completed cycle, and was forthwith used to denote the divisions of the day. A report of the astronomer royal to the king, from the library of Ashurbanipal, reads:

> On the sixth day of Nisan
> Day and night were balanced
> There were six "double-hours" of day
> Six "double-hours" of night.
> May Nabu and Marduk
> Be gracious to the king, my lord.[47]

In the *Epic of Gilgamish*, 12 and 7, rather than 10, are

42. Webster, *op. cit.*, p. 226.
43. McLean, *op. cit.*, p. 11.
44. Cumont, *Astrology and Religion*, p. 7.
45. Webster, *op. cit.*, p. 62.
46. McLean, *op. cit.*, p. 235. A Nippur text from about 2000 B.C. mentions the zodiac, and pictures of the zodiac were made as early as 1117 B.C.
47. Jastrow, *op. cit.*, p. 356.

recognizable as round numbers. It could not have been long before 12 stars were selected as objects of devotion, and the dualism of good and evil, which we have seen at work in the 7 gods and 7 devils, made a distinction between 12 stars in the northern and 12 in the southern hemisphere, sometimes invisible, which became the 24 judges of the living and the dead.[48] They live on, perhaps, as the 24 elders in the highly astrological Book of Revelations. It was a simple enough sequence from the 12 "double-hour" division of the day to the 24 single hours, 12 of daylight and 12 of night.[49]

Meanwhile, in astrological development the ancient number 3 was by no means neglected. The old Babylonian pantheon (in the time of Gudea, *ca.* 2700 B.C.) includes two triads; the first and highest of Anu, Bel, and Ea, rulers of heaven, earth, and water; the second of Sin, Shamash, and Raman, who governed the moon, the sun, and storms.[50] The latter triad is sometimes varied by the substitution of Ishtar, the morning and the evening star, for Raman.[51] On boundary stones dating from the fourteenth century B.C., the crescent and the disc containing a star, symbols of the moon, sun, and Venus, are found appealing to the power of the rulers of the zodiac.[52] The adoption of a 10-day week and a 30-day month provided another 3 in the weeks of the month, ruled over by the decan stars or, as they were named, the Councillor Gods:

> He constructed stations for the great gods
> The stars in their likenesses he fixed, even the Lumasi,
> He fixed the year and designed the signs of the zodiac,
> For the twelve months he placed three stars each.[53]

That the complex symbolisms embodied in Babylonian theology did not, like the tablets on which they were en-

48. Cumont, *Astrology and Religion*, p. 33.
49. McLean, *op. cit.*, p. 18.
50. Jastrow, *op. cit.*, pp. 107-8.
51. Farbridge, *op. cit.*, pp. 101-2; Cumont, *op. cit.*, p. 22.
52. Cumont, *ibid.*, p. 47.
53. *Epic of Creation*, V, 1-4.

graved, disappear, is evidenced by the reappearance of these same numbers, in much the same connections, wherever number symbolism was later practiced. The gift of astrology was accepted by all the later civilizations. The Egyptians adopted a 12-month year, with the amendment of 5 intercalary days at the end of the year.[54] The 36 decans became the "Horoscopi," who determine all human events.[55] At the same time, tribute was paid to the 28 "lunar mansions" [56] and the 28 constellations.[57] Lewis suggests that the varying accounts of the life of the phoenix represent approximations of the Great Year.[58] Three hundred and sixty or 365 lights were burned in honor of Osiris.

Every ancient civilization seems to have had its prominent duodecads. The 12 spokes in the wheel of the Hindu Rta [59] are balanced by the 12 gates of hell, in which the Egyptian Ra must spend the 12 hours of the night.[60] Who has not heard of the 12 labours of Hercules, the 12 gods of Greece,[61] the 12 winds,[62] the 12 tribes of Israel, the 12 gods of Rome, or the 12 tables of Roman law? The strength of this superstition receives comment by Herodotus: "The Ionians founded 12 cities in Asia and refused to enlarge the number, on account (as I imagine) of their having been divided into 12 states when they lived in the Peloponnese." [63] Whether Herodotus imagines correctly or not, his statement is an excellent example of the superstitiously conceived necessity for preserving a traditional number.

54. Tannery, *Recherches sur l'histoire de l'astronomie ancienne*, p. 22; Müller, *op. cit.*, p. 57; Moret, *op. cit.*, p. 446.

55. *The Perfect Sermon*, XIX, 3, in Mead's *Thrice Greatest Hermes*.

56. Narrien, *Historical Account of the Origin and Progress of Astronomy*, p. 82.

57. Blake, *op. cit.*, p. 97.

58. Lewis, *Historical Survey of the Astronomy of the Ancients*, p. 29.

59. Keith, *op. cit.*, p. 24.

60. Conway, *Demonology and Devil-Lore*, p. 344.

61. Herodotus, II, 43.

62. Seneca, *op. cit.*, V, 16-17.

63. *Op. cit.*, I, 145.

Meanwhile the use of astrology for prognostication [64] assumed great prominence in Babylon, Persia, Egypt, Greece, and Rome.[65] One of the principal medieval textbooks of astrology was the *Mathesis* of Firmicus Maternus, whose wisdom was derived from *Aegypti veteres sapientes ac divini viri Babyloniique prudentes*.[66] Here one finds the 12 signs, divided into two groups of 6, left and right, and again masculine and feminine. To these are correlated the 7 planets, by assigning a masculine and feminine sign or "home" to each of 5 planets, and by distributing the remaining 2 signs to the sun and moon, the feminine Cancer to the moon and the masculine Leo to the sun.[67] To each sign is assigned 3 decans and accordingly 30 parts. Each part is further divided into 60 minutes.[68] There are 4 directions, or "boundaries of birth," and 4 secondary places: god, goddess, good fortune, and good demon.[69] Influential also are the 5 zones of the earth, by which is explained away the classic objection of the skeptics that all Africans, under whatever sign of birth, are black.[70] In casting the horoscope, various more or less complicated maneuvers are required, including multiplication and division by astrological numbers including 28, the number of the moon.[71] Many additions were made to the science, but no essential changes. Most important, the dominant astrological numbers, together with the belief in the relation of the microcosm to the macrocosm, were preserved intact.

64. To avoid confusion, I have found it necessary to distinguish between astrology as a concept and the professional practice of prognostication by the stars. By the astrological concept, I mean the belief that the stars are gods, intelligences, angels, demons, the handwriting of God, and that they directly influence mundane affairs. This (with its many variations) was a matter of general belief. Astrology as a profession implies a precise and detailed knowledge of this influence.

65. Cf. Cumont, *Astrology and Religion* and *Oriental Religions*.

66. I, proem.

67. II, 1-2.

68. II, 4-5.

69. II, 15-16.

70. I, 10.

71. Agrippa, *Occult Philosophy*, III, 15.

In most of the sciences, pseudosciences, and magics of the Middle Ages may be found the impress of astrological number symbolism. Yet the effect of all of these put together cannot compare with the overwhelming authority of the Old Testament, in which, as has been intimated, the Babylonian numbers are copiously distributed. The separate books comprising the canon range in time from the inclusion of legends of unknown antiquity to the first-century Book of Esther; [72] but the numerical tradition, although sometimes incredibly confused, as in the flood story, where too many contributors and revisers have been at work, is not only remarkably consistent, but is almost purely Babylonian.

The venerable number 7 receives the sanction of Jehovah in the original act of creation. Seven creative acts are specifically given: Light, the Firmament, Plant-life, the Heavenly Bodies, Fish and Fowls, Animals, and Human Beings. At the same time, the divinely ordained 7-day week is instituted.[73] The correspondency between the 7 days and the 7 creations suggests that a separate day had originally been reserved for each creation but that, at some point, cognizance had been taken of the Babylonian "Sabbath," and simultaneously of the inappropriateness of a sabbatical creative act. Man, therefore, lost the dignity of isolated creation and was forced to share his day with the animals. From this legend arose the belief that the creation prefigured the duration of the world, which would therefore endure for 6 ages (6 days of 1,000 years each), to be followed by the great Sabbath of Eternal Rest.

Between the narratives of the creation and the flood are inserted two diverse genealogical tables. The first, which traces Adam's descendants through Cain, is historically disregarded, but is nevertheless numerically important because it is

72. H. P. Smith, *Old Testament History.*
73. Gen. 1-2.

composed of 7 names, the seventh being Lamech, who lives 777 years, and who boasts, "If Cain shall be avenged 7-fold, truly Lamech 70 and 7-fold." [74] In Lamech, who repeats the sin of Cain, the Babylonian 7 of sin and expiation makes its first appearance. It becomes a traditional number of sacrifice, wherefore the clean animals enter the ark by 7's.[75] Sometimes 7 is used as a number of servitude, as in the 7 years which Jacob serves for Leah and again for Rachel.[76] Sometimes it betokens a period of trial and punishment, as in the 7 months during which the Ark of the Covenant remained in the hands of the Philistines,[77] and in the 70 years of bondage.[78] In other instances, 7 is distinctly the number of sin and expiation, as is ordained by Jehovah's "I will punish you yet 7 times for your sins," [79] by the 7 days of uncleanness, and by the reservation of the seventh month for the annual feast of expiation.[80]

The second genealogy [81] which links the creation and the flood is composed of the 10 prediluvian patriarchs whose Babylonian ancestors have been noted.[82] In this table, Enoch, who is translated in reward for his goodness, is the seventh generation. The 7 years of plenty and the 7 of famine in Egypt [83] provide a picturesque version of the antithesis of Lamech and Enoch, the twin 7's of evil and good. The 7 of good is divinely sanctioned by God's 7-fold pronouncement of good in Genesis 1.[84] It is recognized in the 7 days of the creation narrative, the 7 days of Passover, the 7-branched

74. Gen. 4: 24.
75. Gen. 7: 2-3.
76. Gen. 29.
77. I Sam. 6: 1.
78. II Chron. 36: 21; Jeremiah 25: 11; 29: 10.
79. Lev. 26: 24.
80. Lev. 16: 29.
81. Gen. 5.
82. See above, p. 10.
83. Gen. 41: 26-27.
84. The phrase, "God saw that it was good," appears 7 times.

candlestick,[85] the 7,000 righteous in Israel,[86] the 7 bowings of Jacob,[87] and generally in ritual where sacrifice and blessing are necessarily related. Even the 7 seers are remembered in Proverbs 9: 1: "Wisdom hath builded her house, she hath hewn out her 7 pillars." An extension of 7 makes 70 an important Hebrew number. There are 70 nations,[88] 70 who go into Egypt,[89] 70 children of Jacob,[90] and 70 judges of the Sanhedrim.[91]

These few, among the unnumbered heptads which fill the pages of the Old Testament, witness the enthusiasm with which the Israelites received the number lore which perhaps Abram brought from "Ur of the Chaldees." [92] The Hebrews amplified and solidified the importance of 7, and derived from it, apparently independently, the notion already seen of the sanctity of 8.[93] For as in the 9-10 relationship and by the same reasoning which counts 7 times 7 years and hallows the fiftieth, 8 becomes a day of plenty after fasting, a day of purification after uncleanness, and, above all, it is the day of circumcision. For this reason the temple is sanctified in 8 days; [94] and 8 sons are a sign of blessing to Abraham and Obed-edom. In the last instance, the sanctity of 8 is pointed. The sons of the porters are listed. Many have more than 8 sons. Yet we read that Obed-edom had 8 sons "for God blessed him." [95]

Meanwhile, the number 40 retains in the Old Testament its Babylonian insinuation of trial and privation. The flood

85. The 7 stars of Amos 5: 8?
86. I Kings 19: 18.
87. Gen. 33: 3.
88. Gen. 10: 32.
89. Gen. 46: 27.
90. Exod. 1: 5.
91. Num. 11: 18.
92. Gen. 15: 7.
93. See above, p. 18.
94. II Chron. 29: 17.
95. I Chron. 26: 5.

prevailed, in one version, for 40 days.[96] It is recognized by law that stripes must not exceed 40.[97] Unconscious tribute is paid to the "exile" of the Pleiades in the 40 or twice 40 days of purification after childbirth,[98] the 40 years of Philistine dominion over Israel,[99] the 40 years in the wilderness,[100] the 40 days of Moses on Sinai,[101] the 40 days of Elijah's journey,[102] the 40 days of mourning for Jacob,[103] and the 40 days of Jonah's prediction.[104] From its original meaning, 40 comes to be a "fated" period, possibly as a result of the statement that after the flood man's days are to be 120 years,[105] which divides exactly into 3 periods of 40 years each. The life of Moses is so divided; and Solomon,[106] Jehoash,[107] and David [108] reign 40 years each.[109] From the Exodus to the building of the temple are 480 years,[110] which divide into 4 periods of 120 years each, the temple being started in the fourth year of Solomon's reign. As Farbridge points out,[111] the total equals 12 generations of 40 years, a period repeated from this time to the Babylonian exile.

These approximations of time are noteworthy in their recognition of 40, 3, 4, and 12 as logical temporal measurements, as well as highly significant numbers. The use of the instinctive statistical 3 is common throughout the Old Testa-

96. Gen. 7: 17.
97. Deut. 25: 3.
98. Lev. 12: 2-5. The 7 of "uncleanness" also figures in this rite, for in the computation of the periods the first 7 or 14 days are distinguished from the remainder.
99. Judg. 13: 1.
100. Exod. 16: 35.
101. Exod. 24: 18.
102. I Kings 19: 8.
103. Gen. 50: 3.
104. Jonah 3: 4; see also I Sam. 17: 16.
105. Gen. 6: 3. One hundred and twenty is one-third of the astrological 360.
106. I Kings 11: 42.
107. II Kings 12: 1.
108. II Sam. 5: 4.
109. See also Num. 13: 25; Judg. 3: 11; 5: 31; 8: 28.
110. I Kings 6: 1.
111. *Studies*, p. 146.

ment, and there is a slight possibility that the divinity of 3, possibly derived from Egypt, is also recognized. The triple blessing of God in Genesis I [112] is the clearest indication, and several other references might be interpreted as something more than statistical. Ezekiel, who is especially conscious of number symbolism, names 3 men of especial sanctity: Noah, Daniel, Job.[113] The Lord calls Samuel 3 times.[114] Elijah restores the child to life by stretching himself upon it 3 times.[115] There is a possible significance in the circumstance that Gideon's army was successful only after having been reduced from 32,000 to 300 in 3 companies. The author is apparently conscious of number symbolism, since he gives Gideon 70 children, and emphasizes the fact that the 300 carried 300 trumpets, 300 lamps, and 300 pitchers, or 3 things apiece.[116] Three times a year all the males of Israel are ordered to appear before God at the 3 feasts of the year.[117] Finally, as Farbridge has pointed out,[118] God is called by 3 divine names in Psalm 50: 1 and in Joshua 22: 22. It was considered important, at least in the Middle Ages, that 3 angels appeared to Abraham.[119] Some of these triads are of doubtful significance. The 3 feasts were probably of seasonal origin. Others of the 3's may be explained as purely statistical, among these probably the 3 divisions of the earth [120] and Jonah's 3 days in the fish, [121] but even discounting such possibilities there is indication that the divine 3 was known, though not emphasized, by the Hebrews. To the medieval theologian, however, all of these triads were to be of sacred import.

112. The phrase, "God blessed," occurs 3 times.
113. Ezek. 14: 14.
114. I Sam. 3.
115. I Kings 17: 21.
116. Judg. 7.
117. Exod. 23: 14, 17.
118. *Studies*, p. 106.
119. Gen. 18: 2.
120. Gen. 9: 19.
121. Jonah 1: 17.

The meaning of the ancient tetrad is more solidly fixed by its use in the second version of the creation legend.[122] This so-called Jahwistic version, apparently older than the first, is a picturesque story whose only recognition of number is the very old 4 of the 4 rivers, resembling the Egyptian legend, and doubtless referring to the same 4 quarters of the world which are everywhere recognized. These appear in the 4 winds of Ezekiel 37: 9, and Daniel 7: 2; in the 4 parts of heaven in Job 9: 9; in the 4 golden rings of the ark of the covenant [123] and the table; [124] in the 12 oxen, 3 looking in each direction, which support the sea of the temple; [125] and in the constant 4 beasts, birds, or angels in the prophesies. Farbridge, who has noted this usage, adds:

Blessings and curses which are meant to be diffused abroad have a four-fold character. So Balaam in the doom he utters over the heathen nations adopts a four-fold classification (Numbers XXIV: 3, 15, 20, 23) and his last prophecy foretells the victorious supremacy of Israel over all its foes and the destruction of all the powers of the world. This prophecy is divided into 4 different prophecies by the four-fold repetition of the words: "And he took up his parable." [126]

Since the year was known to be divided into 12 months, it was natural to use the number 12 in other time and space divisions. Solomon conveniently divided his kingdom into 12 sections for taxation purposes, and it was probably by analogy that the myth of the 12 tribes, which were never 12 in fact, was invented.[127] But such was the strength of the tradition that whenever the number is mentioned, as in I Kings 17: 31-34 or I Kings 19: 19, it refers directly to the 12 tribes. It is only with the adoption of the 12-hour day and night that it re-

122. Gen. 2.
123. Exod. 25: 12.
124. Ibid., 26.
125. I Kings 7: 25.
126. Studies, p. 115.
127. H. P. Smith, op. cit., p. 157.

ceives any amplification. Then the priestly author of Chronicles (fourth century B.C.) has David divide the sons of Aaron into 24 orders so that no hour of the day or night be neglected. Twenty-four singers are also appointed, each of whom has 12 sons and brethren. Another 12 are made captains, one for each month, each to rule over 24,000 men.[128] By analogy, the author of II Esdras divides the duration of the world into 12 periods, 10½ of which he conceives to have already passed.[129] This late elaboration, together with the generally naïve usage of number in the earlier books of the Old Testament, indicates that the Babylonian number symbols had filtered into Israel in a legendary form long before the Hebrews had any knowledge of the astrology from which they were derived.

As the legend of the 12 tribes, rather than any cosmic theory, established finally the importance of the number 12, so the 10 commandments, wherever derived, placed upon the decad the stamp of divine approval. In numerous passages 10 is used, as in Homer, as a symbol of infinity or of very great quantity. The best example of this is the assignment of 700 wives and 300 concubines to Solomon. As has been suggested,[130] 70 wives and 300 concubines would be a more customary proportion, but Solomon's splendor would not be recognized by any less significant number than 10, 100, or 1,000. Perhaps by later revisions, influenced by Pythagorean mathematics, 10 became more specifically a number of perfection. Noah was of the tenth generation and "was perfect in his generations."[131] The 10 repetitions of the phrase, "God said," in the creation narrative were doubtless derived from God's commandments, listed in any of the 3 versions of the Decalogue.[132] The 10 plagues, built up from

128. I Chron. 24-25.
129. II Esd. 14: 10 ff.
130. H. P. Smith, op. cit., p. 160.
131. Gen. 6: 9.
132. Exod. 34: 1-28; Exod. 23: 1-19; Deut. 5: 6-21.

the 7 of the earliest document,[133] attest the power of Jehovah, and the tithe is given in token that the entire 10 tenths belong to God. Job's possessions are also pertinent, for they are listed in groups of 7 sons and 3 daughters, 7,000 sheep and 3,000 cattle, 500 yoke of oxen and 500 she asses, "and that man was perfect and upright."[134] In ceremonial, 10 is a very prominent number. In Solomon's temple are 10 lavers, 10 candlesticks, 10 tables. The cherubim are 10 cubits high, with an identical wing span from tip to tip. The molten sea is 10 cubits in diameter. Ten Levites "minister before the ark of the Lord."[135]

Although the record of Hebrew adherence to number symbolism has by no means been exhausted in this rapid survey, we need not here concern ourselves with isolated or doubtful instances which have no direct bearing on later usage. It is far more profitable to turn our attention to a specialized group of Hebraic writings which may be denominated by the term *apocalyptic*, and which, by the use of newly discovered astrological lore, inaugurate a new stage in the history of number symbolism.

With the loss of political independence, the Jews sought to hold their scattering members together by means of a stringent and formalized religion. As a result, many ancient manuscripts were "discovered" in which ancient patriarchs and prophets warned of future tribulations (now realized) due to moral laxity, emphasized the necessity of strict adherence to the law, and offered the hope of a Messiah who would bring spiritual and, in some versions, temporal redemption to a penitent people. Authority was secured for these utterances by having them delivered in the form of visions which had been granted to the authors in reward for notable piety. The best known of these writings are the books of

133. H. P. Smith, *op. cit.*, p. 57.
134. Job. 1: 1.
135. I Chron. 16: 4-6.

Ezekiel and Daniel, together with the New Testament counterpart in the Revelation of St. John; but a considerable number of these apocalypses are extant, all claiming great antiquity.[136]

Apart from their importance in relating the traditional sacred numbers of the Hebrews to their astrological sources (the 4 of the cardinal points, the 12 of the zodiac), the apocalypses served to emphasize the essential identity of all groups defined by the same number. Thus the fourness of the earth, evidenced by the cardinal points, is repeated in the temporal sphere by the 4 seasons,[137] the 4 phases of the moon,[138] named for the cardinal points, the 4 intercalary days.[139] That all of these quaternities are felt to be related expressions of the same fundamental truth may be seen in the naming of the lunar phases from the cardinal points. Four might be said to represent the archetypal pattern for the macrocosm which the microcosm naturally reproduces: "And I gave him a name from the 4 substances, the East, the West, the North, and the South." [140] Fortunately, we are not under the necessity of interpreting this statement, for it is explained in the *Sibylline Oracles* [141] that the Greek directions, taken in the order given, ἀνατολή, δύσις, ἄρκτος, μεσημβρινός, produce by their initial letters the name Adam.

The interrelationship of all things made prognostication possible, and the duration of the world might be predicted by knowledge of the eternal pattern. The great astrological numbers being 4, 12, and 7, the age of the world was known to be

136. These include the Ethiopic *Book of Enoch* and the Slavonic *Book of the Secrets of Enoch, The Testaments of the Twelve Patriarchs, The Ascension of Isaiah, The Apocalypse of Baruch, The Assumption of Moses, The Apocalypse of Abraham,* and, in the same tradition, the *Sibylline Oracles.*

137. En. 82.

138. En. 77.

139. En. 76: 1.

140. Secrets 30: 13.

141. *Op. cit.,* 3: 24-26.

divided into 4 periods,[142] into 12 parts,[143] or into 7,000 days,[144] 70 generations or 7 weeks.[145]

The numbers of the apocalypses were not intended to be readily understood. Originating in astrology, they represent the plan of the world. As such, they are known to God and to the few to whom, like Enoch, special grace has been shown. To the devout they are subjects of adoration beyond mortal comprehension. The halo of mystery surrounding number is especially well illustrated by the sacred number, known only to God, which will determine the Messianic Age:

And then shall righteous men of thy seed be left in the number which is kept secret by me.[146]

4. Because when Adam sinned and death was decreed against those who should be born, then the multitude of those who should be born was numbered, and for that number a place was prepared where the living might dwell and the dead might be guarded.
5. Unless therefore the number aforesaid is fulfilled, they will not live again.[147]

When the number was finally revealed to St. John, it proved to be an astrological compound:

And I heard the number of them that were sealed: and there were sealed a hundred and forty and four thousand of all the tribes of the children of Israel.[148]

142. En. 89: 72; 90: 5; Apoch. Bar. 24: 3-6; Abraham 28; Dan. 2: 31-45.
143. Bar. 27.
144. Secrets 33: 2.
145. En. 10: 12; 93: 10.
146. Abraham XXIX, p. 81.
147. Apoch. Bar. 23: 4-5.
148. Rev. 7: 4.

III. PYTHAGOREAN NUMBER THEORY

WHILE the astrological numbers of ancient Babylon, with all of their massed associations, were being carried down to the Christian Era, there grew up in Greece an independent philosophy of number, which in any of its variations was known to the Middle Ages as Pythagoreanism. Of Pythagoras himself (580?-500? B.C.), whom Herodotus called "the most able philosopher among the Greeks," [1] nothing is certainly known. Tradition has it that after travel and study in Babylon and Egypt, he returned to the West and founded in southern Italy a secret cult based on a numerical explanation of the universe. The members of the Brotherhood were united for life by oath, and were further insulated by the practice of certain of the eastern mysteries and the observance of strict ethical and dietary regulations. The school grew rapidly and became of considerable political importance, but either its politics or its religious observances, or both, led to a fierce persecution, during which Pythagoras is supposed to have perished.[2]

The most complete extant survey of early Pythagoreanism is given by Aristotle:

The first to take up mathematics . . . [they] thought its principles were the principles of all things. Since of these principles numbers are by nature the first, and in number they seemed to see many resemblances to the things that exist and come into being — more than in fire and earth and water (such and such a modification of numbers being soul and reason, another being opportunity — and similarly almost all things being numerically expressible) ; since,

---

1. T. L. Heath, *A Manual of Greek Mathematics*, p. 23.

2. For hypothetical reconstructions of the original Pythagorean philosophy, as well as for more detailed information, consult Zeller, *A History of Greek Philosophy*; Scoon, *Greek Philosophy before Plato*; Ritter, *Geschichte der Pythagorischen Philosophie*.

again, they saw that the modifications and ratios of the musical scales were expressible in numbers; — since, then all other things seemed in their whole nature to be modelled on numbers, and numbers seemed to be the first things in the whole of nature they supposed the elements of number to be the elements of all things, and the whole heaven to be a musical scale and a number. And all the properties of numbers and scales which they could show to agree with the attributes and parts and the whole arrangement of the heavens, they collected and fitted into their scheme; and if there was a gap anywhere, they readily made additions so as to make their whole theory coherent.[3]

It is evident that Aristotle is not over sympathetic; but Philolaus (*ca.* 450 B.C.), whose book on the Pythagorean doctrines survives only in fragments, corroborates this statement of the basic Pythagorean premise. "All things have a number," he writes, "and it is this fact which enables them to be known." [4]

The originality of the Pythagorean treatment of number lay in the enunciation of two fundamental principles: the exaltation of the decad as containing all numbers and therefore all things, and the geometric conception of mathematics. From the first was derived their cosmic theory as reported by Aristotle. At the center of the universe was placed a central fire about which revolved earth, sun, moon, planets, and fixed stars. The resulting total of 9 spheres was so repugnant to their faith in an ordered and mathematical universe that an invisible "counter-earth" was postulated to complete the decad.[5] Not only is the number 10 necessary to realize completeness, but all things are contained within the decad, since after 10 the numbers merely repeat themselves.

On the other hand, the geometric approach to mathematics provided a link (other than astrological) between abstract number and concrete reality. It is by numbers, said Philolaus,

3. *Metaphysica*, A, 5.
4. T. L. Heath, *op. cit.*, p. 38.
5. Aristotle, *De caelo* II, 13; *Metaphysica*, A, 5.

that things become known. The number 1, therefore, is represented as a point. The number 2 gives extension, since by joining 2 points a line is produced. But neither point nor line are tangible objects. The triad, however, is represented by the triangle, the first plane figure, and is therefore the first *real* number. The triangle becomes thereby the basis of all objects perceptible to the senses. This is the meaning of Plato's remark that surface is composed of triangles.[6]

As the number 3 is the most fundamental representation of surface, so from the number 4 the first solid is produced. For if a fourth point is centered directly over the triangle, and joined by lines to the 3 points of the triangle, the pyramid or tetrahedron, composed of 4 triangular surfaces, is produced. Or, as a later commentator put it, surface bounded by 3 points ascends to a point placed above.[7] Five such "regular" solids were discovered, all composed entirely of triangles. The first four, the tetrahedron, octahedron, icosahedron, and cube, were related respectively by Plato to fire, air, water, and earth.[8] It is worth noting that fire, the first principle of Pythagorean cosmography, is described by the first solid, and that the fourth solid, the only figure whose surfaces are quadrangular, is assigned to earth, thus adding philosophical support to the traditional belief in the foursquaredness of earth. Since there were only 4 elements, it would have added greatly to the peace of mind of many of the Greek philosophers had there been only 4 instead of 5 regular solids. Plato either implies that the fifth includes and masters the other 4 or else is completely sidestepping the issue when he says that the dodecahedron with its 12 pentagonal faces is "used to embroider the universe with constellations." [9] Later philoso-

6. *Timaeus*, 53 c. On the geometric aspect of Pythagoreanism, cf. Grace Murray Hopper, "The Ungenerated Seven as an Index to Pythagorean Number Theory," *American Mathematical Monthly*, XLIII, 409-13.

7. Sextus Empiricus, *Outlines of Pyrrhonism*, III, 20.

8. *Timaeus*, 55-56.

9. *Ibid.*, 55 c.

phers were much concerned to define the nature of the "quintessence."

Plato's procedure and terminology here, as in the *Republic*, is seen to be entirely geometric in nature. The "marriage number" of the *Republic* [10] is derived from the famous 3, 4, 5 right triangle, which was known to the Egyptians at least as early as 2000 B.C.,[11] and was traditionally a favorite figure of Pythagoras himself.[12] It may well have been so in actuality, since tribute must inevitably have been paid to a figure whose dimensions are entirely rational and whose sides, 3 and 4, the first plane number and the first solid number, unite to produce the hypotenuse, 5, the number of the regular solids.[13] The summary of Greek mathematics in Euclid also testifies to the predominance of geometric thinking over arithmetical, and the discovery of harmonic proportions, ascribed to Pythagoras, must have originated in the geometric experiment of stopping down a taut string or observing the relative weights of a blacksmith's hammers. From geometry came the Pythagorean conception of the perfect number which was the sum, not of its divisors, but of its aliquot parts. It must have added great weight to their philosophy to discover that the first perfect number, 6, $(= 1 + 2 + 3)$ was also the area of the great 3, 4, 5 right triangle, and that the second perfect number was the astrologically significant 28.

This combination of philosophy and geometry caused "mathematics" and "Pythagoreanism" to be considered as almost convertible terms.[14] Some of the Pythagorean discoveries, such as the distinctions of even and odd numbers, and

10. *Op. cit.*, 545 c.

11. D. E. Smith, *History of Mathematics*, II, 288.

12. Cajori, *History of Mathematics*, p. 18.

13. For an interpretation of the marriage number, cf. Grace Chisholm Young, "On the Solution of a Pair of Simultaneous Diophantine Equations Connected with the Nuptial Number of Plato;" also James Adam, *The Nuptial Number of Plato*.

14. Scoon, *Greek Philosophy before Plato*, p. 344.

of primes, were purely mathematical. Another attempt to organize the rational integers took its cue from the discovery of perfect numbers, and proceeded to classify numbers as perfect, deficient, or abundant from the relationship of a number to its aliquot parts. This is also a geometric conception. In algebraic terminology, the aliquot parts of a number are its divisors, exclusive of itself. A perfect number is therefore one whose divisors add up to the number itself; for example, the divisors of 6 are 1, 2, 3, and $1 + 2 + 3 = 6$. A deficient number is one whose parts sum up to less than the number; the aliquot parts of 14 are 1, 2, 7, whose total is only 10. Similarly an abundant number has parts to spare: the parts of 12 are 1, 2, 3, 4, 6, whose sum is 16.

Numbers were also classified by means of figured representations. It was discovered that the sum of any number of successive arithmetic terms (beginning with 1) forms a triangle: $1 = .,\ + 2 = \therefore, + 3 = \ldots$, and so on. Hence the recognition of triangular numbers. Square numbers are built up by adding any number of successive terms of the series of odd numbers starting from 1. The successive addition of even numbers, following the same scheme, creates oblong numbers, with sides differing by 1. An oblong number is also the double of a triangular number. Finally, 8 times any triangular number plus 1 equals a square.[15]

Meanwhile, the purely philosophical implications of number had not been lost sight of. There must have been many who, following the lead of Plato and possibly Pythagoras himself, continued to see in the decad the archetypal pattern of the universe and in the members of the decad the expression of divine ideas. Such, at any rate, is the doctrine of the so-called Neo-Pythagoreans, who, flourishing from the first century B.C. to the fifth century A.D., built upon a tradition which had apparently been preserved and amplified in the now-

15. T. L. Heath, *op. cit.*, p. 50.

vanished writings of their predecessors. The record of this school is preserved in the writings of Philo Judaeus, Nicomachus of Gerasa, and Plutarch, who lived in the first century A.D.; of Plotinus, Diogenes Laertius, Porphyry, and Iamblichus of the third century; and of Proclus, Macrobius, and Capella of the fifth, with a late ninth-century echo in Photius of Constantinople.

These writers, who represent the Pythagoreanism of the Middle Ages, are in general agreement as to the importance and properties of numbers. By them number is held to be the first principle, and arithmetic, accordingly, the key to cosmic secrets. Nicomachus gives a concise statement of the theory in his *Introduction to Arithmetic*:

All that has by nature with systematic method been arranged in the universe seems both in part and as a whole to have been determined and ordered in accordance with number, by the forethought and the mind of him that created all things; for the pattern was fixed like a preliminary sketch, by the domination of number preexistent in the mind of the world-creating God, number conceptual only and immaterial in every way, but at the same time the true and eternal essence, so that with reference to it, as to an artistic plan, should be created all these things, time, motion, the heavens, the stars, all sorts of revolutions. It must needs be, then, that scientific number, being set over such things as these, should be harmoniously constituted in accordance with itself; not by any other but by itself.[16]

Since the numerical terms after 10 are simply outgrowths of the decad and since, "clearly and indisputably," [17] the ordered and the finite takes precedence over the unlimited and the infinite, it follows that a thorough analysis of the properties of the first ten numbers will reveal not only the whole nature of numbers, but also the pattern of the universe as it exists in the mind of God.

The observable efforts of Greek philosophy were generally

16. *Op. cit.*, I, vi, 1-2.
17. *Ibid.*, I, xxiii, 4.

directed toward the resolution of multiplicity into unity.[18] Empedocles is reported to have said, "the universe is alternately in motion and at rest — in motion when love is making one out of many, or strife is making many out of one, and at rest in the intermediate periods of time." [19] Even here, where two states are posited, the unifying impulse is obviously felt to be the more desirable. Hence it is very natural that the Pythagoreans should have considered the monad as the first principle from which the other numbers flow.[20] Itself not a number, it is an essence rather than a being [21] and is sometimes, like the duad, designated as a potential number, since the point, though not a plane figure, can originate plane figures.[22] As first originator, the monad is good and God.[23] It is both odd and even, male and female,[24] for when added to odd it produces even, and when added to even it produces odd.[25] It is the basis and creator of number, but, although it is actually the great Even-Odd, its nature is considered to be more akin to masculine oddness than to feminine evenness. In short, it is always taken to represent all that is good and desirable and *essential*, indivisible and uncreated.[26]

If 1, the point, is the Father of number, it follows that the duad, the line, is the Mother of number.[27] As a line it is generated by expansion of the monad,[28] and since each number, however large, is unified as a group,[29] the duad is mysti-

18. Xenophanes, Parmenides, Melissus, Plato, and Aristotle all sought one principle.

19. Aristotle, *Physica*, VIII, 1.

20. Nicomachus, *Introduction*, II, vi, 3; Plotinus, *Enneads*, V, 1, 7; Photius, *Biography of Pythagoras*, 7; Proclus, *Elements of Theology*, A; C, 21.

21. Plotinus, *Enneads*, VI, 9, 3.

22. Nicomachus, *op. cit.*, II, vi, 3.

23. *Enneads*, VI, 1; 9, 6; V, 1, 7.

24. Macrobius, *In Somn. Scip.*, I, 6.

25. *De E apud Delphos*, 8.

26. Capella, *De nuptiis*, VII.

27. Capella, *ibid.*; Plutarch, *De animae procreatione in Timaeo*, II.

28. Sextus Empiricus, *op. cit.*, III, 20.

29. *Enneads*, VI, 6, 5.

cally known as the "Manifold One."[30] The line is neither spatial nor concrete, and consequently the duad, like the monad, is a principle rather than an actual number. As such it represents diversity, a breaking-away from unity,[31] and for that reason was sometimes given the epithet of "daring."[32] It is therefore the representative of matter or existence, mother of the elements,[33] eternal but not immutable, as opposed to Essence or Idea,[34] since everything divisible is mutable and material.[35] It is the number of excess and defect,[36] of manifoldness and of man, because he is both animal and reasonable.[37]

These first two principles are conceived to be in eternal opposition, wherefore they represent respectively the intelligible and the sensible, the immortal and the mortal, day and night, right and left, east and west, sun and moon, equality and inequality.[38]

From the unstable duad marches the procession of the even numbers, called feminine because they are weaker than the odd. For they are empty in the center, whereas when the odd numbers are divided, a middle is always left.[39] Furthermore, the odd number is always master, because odd and even mixed (added) produce always odd. An even plus an even never produces an odd number, but odd numbers produce evens.[40] The even numbers are of ill omen[41] and are delegated to the gods below.[42] As if the feminine numbers were

30. *Enneads*, V, 1.
31. *Enneads*, V, 1, 4.
32. Robbins and Karpinski, *Studies in Greek Arithmetic*, p. 105.
33. Capella, *op. cit.*, VII.
34. Timaeus Locrus, *On the Soul of the World*, 1-6; *Enneads*, V, 1, 8-9.
35. Porphyry, *Biography of Pythagoras*, 50.
36. Photius, *Biography*, 4.
37. *Enneads*, VI, 6, 16.
38. Porphyry, *On the Cave of the Nymphs*, 13; *Biography*, 38.
39. Plutarch, *De E apud Delphos*, VIII, 4; Capella, *op. cit.*, VII.
40. Plutarch, *ibid.*
41. Plato, *Laws*, V, 100. Trans. by Jowett.
42. Plutarch, *Life of Numa*, 14.

not already sufficiently in disfavor, the stigma of infinity is attached to them,[43] apparently by analogy to the line. So strong, in fact, was the repugnance of the idea of infinity that it may be said that the principle of limit and unity was the most important contribution of Pythagoreanism to medieval thought, since, by analogy to Pythagorean mathematics, the belief in an ordered and limited world was largely sustained.

The infinite [says Proclus], is not cognate with the One but alien from it. . . . The manifold of gods is therefore not infinite but marked by a limit.[44]

Plotinus adds, "Doubtless the universe is both great and beautiful; but it is beautiful only so far as the unity holds it from dissipating into infinity." [45]

Since 1 and 2 are only principles or potential numbers, 3 becomes the first real number.[46] It represents all reality not only as the image of "surface," but also as having beginning, middle, and end.[47] By virtue of the triad, unity and diversity of which it is composed [48] are restored to harmony, "because the mean acting as a mediator links the other two into a single complete order.[49] A somewhat more mystical explanation is given in the *Theologoumena arithmeticae*: "For as rennet curdles flowing milk by its peculiar creative and active faculty, so the unifying force of the monad advancing upon the duad, source of easy movement and breaking down, infixed a bound and a form, that is, number, upon the triad; for this is the beginning of actual number, defined by combination of monads." [50] In the Pythagorean triad may be

43. Aristotle, *Metaphysica*, A, 5.
44. *Elements*, L, 149.
45. *Enneads*, VI, 6, 1.
46. Iamblichus, *Biography of Pythagoras*, 28; see above, p. 35.
47. Aristotle, *De caelo*, I, 1; Plato, *Phaedrus*, 473, trans. by Jowett; Philo, *Questions and Solutions*, III, 3; Porphyry, *Biography*, 50; Capella, *op. cit.*, VII.
48. *Enneads*, V, 1, 8-9; VI, 6, 4.
49. Proclus, *Elements*, L, 148.
50. Robbins and Karpinski, *op. cit.*, p. 117.

found the logic of the Christian Trinity. For although God is essentially One, yet "every divine order has an internal unity of 3-fold origin from its highest, its mean, and its last term." [51] Perhaps the best definition of the triad is perfect unity as it is comprehensible to human experience by virtue of "form." For this reason, it is referred by Plotinus [52] and Diogenes Laertius [53] to the soul. Three is also the first of the odd numbers, which are masculine, finite, and godlike. In addition to these qualities, it was observed that the progression of the odd numbers from the monad always produces squares. [54]

The tetrad completes the list of the "archetypal" numbers, representing the point, line, surface, and solid. [55] But the particular glory of the archetypal numbers is that they produce the decad, either as a sum ($1 + 2 + 3 + 4 = 10$) or in the figured representation of 10 as a triangular number. This figure was known as the tetraktys, [56] the legendary oath of the Pythagoreans. [57] Lucian, in the *Sale of Philosophers*, represents the Pythagorean as asking the prospective buyer to count. When he has counted to 4, the philosopher interrupts, "Lo! what thou thinkest four is ten, and a perfect triangle, and our oath." [58] Philo adds that there are 4 boundaries of number, the unit, decad, century, and thousand, all of which are measured by the tetraktys. For just as $1 + 2 + 3 + 4 = 10$, so $10 + 20 + 30 + 40 = 100$, and $100 + 200 + 300 + 400 = 1,000$. [59] Four is also the number of the square, [60] and is represented in the elements, the seasons, the 4

51. Proclus, *Elements*, L, 148.
52. *Enneads*, V, 1, 10.
53. *Biography*, 19.
54. That is: $1 + 3 = 4 + 5 = 9 + 7 = 16$, and so on; Capella, *op. cit.*, VII.
55. Philo, *On the Ten Commandments*, 7.
56. Photius, *Biography*, 4; Iamblichus, *Biography*, 28; Capella, *op. cit.*, VII.
57. Iamblichus, *Biography*, 28.
58. Harmon trans., II, 457.
59. *On the Ten Commandments*, 7.
60. Plutarch, *De animae procreatione*, 1,

ages of man, the 4 principles of a reasonable animal, the lunar phases, and the 4 virtues.[61]

The addition and multiplication of the masculine 3 and the feminine 2 produce the marriage numbers, 5 and 6.[62] Both imitate the first cause, since they are incorruptible by multiplication, and always return to themselves.[63] Five is the type of nature, embracing all living things.[64] There are 5 essences, 5 parts of musical harmonies, 5 zones, 5 inhabitants of the world (plants, fishes, birds, animals, humans), and 5 senses.[65] Capella designates it as the number of this world, since from the perfect circle, represented as 10, is removed this hemisphere.

Six is the female marriage number.[66] Its imperfection as female is overlooked in view of the fact that it is the only perfect number within the decad and partakes of the basic numbers, 1, 2, and 3.[67] It is called *Venus* by Capella.[68]

The Pythagorean philosophy of number could scarcely have justified itself unless it had reserved special tributes for the powerful heptad. To 7, accordingly, is granted the distinction of absolute isolation and therefore first cousinage to the monad. One cycle has been completed by the perfect number 6. Eight is the cube of 2; 9 the square of 3. Ten is the sum of the first 4 numbers. The number which Plato had distinguished in the planets as "the movable image of eternity" [69] is known, therefore, as Pallas, the virgin number, neither generated nor generating within the decad.[70] Macrobius calls

---

61. Diogenes Laertius, *Biography of Pythagoras*, 19, 7; *Theolog. Arith.*, 22; *Enneads*, VI, 6, 16; Capella, *op. cit.*, VII.

62. Plutarch, *De E apud Delphos*, 8.

63. 5 x 5 = 25 x 5 = 125; 6 x 6 = 36, and so on.

64. Macrobius, *op. cit.*, I, 6.

65. Plutarch, *De E apud Delphos*, 8; Philo, *On Who Is the Heir of Divine Things*, 29; *Abraham*, 41; Capella, *op. cit.*, VII.

66. Plutarch, *De E apud Delphos*, 8.

67. Plutarch, *De animae procreatione*, 13; Iamblichus, *Biography*, 28.

68. *De nuptiis*, VII.

69. *Timaeus*, 38.

70. Macrobius, *op. cit.*, I, 6; Philo, *On the Festivals*, I; *Questions and Solutions*, II, 12; Capella, *op. cit.*, VII.

it the universal number, because of the innumerable heptads in the microcosm and macrocosm.[71] It is especially the number of harmony, because of the 7 tones presumably caused by the varying velocities of the planets, and is similarly related to the 7 vowels and the 7 Pleiades,[72] called by Porphyry the "lyre of the muses." [73] In Neo-Pythagorean commentaries on this number may be seen the increasing weight of astrological influence. Capella is at great pains to explain this ancient lunar symbol as composed of the 4 phases and 3 forms; only 3 forms because one repeats. Furthermore, by another of those uncanny coincidences which still brings converts to the altar of numerology, the sum of the first 7 numbers is found to be exactly 28! [74]

Eight is the first cube,[75] considered perfect by virtue of its 6 surfaces.[76] Nine is the first masculine square,[77] and is the perfect form of the perfect 3.[78] Nearly any number, it becomes apparent, may be considered "perfect" for one reason or another. Another "perfection" of 9 results from its propinquity to 10. The 9 orbs of the fixed stars, 7 planets, and earth are completed only by God, who is the first and the tenth.[79]

Ten and 1 are mystically the same, as are also 100 and 1,000, the "boundaries" of number. In the decad, multiplicity returns again to unity. Ten are the categories,[80] for 10 is the total of all things, embracing the entire world.[81] It is the most perfect of all "perfect" numbers and is called

71. *In Somn. Scip.*, I, 6.

72. Plutarch, *De E apud Delphos*, 4; Macrobius, *op. cit.*, I, 6; Capella, *op. cit.*, VII.

73. *Biography*, 41.

74. Capella, *op. cit.*, VII.

75. Philo, *Questions and Solutions*, III, 49.

76. Macrobius, *op. cit.* I, 5; Capella, *op. cit.*, VII.

77. Plutarch, *De animae procreatione*, 1.

78. Capella, *op. cit.*, VII.

79. Philo, *On Seeking Instruction.*

80. Photius, *Biography*, VI; Aristotle, *Metaphysica*, A, 5.

81. Aristotle, *ibid.*

by Porphyry "comprehension," as "comprehending all differences of numbers, reasons, species and proportions." [82]

All higher numbers are generated by the members of the decad and from their "parents" derive their virtues and qualities. A few larger numbers were especially venerated. Twenty-seven is the first odd or masculine cube.[83] Twenty-eight is the second perfect number and the lunar month. The number 35 is called "harmony" by Plutarch, as representing the sum of the first feminine and the first masculine cube: $8 + 27$.[84] Plutarch is, in fact, a superb demonstrator of the operations of Pythagorean mathematics. He finds that 36 is the first number which is both quadrangular (6×6) and rectangular (9×4), that it is the multiple of the first square numbers, 4 and 9, and the sum of the first three cubes, 1, 8, 27.[85] It is also a parallelogram (12×3 or 9×4) and is named "agreement" because in it the first four odd numbers unite with the first four even: $1 + 3 + 5 + 7 = 16$; $2 + 4 + 6 + 8 = 20$; $16 + 20 = 36$.[86]

Lest there be any apprehension that the old number 40 is being neglected, it is only just to add that 40 is a sort of glorified tetraktys. For if each of the first 4 numbers be multiplied in turn by 4, and the 4 products added, the result will be found to be 40. It is also derived as the sum of the first two tetragons, 1 and 4, and the first two cubes, 8 and 27.[87]

Such extravagant manipulations were to be duplicated by the most serious of medieval scholars. The pyrotechnics of a Plutarch are not, however, of great importance. The abiding power of Pythagoreanism lay in its unchanging faith in mathematics as the representation of fundamental truth.

82. *Biography of Pythagoras*, 52.
83. Plutarch, *De animae procreatione*, 1.
84. *De animae procreatione*, 12.
85. It does not do to follow too closely the reasoning of most Pythagorean practitioners. Thirty-six is not rectangular according to precise definition. The monad is counted as a square or cube only when desirable.
86. *De animae procreatione*, 13.
87. *Ibid.*, 14.

Never could error slip into number, for its nature is hostile thereto. Truth is the proper innate character of number.[88]

These words were engraved in medieval minds, and supplementing them was the dictum of Plotinus:

Number exists before objects which are described by number. The variety of sense-objects merely recalls to the soul the notion of number.[89]

Although astrology and Pythagoreanism followed divergent modes of procedure, there was actually little quarrel between them. The Pythagoreans were quite willing to accept 4 as the basic number of the cosmos or 7 as the universal prototype. Consequently, although each of these two theories had developed in the main independently, their eventual reunion was marked by every sign of concord and amity.

The result of the juncture of astrology and Pythagoreanism is graphically detailed in the writings of Philo Judaeus. Living in the first century A.D., Philo was thoroughly versed in the current doctrines of Platonism; so much so, in fact, that the saying is said to have arisen that "either Plato Philonizes or Philo Platonizes." [90] A review of his extant writings reveals him to have been, like the majority of the Neo-Platonists, keenly alive to the philosophic implications of Pythagoreanism. His comprehension of the sanctity of number is clearly shown in his treatise *On the Posterity of Cain*, where he states: "for that which is not accounted worthy of being comprehended under number is profane, not sacred; but that which is according to number is approved, as having already been tested." [91]

At the same time, Philo was a devout Jew whose energies were devoted to scriptural exegesis and whose resultant com-

88. Stobaeus, I, 3, 8.
89. *Enneads*, VI, 6, 4-5.
90. Yonge, in *Works of Philo*, I, 3.
91. *Op. cit.*, 28.

mentaries made so strong an impress upon his time that his writings became the accepted model of biblical commentary for the later Christians as well as the Jews. Philo's revolutionary "discovery" of Pythagorean elements in the books of Moses led to the theory that the Greeks had themselves derived their learning from these books in an earlier age. By this ingenious sophistry, Divine Authority, which was already claimed by astrology, was added to Pythagoreanism as well.

Philo bases his speculation on a twofold world, intellectual and physical; the latter patterned upon the former and revealing to the senses the physical counterpart of invisible ideas. Between the incomprehensible Deity and the material world, he posits the intermediary Logos of the Gnostics who formed the gross, chaotic matter of earth into patterns which represent in material form the intangible Divine Idea. Allegory is the method by which Essence may be derived from Appearance.

Every line of Scripture is therefore scrutinized by the analytical eye of Philo, with gratifying results. An excellent example of his method, as well as his philosophical approach, may be seen in his commentary on the creation:

When, therefore, Moses says, "God completed his works on the sixth day," we must understand that he is speaking not of a number of days, but that he takes six as a perfect number. Since it is the first number which is equal in its parts, in the half, and the third, and sixth parts, and since it is produced by the multiplication of two unequal factors, two and three. And the numbers two and three exceed the incorporeality which exists in the unity because the number two is an image of matter, being divided into two parts and dissected like matter. And the number three is an image of a solid body, because a solid can be divided according to a threefold division. Not but what it is also akin to the motions of organic animals. For an organic body is naturally capable of motion in six directions, forward, backwards, upwards, downwards, to the right, and to the left. And at all events he desires to show that the races of mortal, and also of immortal beings, exist according to their appropriate numbers; measuring mortal beings, as I have said, by the number six, and the blessed and immortal beings by the number seven. First, therefore, having desisted from the creation of mortal creatures on the seventh day, he began the formation of other and more divine beings.[92]

As God sanctified the heptad in the "Sabbath," so he added to its glory by making his seventh creation that of light, incorporeal and, like 7, perceptible only to the intellect.[93] Pages are devoted to this sacred integer. Its prominence in the Old Testament, as well as in the macrocosm and microcosm, is explained by its archetypal position as "Lord of the Universe," the image of God, "being one, eternal, lasting, immovable, himself like to himself, and different from all other beings."[94] Not content with detailing its geometric, astrological, and harmonic properties, Philo adds what is apparently his own discovery, that the virgin number is related to the sacred tetraktys. This is evidenced in the 4 lunar phases, each of 7 days duration.[95] It is further noted with a mingling of wonder and satisfaction that the seventh power of any number is both a square and a cube.[96]

Always the number itself, rather than its concrete representation, is considered the ultimate reality. Accordingly, the fact that the stars were created on the fourth day leads to an extended peroration on the beauties of 4, the potential decad, which is the source of both matter and time.[97] That number was the basis of the design of the Creator is also observed in his creation of the first of mortal creatures on the fifth day, "thinking that there was no one thing so akin to another as

92. *On the Allegories of the Sacred Law*, 2.

93. *Creation*, 7.

94. *Ibid.*, 23.

95. *Ibid.*, 34.

96. *Ibid.*, 30. This is necessarily so, since the Pythagorean view of unity as the first power of any number makes the seventh Pythagorean power of a number actually the sixth, which may, of course, always be expressed as a square and a cube.

97. *Ibid.*, 15-19.

the number 5 was to animals." [98] The 5 senses provided the basis of this affinity.

No scriptural number is too large or too recalcitrant to be resolved by Philo into first principles. The explanation of the 365 years of Enoch taxes his powers severely, but a long series of intricate maneuvers eventually reduces even this number to its archetypal form.[99] The effort expended in this and similar tortuous computations is eloquent testimony to the high seriousness of the numerical expositor, as well as to the strength of number veneration at the dawn of the Christian Era.

98. *Ibid.*, 20.
99. *Questions and Solutions*, 82-83.

IV. THE GNOSTICS

WE HAVE seen in the preceding chapters the fascination which number exerted over the philosophical and the scientific minds of the ancient world. It is of particular significance to observe that the centuries at the beginning of the Christian Era (first century B.C. to fifth century A.D.) were especially dominated by that exaggerated kind of number mysticism which informs the pages of Philo, Plutarch, and the Neoplatonists.

The sacrosanct character with which number became invested during these centuries appears to have been the result of a gradual but powerful influx of Eastern "mysteries" into the Roman Empire.[1] The spiritual emptiness of official Roman paganism (empty partly because of its official character) provided a void which made the extreme mysticism of the Orient doubly attractive. In close succession, one new deity after another was introduced into the Roman Pantheon, waxing and waning in popularity, until all were submerged by the superior power first of the Egyptian Isis and Osiris, then by Mithraicism from Persia, and at long last by Christianity.[2]

Imbedded in all of these creeds was the ancient union of science and religion, a connection novel to the western mind but the inevitable result of the astral character of Egyptian, Persian, and Babylonian religions. In the East the formation of the calendar was a priestly prerogative, prognostication was a priestly duty, and the records of centuries of astronomical discoveries and hypotheses were zealously guarded in the temples. This meant that many of the astrological numbers were reintroduced to the West not as subjects for philosoph-

---

1. Cumont, *Oriental Religions in Roman Paganism*.
2. Mithraicism, introduced into Rome about 70 B.C., was the most formidable rival of Christianity. Dill, *Roman Society in the Last Century of the Western Empire*, p. 78.

ical inquiry, but as Divine Revelation, and were accordingly invested with all the mystery and power of Holy Secrets.

A further eastern innovation, which affected religious thought, was the removal of Godhead far from the sphere of mundane affairs. The creation of the universe, instead of being attributed directly to Godhead, was assigned to a Demiurge who was himself created as a result of a series of emanations. If the series is traced back to its source, the emanations are found to become successively more abstract in character until the incomprehensible, uncreated First Cause is finally reached. No anthropomorphic Jahveh or Jove consorts with earthly creations, nor do the gods and goddesses procreate as a result of carnal relations with one another. Instead, a definite dualism of matter and spirit is posited, and the chasm is bridged only by abstract qualities which emanate mystically from the First Cause. These, by producing in turn successive emanations, eventually succeed in bringing form and order to the chaos, and spiritual animation to the lifelessness of matter.

While the mass of proselytes was probably attracted by the picturesque qualities of eastern legends and the ecstasies in the performance of the mysteries, many of the learned, already steeped in Hellenic philosophy, felt the attraction of eastern astrology and the subtlety and abstraction of a theology essentially Platonic in character. By such men was Gnosticism created, and the original Gnostics may be broadly described as philosophers, living principally in Alexandria, who attempted to combine Greek philosophy with eastern science and religion. In this combination, Pythagoreanism plays a dominant part. The doctrine of emanations is entirely germane to the generation of the decimal system by the monad. Astrology had already been recognized by Pythagoreanism in the 4 elements, 7 planets, and 10 spheres. Thus from a mixing bowl into which all varieties of revelation, science, and philosophy were poured, emerged a host of variant sects which preserved certain commonly derived essentials and which were alike in apparently subordinating morality and devotion to the "gnosis" of highly intricate and occult philosophical systems.

Before proceeding to a discussion of the different varieties of Gnosticism which contributed to the formulation of medieval number symbolism, it would be well to admit that in most cases we are skating on rather thin ice. Survivals of Gnostic literature are few and far between, and there is no certainty that even those that remain are not vulgar popularizations or heretical offshoots. The principal fund of information is contained, ironically enough, in the Church Fathers, who were zealous in combating these heresies. But although we cannot entirely trust the soundness of their knowledge nor the impartiality of their presentation, we cannot fail to sense in them a sufficient interest in philosophical speculation to have forced them to take a certain pride in their abilities to fathom the subtleties of Gnostic theology. Finally, the basic implications of all Gnostic creeds were so widespread that no learned man could have escaped some knowledge of the distinctive philosophical tendencies of his age.

So attractive, in fact, was the doctrine of emanations that even the Greek pantheon was divided into a series of successive triadic groups representing the several stages from the Uncomprehended and Incomprehensible to the less remote Creators of the cosmos. As a result of the infusion of Neo-Pythagorean elements, 3 and 4 became the basic numerical symbols of the theology. As in Pythagoreanism, all proceeded from the One, but the sensible world was produced from the triadic harmony of Being, Life, and Intellect in association with the 4 creative elements or the 4 elementary kingdoms.[3] The sanctity of the 3 received new emphasis from the triadic groupings of Egyptian and Babylonian gods.

3. Mead, *Orpheus*, p. 167.

Further generation was produced by addition and multiplication of the triad and quaternary to form a series of hebdomads and duodecads. By these computations, the Pythagorean 3 and 4 are directly generative of the astrological 7 and
12. In general, the hebdomads, related to the planets, apply
to the established order of worlds and gods. The duodecads,
imaging the zodiac, are less common and, oddly, appear to
hold a more exalted position. The particularly sacred number
of Orphism is composed of 7 septenaries. We might hazard
the guess that knowledge of 7 orders (groups of 7, such as the
7 planets, vowels, parts of the human body) of the macrocosm and the microcosm distinguished the initiate who possessed the gnosis of the 49 "Fires" of the Secret Doctrine.[4]

The introduction of this same religio-philosophical ferment
into Egypt resulted in the long venerated Hermetic writings.
The mythical author, Hermes Trismegistus, is generally identified with the god Thoth, whose name was used to give
authority to the profundities of a group of Alexandrian
scholars.[5] The traditional "42 books" were reputed to have
contained all knowledge concerning religion, astrology, cosmography, geography, law, medicine, and other minor subjects.[6] There is no very good reason to suppose that these 42
books, or indeed any given number of works, ever existed,
since 42 is a traditional Egyptian number. The surviving
records, such as the *Poimandres* which is not in the list, concern themselves with a combination of theology and astrology.
Much of the religious doctrine found its way into other
gnostic sects, while the astrology accounts for the superstitious veneration paid to the thrice-greatest Hermes by centuries of alchemists and other workers in magic.

Although no consistent "system" may be deduced from

4. A brave attempt to reconstruct Orphic theology has been made by Mead,
in his *Orpheus*.

5. Scott, *Hermetica*, I, 4-5.

6. Mead, *Thrice Greatest Hermes*, III, 222-25.

the existing fragments and commentaries, it is possible to
discern bits of typically Gnostic terminology, together with
a generous use of astrology and number symbolism. Naturally
the traditional Egyptian Triad and Ennead are retained and
expanded,[7] but the historic aspects of Egyptian religion were
submerged in a mass of astrological doctrine.

The material or mechanical ordering of the universe is
understood to be organized by the working of the zodiac.
The 12 signs are forces of evil. They are designated, accordingly, as the 12 "torments of matter" or the 12 "tormentors."[8] The contrary spiritual force which works in all
human events proceeds from the 36 Decans or "Horoscopi."[9]
The Decans rule over the 7 planets or 7 Administrators, in
whose control are the workings of fate.[10] The planets are
assigned to 7 gods severally controlling tears, birth, reason,
courage, sleep, desire, and laughter.[11] By extension, 7 spiritual
and 7 cosmic worlds are named.[12] The year of twelve 30-day
months plus 5 intercalary days, or the 365 "zones," is assigned
to Abraxas or Abrasax, whose mysterious name is composed of
7 letter or elements, and gives a numerical value of 365.[13] The
5 intercalary days are related to the heavenly scheme by
separating the sun and moon from the 5 other planets.[14] The
Poimandres further emphasizes the number by giving a 5-fold
scheme of emanations from *God* to *Aeon* to *Cosmos* to *Time*
to *Becoming*.[15]

In Hermetic theology as in the Old Testament, consid-

7. Mead, *ibid.*, I, 94, 146-47, 152, 164-65; *Poimandres*, I, 3.
8. *Poimandres*, XIII, 7.
9. *Perfect Sermon*, XIX, 3.
10. Stob., VI, 9; *Poimandres*, I, 9, 17-18. These are the 7 Hathors of
Egyptian religion.
11. Mead, *Thrice Greatest Hermes*, III, 91-92.
12. *Poimandres*, XI, 7.
13. Mead, *op. cit.*, I, 402.
14. *Ibid.*, III, 46.
15. *Poimandres*, XI, 2.

erable importance is attached to the number 8. This Ogdoad is derived by the breaking down of the Ennead into one Chief God, Thoth, and 8 minor attendant or warder gods.[16] In the heavens Thoth is identified with the sun, and the necessary concomitant of 8 other spheres is made up by adding to the remaining six planets the sphere of the fixed stars and an earthly sphere.[17] The influence of Pythagoreanism is seen not only in the separation of the one from the many, but in various extensions of the idea. An inscription of the twenty-second Dynasty reads, "I am 1 who becomes 2, I am 2 who becomes 4, I am 4 who becomes 8, I am the 1 after that."[18] This same inscription gives the method of the generation of the Ogdoad, 4 pairs of powers, each syzygy representing male and female, positive and negative, active and passive principles.[19] A substantiation of this derivation may be found in Plutarch's *Of Isis and Osiris*,[20] where the tetraktys is given not as 4 or 10 but as 36, called Cosmos, and generated by adding the first 4 even and first 4 odd numbers. By what a perfect coincidence of Pythagoreanism, astrology, and religion, then, are the Decans made the Spiritual Rulers over even the 7 Fates! Three decans are assigned to each month. Here is the Egyptian triad. Their very name is an image of the perfect decad. Finally, the 36 Decans of the year are precisely drawn from the Pythagorean quaternary and incidentally proceed from the addition of the members of the Ogdoad $(1 + 2 + 3 + 4 + 5 + 6 + 7 + 8 = 36)$.

A common practice of Gnosticism is seen in this constant effort to relate science and religion and to discover affinities between the spiritual and material worlds. A resemblance is proved merely by the identity of number, a practice which

16. Mead, *op. cit.*, I, 57, 121.
17. *Definitions of Asclepius*, 17.
18. Mead, *op. cit.*, I, 120.
19. *Ibid.*, I, 57.
20. *Op. cit.*, LXXV, 12-15.

hints again at number as a first principal. The Ogdoad is therefore found to be duplicated in the 8 parts of the human body.[21] In astrology the eighth sphere is that of the fixed stars.[22] Theologically it is identified with Asclepius, the brother of the 7 Administrators.[23] Spiritually it is the goal of the initiate who has passed through the 7 successive heavens.[24] Thus in Egypt, as in Judea, 8 becomes a symbol of Blessedness.[25]

A further Pythagorean aspect of Hermetic philosophy is revealed in the dominating importance of the decad. It was not coincidence that made the Decans, the Councillor Gods of Babylonia, the highest controllers of the heavens. In a very interesting passage of the *Poimandres*, Tat explains to Hermes that these 10 powers of God drive out the 12 tormentors, because of the superiority of the decad to the number 12.[26]

The origin of Christian Gnosticism is universally ascribed by the early Fathers to Simon Magus, who had asserted himself to be "a great Power of God." [27] To him, Hippolytus ascribes a comparatively simple system of emanations. Fire, possessed of 2 natures, secret and manifest, is stated as the First Cause, whence proceed 3 creative pairs which complete the mystic Hebdomad by which the world is generated.[28] In this simplified version are to be recognized the essential traits of most of the Gnostic "heresies." Here are the 2 levels, secret and manifest, spiritual and material. Here is the essential scheme of creative pairs. Here also is a recognition of the divine triad, which, in one form or another, is venerated by

21. *The Perfect Sermon*, XI, 3.
22. *Definitions*, 17.
23. Mead, *op. cit.*, I, 127.
24. Mead, *op. cit.*, II, 42; *Poimandres*, I, 24-26.
25. See above, p. 25.
26. *Op. cit.*, XIII, 12.
27. Acts 8: 5, 9, 10.
28. Hippolytus, *Refutation of All Heresies*, VI, 9.

the Naaseni,[29] the Sethians,[30] the Justinians,[31] the Docetae,[32] and the Marcions.[33] In many of these doctrines the triad is a trinity. Hippolytus, writing of the Naaseni (Assyrian Gnostics), indicates this sect as a possible source, "for the Assyrians first advanced the opinion that the soul has 3 parts, and yet [is essentially] one." [34]

The above listing gives something of an idea of the diversifications of Christian Gnosticism. A reading of Hippolytus leaves one with the impression that there were as many different theologies as there were Gnostics. The doctrines are often all but indistinguishable, and the Fathers themselves betray some confusion in their presentations.

The most fully presented variety of Gnosticism is that of Valentinus, to whom is credited the compilation of the principal surviving Gnostic document, the *Pistis-Sophia*.[35] As in Simonism, the Valentinian "heresy" distinguishes between two worlds, a physical universe and a spiritual order known as the Pleroma.[36] Highest in the *Pleroma* is Bythos (Profundity, First Cause) who is coëxistent with *Eunoe* (Idea). From them proceed *Nous* (Intelligence) and *Alethia* (Truth), to complete the first Pythagorean tetrad. The latter pair produce *Logos* (Word) and *Zoe* (Life), who in turn create *Anthropos* (Man) and *Ecclesia* (Church). All of these together form the first begotten Ogdoad, similar to the creative pairs of Hermes. Thereupon *Nous* and *Alethia* offer to the Father a perfect number by the creation of 10 Aeons.

Logos himself also, and *Zoe*, then saw that *Nous* and *Alethia* had celebrated the Father of the universe by a perfect number; and *Logos* himself likewise with *Zoe* wished to magnify their own

29. *Ibid.*, V, 3.
30. *Ibid.*, V, 14.
31. *Ibid.*, V, 21.
32. *Ibid.*, VIII, 1.
33. *Ibid.*, X, 15.
34. *Ibid.*, V, 2.
35. King, *The Gnostics and Their Remains*, p. 21.
36. Greek πλήρωμα, a complete measure, a full number, sum.

father and mother, *Nous* and *Alethia*. Since, however, *Nous* and *Alethia* were begotten and did not possess paternal [and] perfect createdness, *Logos* and *Zoe* do not glorify *Nous* their father with a perfect number, but far from it, with an imperfect one. For *Logos* and *Zoe* offer 12 Aeons unto *Nous* and *Alethia*.[37]

Two of these Aeons are *Pistis*, Faith, and *Sophia*, Wisdom. Thus is completed the triacontad of the Pleroma, tripartite, recognizing the astrological 30 and 12, the Hermetic 8, and the Pythagorean 4 and 10. Various scriptural passages are cited, including the 30 years of Christ's preparation for teaching, as illustrating enigmatically the formation of the Pleroma.

The absence of the heptad from this scheme is quickly supplied by the creation of 7 heavens or angels, the seventh being the abode of the *Demiurge*, whose mother, *Achamoth*, completes the number of the Ogdoad. A further mystery is stated in the symbolic emanation of the letters of the Greek alphabet from the 3 powers. Of these the 9 mute letters were produced from the original duad; the 8 semivowels from *Logos* and *Zoe* midway in the Ogdoad; and the 7 vowels by *Anthropos* and *Ecclesia*. The total is 24, but by the addition of the 3 double letters, δs, χs, πs, which are the images of the images of the 3 powers, the complete 30 is produced.[38]

The *Pistis-Sophia* represents the teachings of Christ to his disciples during the eleven years (sic) after the Resurrection. In mysterious terminology incomprehensible to the uninitiated, Christ promises (he never does) to tell his disciples about the 24 mysteries, the 24 spaces, the 24 laudables, the 3 Powers, the 24 invisibles, the 5 impressions, the 5 trees, the 7 voices, the 7 Amens and the 3 Amens, the 12 powers, the 12 unmanifestables, the 12 unrevealables, the 5 supporters, the 7 virgins of light, the 5 rulers, the 365 workmen, the 12 Saviours. Numbers are the principal clue to the identity of these cryptic inhabitants of the Pleroma. It is easy to discern

37. Hippolytus, *Refutation*, VI, 25.
38. Irenaeus, *Against Heresies*, I, 1-14.

in the 24 invisibles, laudables, etc., the alphabet; and in the 12 powers and the 3 powers, references to the formal scheme of the Pleroma, or the Zodiac. The 7 voices are the 7 vowels. The "7 virgins of Light" is descriptive of the sun, moon, and 5 planets, or rulers who govern the 365 workmen. Pliny mentions 5 divine trees [39] consecrated to Roman deities, and it is probable that the impressions, supporters, and so forth are derived or invented embellishments of the central scheme, since it was a part of the Gnostic theory to find the image of the Divine Order reproduced in all phases of the material world, this being the legacy of astrology.

The most powerful and longest-lived of the Gnostic heresies arose in the third century. Named after its founder, Mani, Manicheanism arose as a schism in Zoroastrianism, with which was mingled the usual Babylonian astrology. Astrology, however, was especially virulent in Manicheanism by virtue of its origin and from the fact that Babylon continued to be the chief headquarters of the sect, to which it returned after successive persecutions.[40] As it is referred to by the Church Fathers, it appears to have contained phraseology and ideas borrowed from or common to other branches of Gnosticism, and thus to have kept alive the elements of otherwise defunct Gnostic creeds.

The essential departure of Manicheanism from other varieties of Gnosticism is in the prominence of the Zoroastrian duality, which is preserved in the 2 uncreated and opposing deities known as "the Ruler of Light" and "the Ruler of Darkness." In the successive emanations and creations of these rulers is the usual blend of Pythagorean and astrological numbers, with, however, particular emphasis on the eastern holy number 5.[41] This is not surprising, if, as Archelaus

---

39. *Naturalis historia*, XII, 2.
40. Newman, *Introductory Essay on the Manichean Heresy*.
41. Jackson, *Researches in Manichaeism*; Archelaus, *Disputations*, VI; Augustine, *Contra epistolam Manichaei*.

informs us, one of the three disciples, Hermeias by name, "directed his course towards Egypt." [42]

The Jewish acceptance of Gnosticism, prefigured in Philo and the apocalypses, resulted in the speculations of the cabala. The two great documents, the *Sefer Yezireh* (*Book of Creation*) and the *Zohar* (*Splendour*), were compiled in the ninth and thirteenth centuries respectively,[43] but they represent centuries of growth and elaboration. The doctrine is in most respects germane to that of the other Gnostics, so that its commentators agree in pushing its origin back to the opening of the Christian Era and some, like Maeterlinck, believe it to antedate both Gnosticism and Neoplatonism.

In its present form it is the most completely formulated of all of these related philosophies. The "Aeons" of Christian gnosis become the "Sephiroth," which may be translated as "numerical emanations." Ten in number, they represent the most abstract forms of the Pythagorean decad.[44] The first Sephira, the monad, is the First Source of the other nine. It is indivisible and incapable of multiplication, but it may *reflect* itself to produce a duad (Jahveh) representing itself and its reflection.[45] The third Sephira (Elohim), coequal with the second, is called the Mother [46] and completes the great primal trinity which is the origin of all things.

By the union of Jahveh and Elohim, 6 more Sephiroth are successively emanated to compose what is known as "The Lesser Countenance" or the Microprosopus. These 6 are described in the 6 words of the first verse of Genesis, where the initial word, BRASHITH (*In the beginning*) may be divided into two words, BRA SHITH, "He created the 6." The 9 Sephiroth are considered as being composed of 3 trinities, each of which is an image of the original trinity of

---

42. *Disputation*, VI.
43. Maeterlinck, *Le Grand Secret*, p. 184.
44. Mathers, *The Kabbalah Unveiled*, p. 21.
45. *Ibid.*, pp. 22-23.
46. In the cabala, even numbers are masculine; odd, feminine.

male and female principles combined with a uniting intelligence. The trinity of trinities is, in turn, described as Upper (Intellectual), Middle (Moral), and Lower (Material World); Crown, King, and Queen; whose physical counterparts are the Primum Mobile, Sun, and Moon. Furthermore, each Sephira is identified with a heavenly sphere. The tenth Sephira, Adoni, or "the Kingdom," represents the mystic return of the 9 to unity. In their totality and unity, the 10 Sephiroth are called the Macroprosopus or "Greater Countenance," and prefigure the archetypal man, Adam Cadmon.

The image of the decad runs through the entire cabalistic theology. It is repeated in the 10 divine names, the 10 archangels, the 10 orders of angels, the 10 divisions of the material world, 10 orders of demons, and 10 archdevils. For no numerical distinction is made between angels and devils, and the divine trinity is matched by an infernal trinity composed of Samael (Satan), the Harlot, and the Beast. It is a dominant cabalistic idea, directly Pythagorean in origin, that unity expands to trinity, which is always completed by the quaternary, which ideally returns to the decad or unity again. Study of the first Sephira, the Ancient One, leads to a discovery of the Pythagorean 7, or Harmony in the 7 conformations of the cranium, and a new representation of Unity in the 13 divisions of the Beard, since the numerical value of *Achad*, unity, is 13; and 13 weeks equal one season. The 13 conformations of the Holy Beard are variously referred to as 13 fountains, 13 gates of mercy, and so on.[47]

The resemblance of the cabala to Christian Gnosticism is even more pronounced in the concomitant exposition of the 32 marvellous paths of wisdom with which God founded his name. These 32 paths are the decad and the 22 letters of the Hebrew alphabet. The letters are divided into 3 Mothers, 7 Doubles, and 12 Simples, which are everywhere apparent in

47. *Ha Idra Rabba Qadisha*; Mathers, *op. cit.*, pp. 213, 233, 259.

symbolic representation. The Mothers are the 3 elements (water, air, fire), the 3 divisions of the year (hot, cold, temperate), the 3 parts of the human body (head, heart, stomach). The Doubles include the planets, the week, the 7 degrees of existence, the 7 tabernacles of hell, the 7 attributes of Divinity, the 7 gates of the human body. The Simples are duplicated in the signs of the zodiac, the months, and the 12 principal parts of the body. In all Gnosticism the scheme of the world, Intellectual, Macrocosm, and Microcosm, is considered to be founded on a few simple numbers, which are the same no matter what the philosophy.

One result, or rather concomitant, of Gnosticism in all its branches was the development of the science known as gematria, which consisted in assigning numerical values to the letters of the alphabet and thereby deriving from names, words, and whole passages of Scripture new meanings and relationships. Casper Lewis, in the *Jewish Encyclopaedia*, has dated the first actual appearance of the word, *gematria*, at about 200 A.D.,[48] but the use of the system is undoubtedly much older. Farbridge has, in fact, unearthed a single instance of Babylonian gematria in Sargon's directions for building the wall of Khorsabad, which wall was to be made equivalent to the value of Sargon's name.[49]

The discovery of gematria was all but inevitable among the Jews, since the letters of the Hebrew alphabet were used as numerals, so that any given word actually was a number. The numerical system was built up by using the first 10 letters as units, the second 10 as tens, and the remainder plus variant forms of the letters from 3 to 9, as hundreds.[50] This became the method of all gematria, applicable as it is to any language. Lewis gives three instances of possible gematria in the Old Testament. The most convincing is the preservation

48. Vol. V, 589.
49. *Studies*, p. 94.
50. *Ibid.*, p. 93.

of the name of only one of Abraham's servants, Eliezer, whose name has the numerical value of 318, the number of the servants.[51] Philo Judaeus shows acquaintance with the science in remarking that Sara's name was changed to *Sarra* because in Greek the letter *rho* equals 100.[52] In the Talmud, also, a "ripe age" is defined as 60, since that is the numerical value for the Hebrew word.[53]

The Gnostics appear to have employed gematria constantly in scriptural exegesis. Tertullian charges Marcus with the statement that Christ, in calling himself the Alpha and Omega, authorized the search for numerical values.[54] Incidentally this statement of Christ's is the explanation of the cryptic remark in the *Pistis-Sophia* that the twenty-fourth mystery (letter) is also the first mystery. Christ is known among the Gnostics as 801 from the "dove," [55] or as 888 from "Jesus." [56] "These men," remonstrates Tertullian, "run through the whole alphabet . . . and compute ogdoads and decads." [56] A further ramification of the theory was in use among the Ophites and Sethites, whereby all names whose sum was below 100 belonged to the left hand (material, destructible), while to the right hand (spiritual, eternal) were assigned all names adding up to 100 or over.[57] By another rule, simple numbers or units were understood to signify divine things; numbers of 10, celestial things; numbers of a hundred, terrestrial things; and thousands, the future.[58]

By the use of gematria, the cabala establishes many hidden relationships, such as the proximity of the word *Amen* to

51. Gen. 14: 14; *Jewish Encyclopaedia*, V, 589.
52. *Questions and Solutions*, III, 54.
53. Tract *Ebel Rabboth*, 9, in *The Babylonian Talmud*, VIII.
54. *Against Heresies*, III.
55. Hippolytus, *Refutation of All Heresies*, VI, 45.
56. Tertullian, *Against Heresies*, III.
57. Irenaeus, *Against Heresies*, II, 24.
58. Mathers, *op. cit.*, p. 48.

God, since both *Amen* and *Jahveh Adonai* equal 91.[59] The meanings of certain numbers were also established. The number 13 is contained in *Achad*, or unity. It is also contained in *Ahebah*, love. Therefore 13 signifies love of unity.[60] The principal employment of gematria, however, is in scriptural exegesis. A simple example is the interpretation of Genesis 14: 10, "Shiloh shall come." The Hebrew letters of the phrase sum up to 358. But the word *Messiah* is also equal to 358. Therefore the verse is to be interpreted as a prophecy.[61]

It should be obvious from the foregoing that gematria is not an exact science. By choice of alphabet, word, and system, it is possible to derive nearly any desired meaning from any given word or passage. Interpretation depends entirely on the fancy and ingenuity of the practitioner. It should be equally obvious that no deliberately symbolic numerical value can be interpreted with any degree of accuracy, unless a hint is given of the alphabet employed and the intent of the author. Even then, various equally feasible solutions may be found, because any large number may be split up into several meaningful combinations of the alphabet.

The number of the beast in Revelations has exercised the ingenuity of countless commentators, without any possibility of final solution. The favorite medieval interpretations were TEITAN, from Greek gematria, and DICLUX, from rearrangement of the Latin numerical symbols.[62] The number is especially curious, inasmuch as it is produced by setting down in order the Latin numerical symbols beginning with 500: DCLXVI. It is therefore remotely possible that no exact name is implied, but that the author is repeating in a graphic manner the statement in Mark 5: 8-9 and Luke 8: 30 that his name is *Legion*. The only thoroughly sensible disposal of the subject is still that of Irenaeus: "It is therefore more certain

59. Mathers, *op. cit.*, p. 89.
60. Mathers, *op. cit.*, p. 166.
61. Mathers, *op. cit.*, p. 7.
62. Sanders, "The Number of the Beast in Revelations."

and less hazardous to await the fulfillment of the prophecy than to be making surmises, and casting about for any names that may present themselves, inasmuch as many names can be found possessing the number mentioned; and the same question will after all remain unsolved." [63]

The same remark might be made with equal pertinence concerning the prophetic *"un cinquecento diece e cinque"* of the *Divine Comedy*.[64] Since Dante's most certain models were the solutions proposed for the number of the beast, it should be ideally possible to find both a Latin and a Greek name or word, summing up to 515. In actual practice, however, the creation of an enigma which would be soluble by two different systems would present all but insuperable difficulties. The Latin DVX is certainly implied by analogy to DICLUX. Whether or not there is a Greek solution is impossible to say. I must confess that I have wasted much valuable paper in "casting about for any names that may present themselves."

The proposal of Dr. Moore,[65] who derives Arrico (Arrigo, Henry VII) by using the Hebrew alphabet, depends, apart from its confessed internal weaknesses, on the supposition that Dante would complicate an already sufficiently complex problem by using a system of gematria which was virtually unknown to his contemporaries. If two interpretations are indeed intended by Dante, one of them is almost certain to be forced. Dr. Moore weakens his own case immeasurably by considering the DVX as a secondary and unimportant meaning. If the 515 were not important for the sake of the Latin, no reasonable motive is left for resorting to an unknown and dubious system in preference to the accepted procedure. Any gematria is uncertain enough! The fact that no even reasonably simple solution offers itself in Greek or Hebrew makes the DVX interpretation all but mandatory. For the rest, we must either accept DVX as the entire meaning, or be willing

63. *Against Heresies*, V, 30.
64. *Purg.*, XXXIII, 43.
65. "The DXV Prophecy," *Studies*, 3d ser., pp. 253-83.

to allow an indirect or forced secondary meaning, to which no final certainty can be attached.

The use of Latin letters ("Roman numerals") to indicate dates has actually nothing in common with gematria; yet Ariosto was undoubtedly influenced by Dante's cryptic prophecy, when, in the thirty-fifth canto of *Orlando Furioso*, he sought to infuse into his own prediction the atmosphere of oracular mystery by the pronouncement that:

> Che venti anni principio prima avrebbe
> Che coll'M e col D fosse notato
> L'anno corrente dal Verbo incarnato.[66]

> This . . .
> Shall have existence twenty years before,
> Dating from The Incarnate Word, the year
> Shall marked by men with M and D appear.

John Skelton used and probably invented an English code gematria by numbering the vowels from 1 to 5 and then giving the consonants their correct numerical positions in the alphabet. By this system, A = 1, B and E are both 2; C = 3; D = 4; F = 6; and so on. (I and J count as the same letter, which is numbered 3.) In *The Garland of Laurel*, therefore, the numbers

> "17.4.7.2.17.5.18
> 18.19.17.1.19.8.5.12"

spell the name of ROGERUS STRATHAM.[67] The still un-interpreted "verse or twain," which Pensitate writes in *Ware the Hawk*, contains in its unfathomable midst a numerical puzzle which even the application of this code fails to solve completely:

> "18.10.2.11.19.4.13.3.3.1 ten valet"
> S K E L T O N I I A K
> J J
> C C

66. Stanza 4; Rose trans.; cf. Dante, *Par.*, XIX, 127-29.
67. The solution of this code was the work of Mr. Richard Hughes; cf. his edition of *Poems* by John Skelton (Heinemann, 1924).

Allowing for errors in copying a meaningless string of figures, one might reasonably guess the intention to have been *Iak Skelton*. The *valet* may be part of the entire sentence of which this is the conclusion.[68]

Closely allied to gematria is an equally revered Gnostic secret, the mystery of the Ineffable Name. If the belief in the importance of number seems to derive from Babylon, the origin of the devotion paid to the name may, with much greater certainty, be traced to Egypt. In a comprehensive study of Egyptian religion and folklore, E. A. Wallis Budge remarks, "To the Egyptian the name was as much a part of a man's being as his soul, or his double, or his body, and it is quite certain that this view was held by him in the earliest time."[69] The names of the gods were held in secrecy and were considered to be of awful potency. One papyrus reads, "He is the king of men and of gods . . . his names are manifold and unknown, the gods even know them not."[70]

It is not to be wondered at that the Hermetics should have included the tradition among their mysteries, and the Gnostic Logos was often used in the same sense.[71] As among the Egyptians, the Name of God was never to be uttered. In the manuscripts it is indicated by blank spaces, crosses, or the term *Tetragrammaton*.

The composition of the Name is variously given. According to Valentinus, it is made up of 22, 42, or 72 letters or

68. Skelton is, even numerically, a puzzling author. In his prayer *To the Second Person* he uses the refrain, "Defend me with they piteous woundes five," which is conventional enough. But I can make nothing of the fourth stanza of *Now Sing We, as We Were Wont*:

> "Man, thou shalt now understand,
> Of my head, both foot and hand,
> Are four c. and five thousand
>   Woundes and sixty;
> Fifty and vii.
> Were told full even
>   Upon my body."

69. *Egyptian Magic*, p. 157; cf. Cumont, *Oriental Religions*, pp. 29-30.
70. *Papyrus of Ani*, Budge, *op. cit.*, pp. 137-41.
71. Mead, *Thrice Greatest Hermes*, I, 165.

parts or words.[72] The *Revelation* of Marcus defines it as containing 30 letters and 4 syllables.[73] Archelaos, on Manes, also speaks of the Names which only the 7 elect know.[74] The Ineffable Name of the cabala is likewise composed of 4, 22, 42, or 72 letters: "He who can rightly pronounce it causeth heaven and earth to tremble, for it is the name which maketh the universe." [75]

In this résumé of Gnosticism we have seen in its fullest development the philosophical conception that there is a strict order in the working of the universe, that this order is expressible in terms of number, which is a sort of abstract prototype of reality, and that the Divine plan mirrored in the heavens is repeated *ad infinitum* in the spiritual, sensible, and material worlds. Number, as in Pythagoreanism, is not so much a symbol as an essence. It is, therefore, of the gravest importance.

Succeeding centuries continued to be ruled by this philosophy, while the Gnostics themselves, though frowned upon and suppressed wherever possible by the True Church, continued to hoard and transmit their mysteries. Manicheanism, the strongest of the sects, seems never to have been thoroughly suppressed, and the powerful medieval organization of catharism drew much from Manichean theology. Gnostic formulae, meanwhile, persisted in magic, astrology, alchemy — in all of those realms where cosmic secrets were at a premium. Concurrently, the crusaders in one direction and the adventurous scholars who flocked to the school of Toledo in the other were coming directly into contact with cabalistic doctrines.[76]

72. Gaster, *Studies and Texts*, I, 291-93.
73. King, *op. cit.*, p. 286.
74. *Acts of the Disputation*, AN XX, 289.
75. Mathers, *op. cit.*, p. 30.
76. Lea, *A History of the Inquisition of the Middle Ages*, *passim*, Gebhart, *Mystics and Heretics in Italy, passim.*

V. THE EARLY CHRISTIAN WRITERS

THE fact that the number symbolism of the European Middle Ages never reached the extravagant complexity of Gnosticism is attributable directly to the marked simplicity of the original Christian Faith. Whether "Gnostics" or "Christians" were earlier in point of time is still an open question, but it is certain that first-century Christianity was unique among the welter of contemporary religious and philosophical creeds. For in the midst of emanations, aeons, and learned though cryptic disquisitions on cosmology and eschatology was born a faith rather than a "gnosis," adoring a personality rather than a principle, and as wholly isolated as possible from the speculative habit of the time.

To be sure, later New Testament exegeticists were able to discover numerical secrets everywhere in the life and preachings of Jesus, but it is obvious to the most casual reader that such scholarly interpretation is utterly at variance with the spirit of naïveté and directness which distinguishes the scriptural accounts. The Pauline epistles, earliest and most certainly authentic of the original records, are completely innocent of number theory. The synoptical Gospels, together with the more disputable account of John and the Acts, all first-century compositions, do contain numbers, but these are "symbolic" numbers only in the most elementary sense.

The number 10, for example, with its Pythagorean connotations, is a very natural expression of totality. It is not necessarily more meaningful than an everyday reference to a "dozen" or a "score" as an approximation of a group. In telling a story, then, it was natural to speak of 10 virgins (Matthew 25), 10 pieces of silver (Luke 15: 8), 10 lepers (Luke 17: 12-17), 10 servants (Luke 19: 12-25). The same common propensity for round numbers accounts for the 100 sheep of Matthew 18: 12 and Luke 15: 4.

Later theologians were to find intimations of the Trinity in the 3 gifts of the magi, in Peter's 3-fold denial, in the 3 days between death and resurrection, in the 3 figures of the transfiguration and crucifixion, the 3 at Gethsemane awakened 3 times, the 3 temptations of Christ, and the 3 appearances of Christ to his disciples after his death. The list is rather extensive, but a sober judgment will not find in these triads any more advanced symbolism than that of the statistical 3, common to story, fable, and legend the world over, adumbrated here perhaps by the connotations of sanctity which had always clung to the number. Never is there any intimation that obscure first principles are hidden within these numbers.

The Christian abandonment of the philosophical tradition, however, made it necessary to substitute the confirmatory background of some equally venerable "truth." Differing therefore from the Gnostics, who in the main repudiated the Old Testament and its God, the early Christians found in the Hebrew writings a foundation on which to build and discovered in the Hebrew prophecies confirmation of the divinity of Jesus by identifying him with the long-awaited Messiah. Exactly how much of the Gospels is fact and how much devout invention is of no great moment in this connection. Perhaps Jesus actually chose 12 disciples. Perhaps the recorded statement, "Ye also shall sit upon 12 thrones, judging the 12 tribes," [1] is pure fiction. In either case the obvious intention is to continue the Hebrew tradition.

So it is with most of the New Testament numbers. Christ's appointment of 70 missionaries, besides the 12,[2] may have been intended to recall to the Hebrew mind that "thy fathers went down into Egypt with threescore and ten persons; and

1. Matt. 19: 28; Luke 21: 30.
2. Luke 10: 1.

now the Lord thy God hath made thee as the stars of heaven for multitude" (Deuteronomy 20: 22). Even the juncture of the 70 with the 12 harked back to Hebraic lore. For when Moses was called to the mountain to receive the law, 70 elders were delegated to "worship afar off," and 12 pillars were built "according to the 12 tribes of Israel" (Exodus 24: 1, 4). These 12 tribes and 70 elders were readily linked to the 12 fountains and 70 palm trees which solaced the Israelites at Elim.[3]

The 40 days of Christ's temptation similarly harks back to the 40 days of Elijah's solitude, or the 40 days of trial by flood. The ancient 7's of evil and repentance live on in the 7 devils of Mary Magdalen,[4] and in the discussions concerning forgiveness of sin (Matthew 18: 22; Luke 17: 4). In all of these instances the choice of numbers is symbolic only in the sense of continuing a known and accepted idiom. The dominant mood of the New Testament is that of writing new chapters in an old book. "That the Scripture might be fulfilled," the biographers of Jesus write always with one eye on their subject and the other on the sacred texts of the Jews. Guiltless of theological or metaphysical subtlety, they weave their accounts with the thread which they have inherited. What other number of apostles than 12 could have been chosen? How possibly more or less than 7 devils? When, if not on the day of Pentecost, should the Holy Spirit have descended?[5]

The nearest approach to deliberate number symbolism occurs in the Gospel of John. It is this gospel which records the triple appearance of Christ after death and the dividing of the garments into 4 parts,[6] which is to be interpreted in the same sense as the gathering of the elect "from the 4 winds" of

3. Num. 33: 9.
4. Mark 16: 9; Luke 8: 2.
5. Acts 2: 1-4.
6. John 19: 23.

Matthew 24: 31. Again it is possible to find a symbolic inference in Christ's question

Are there not 12 hours in the day? If any man walk in the day he stumbleth not, because he seeth the light of this world.[7]

It is possible that, in view of these indications, some specific significance is involved in the 153 fishes which Peter drew from the sea,[8] though what that significance may be is a complete mystery.

But even if the two numerically compiled genealogical tables appended to Matthew and Luke be included in the record of authentic first-century Christian documents, and the apocryphal gospels and legends be added, there is still the plain and inescapable evidence that the path of numerical theology was not the road chosen by early Christianity. Such isolation might have continued, even though beset on every side, if there had not been left certain vulnerable weaknesses in this armor of simplicity.

The fact that numbers appeared at all in the gospels was in itself a fatal weakness in a numerically minded age, and the necessary inclusion in the canon of the Apocalypse of John, on the basis of its supposed authorship, was an open invitation to commentators to ponder on the mysteries of number. More than that, the acceptance of the book of Revelations foretokened the serious consideration of the *Pastor of Hermas*, similarly filled with numerical allegory and with the added attraction of interpretation within the text. This was to become one of the most popular documents of the Christian Church during the second, third, and fourth centuries. At the same time was promulgated the pseudo-Clementine *Recognitions* (before 231 A.D.), which purports to be the story of Clement's career in company with the apostle Peter. The book is weighted with all varieties of astrological, Pytha-

7. John 11: 9.
8. John 21: 11.

gorean, and Gnostic lore, much of which proceeds from the lips of Peter himself. It was not long before the authority of Hermes was being cited as witness to the True Faith.[9] Simultaneously, the Church admitted to its communion men of scholarly and philosophical dispositions who were concerned with the creation of a consistent body of Christian theology. Among them were the great Alexandrian doctor, Clement (d. A.D. 200), and his pupils, Origen and Hippolytus. These men, living in the greatest of philosophical and Gnostic centers, inevitably drew inspiration from the models with which they were in contact. The paramount doctrinal weakness of Christianity, as the Arian heresy testifies, was the duality of the Godhead. The acceptance of Philo's "logos," and its identification with the Son, was the first step toward a solution, but the addition of a third person, the Holy Ghost, provided indisputable evidence of Unity. The presence of divine triads in all the Gnostic creeds was certainly a determining factor in the creation of the Trinity, but the underlying Pythagorean basis of contemporary philosophy necessitated the doctrine. That the Father and Son were One was questionable on numerical as well as philosophical grounds. But Father, Son, and Holy Spirit were unquestionably One by very virtue of being Three!

Many of the early writers, including Paul, seem never to have heard of the doctrine. For this reason the two New Testament references, one to a triad (Matthew 28: 19) and the other precisely to Trinity (I John 5: 7) are, especially the latter, suspect as interpolations. References to the Trinity do not become common or definitive until the third century and the doctrine was not to receive its final and official formulation until the Council of Constantinople (A.D. 381).[10] The acceptance of this fundamental tenet of Pythagoreanism was in itself a sufficient sponsor for the whole philosophy. The

9. Cyprian (A.D. 200-248), On the Vanity of Idols, 6.
10. Reinach, Orpheus, p. 260.

doctrine of Purgatory, stated by Clement[11] and Origen,[12] created, by addition to Heaven and Hell, another triplicity in the spiritual world.

Meanwhile, philosophical interest in number, in a more than general way, was becoming increasingly common. Irenaeus, in his refutation of the Gnostics, argues that their theology is fallacious not because it is based on number, but because the numerical scheme is incorrect. For do they not completely ignore the number 5, which is everywhere manifest in the True Faith? *Soter* (Saviour) has 5 letters, as has *Pater*. The Lord blessed 5 loaves and fed 5,000. There are 5 extremities of the cross, 5 fingers, 5 senses.[13] In the same way Tertullian defends the number 12, evidencing the numerous duodecads of the Old Testament and asking argumentatively, "What equally good defense of such a number has Marcion's Christ to show?"[14] References to Philo become common, and even Hermes is spoken of with respect. Justin Martyr adds weight to his arguments by citing Pythagoras, who, by stating that "unity is the first principle of all things, and that it is the cause of all good . . ., teaches by an allegory that God is One and alone."[15] Origen is certain that God made the world "according to some definite number, predetermined by himself, for it is not to be imagined . . . that creatures have not a limit."[16] He adds that some passages of Scripture do not contain a "corporeal sense," but are to be interpreted figuratively, illustrating by a numerical passage:

And perhaps on this account the water-vessels containing 2 or 3 firkins apiece are said to be for the purification of the Jews, as we

---

11. *Stromata*, VII, 6.

12. *Against Celsus*, V, 14-15.

13. *Against Heresies*, II, 24, 4.

14. *Against Marcion*, IV, 13; AN VII, 222. That these statements are not intended as a subtle method of discrediting the whole numerical system is evidenced by the serious consideration of numbers in other writings of these same authors.

15. *Hortatory Address to the Greeks*, XIX; AN II, 305.

16. *De principiis*, II, 9; AN X, 127.

read in the Gospel according to John: the expression darkly intimating, with respect to those who [are called] by the apostle "Jews" secretly, that they are purified by the word of the Scripture, receiving sometimes 2 firkins, i.e., so to speak, the "psychical" and "spiritual" sense; and sometimes 3 firkins since they have, in addition to those already mentioned, also the "corporeal" sense, which is capable of [producing] edification. And 6 water-vessels are reasonably [appropriate] to those who are purified in the world, which was made in 6 days.[17]

Following the lead of Philo and finding justification in the apparent meaninglessness of literal interpretation of certain scriptural passages, various of the Church Fathers began to write figurative interpretations of biblical texts. They found precedent for giving importance to numbers in the precise directions given for the dimensions of the tabernacle,[18] and in the testimony of the *Book of Wisdom* that "God has arranged all things in number and measure." [19]

Early interpretation of scriptural numbers is concerned with only the most prominent of them, such as the 12 springs and the 70 palm trees of Elim, the 318 servants of Abraham, and the apocalyptic writings. Something of the attitude of *gnosis*; that is, of scriptural mysteries hidden from the layman, is to be seen in an interpretation of Barnabas:

Learn then, my children, concerning all things richly, that Abraham, the first who enjoined circumcision, looking forward in spirit to Jesus, practised that rite having received the mysteries of the 3 letters. For [the Scripture] saith, "And Abraham circumcised 10, and 8, and 300 men of his household." What, then, was the knowledge given to him in this? Learn the 18 first and then the 300. The 10 and 8 are thus denoted. Ten by I, and 8 by H. You have [the initials of the name of] Jesus. And because the cross was to express the grace [of our redemption] by the letter T, he says also "300." *No one else has been admitted by me to a more excellent piece of knowledge than this, but I know that ye are worthy.*[20]

17. *Ibid.*, IV, 1; AN X, 303-4.
18. Clement, *Stromata*, VI, 11.
19. *Wisdom*, XI, 20; Origen, *De principiis*, II, 9.
20. Epistle IX; AN IV, 117; italics mine.

The interpretation of 318 by gematria becomes traditional and T, or 300, is thereby made the symbol of the cross. According to Ambrose, this was the meaning of Gideon's choice of 300 men [21] and Judas Iscariot's evaluation of the ointment at 300 pence.[22] Hippolytus interprets several of the Psalms in accordance with their numbers, explaining that "the psalms which deal with historical matter are not found in regular historical order, and the only reason for this is to be found in the numbers according to which the psalms are arranged." [23]

Some of the early explanations of scriptural numbers are rather forced, such as the reasoning of Ambrose concerning the 15 cubits of the ark. These, he says, represent the 5 senses triply, as "he *sees* the *sight visibly*"! [24] Nevertheless, there is discernible a growing harmony among the Fathers, as one builds upon another. Particularly prominent numerical associations become definitely established and are carried on unchanged through the Middle Ages, so that it is not unusual to find a statement of Ambrose exactly reproduced by Augustine or by Aquinas. The most enduring of these are drawn from Scripture, Pythagoreanism, and astrology. One result of the apocalypses was to make the astrological implications particularly strong and recognized as such. The Clementine *Recognitions* contains considerable astrological lore, including the oft-quoted "for He is the acceptable year of God, having us apostles as His 12 months." [25] By the same type of reasoning, Victorinus calls the 24 elders of Revelations the 24 angels of the day and night, and distributes the 7 "gifts" of the Holy Spirit among the 7 heavens.[26]

21. *De Spiritu Sancto*, I, Introduction.
22. *Ibid.*, III, 17.
23. *On the Psalms*, 5; AN VI, 501.
24. *De noë*, XV; P. L. 14, 405.
25. *Op. cit.*, IV, 35; AN III, 301.
26. *On Creation*; AN XVIII, 391. Dante may have these hour-angels in mind when he speaks of the hours of the night as winged creatures (*Purg.*, IX, 7-9).

The Hebrew analogy of the creation as a prototype of human history [27] led to renewed inquiries concerning the duration of the world. The repetition in II Peter 3: 8 of the statement in the Ninetieth Psalm (verse 4) that a day is with Him as 1,000 years, reëstablished that interval as the length of an age. Accordingly, Irenaeus [28] and Lactantius [29] agree that the limit of the world shall be 6,000 years.[30] On the other hand, the testimony of astrology points out the 7-fold nature of the world, and the resurrection of Christ on the eighth day, the day of circumcision and the first day of the second week, indicates that the eighth age, endless and timeless, will see the future glory. Such is the conclusion of Clement,[31] Victorinus,[32] and Basil.[33] Neither of these arrangements was entirely satisfactory, since Rest was universally appointed to the Sabbath and Regeneration to the number 8. Both 7 and 8 are therefore symbolic of the Final Glory. It remained for Augustine to resolve the dilemma. There was, in his mind, no doubt that the creation of the world in 6 days foretokened 6 earthly ages. The seventh day of rest symbolized the culminating Eternal Rest. But there was no evening of the seventh day! The eighth day, therefore, represents a return to the original life, not taken away, but made eternal.[34] In other words, the seventh and eighth ages are both spiritual and timeless, but both are used to indicate the com-

27. I am told that the orthodox Jew still anticipates the end of the world in his year 7000, which would be the Gregorian year 3239.

28. *Against Heresies*, V, 28, 2-3.

29. *Divine Institutes*, VII, 14.

30. Without in any way altering the established convention of the 6 ages, it was held by some that an extra or "bonus" day of 1,000 years had been granted though the dispensation of Christ, thereby fulfilling the promise implicit in the Old Testament when Joshua (= Jesus) caused the sun and moon to stand still for the space of a whole day (Josh. 10: 13; Rabanus Maurus, P. L. 108, 1045; Augustine, P. L. 35, 2175-76).

31. *Stromata*, IV, 25.

32. *On the Creation*; AN XVIII, 390.

33. *De Spiritu Sancto*, XXVII, 66.

34. Letter LV, 9, 17.

bined sabbatical and regenerative character of the Last Age. The seventh day is the rest of the saints, spiritually in progress during the sixth earthly age. Both sixth and seventh days will culminate in the Judgment and Eternal Regeneration of the eighth.[35]

It was Augustine who gave the final stamp of approval to number symbolism. A man of towering intellect and broad scholarship, trained in the complexity of Manichean theology, he brought to the study of theology a greater degree of intellectual curiosity and analytical logic than any previous Christian writer. As a philosopher, he saw in number an image of the absolute, for "there is a relation of numbers which cannot possibly be impaired or altered, nor can any nature by any violence prevent the number which comes after one from being the double of one." [36] Again,

Concerning now the Science of number, it is clear to the dullest apprehension that this was not created by man, but was discovered by investigation. . . . It is not in any man's power to determine at his pleasure that 3 x 3 are not 9, or do not make a square or are not the triple of 3. . . . [37]

By investigation, therefore, man may discover the mysteries of God which are set down in Scripture. Consequently Augustine's treatment of the 6 days of creation leads him to an extended peroration on mathematically perfect numbers, explaining that

we must not despise the science of numbers, which, in many passages of Holy Scripture, is found to be of eminent service to the careful interpreter. Neither has it been without reason numbered among God's praises, "thou has ordered all things in number, and measure and weight." [38]

God's use of number is further revealed in Isaiah 11: 26,

35. *Reply to Faustus*, XII, 8.
36. *On the Morals of the Manicheans*, XI, 24; Dods trans., V, 65.
37. *On Christian Doctrine*, II, 38, 56; Dods trans., IX, 73.
38. *Civ. Dei*, XI, 30; Dods trans., I, 475.

"Who bringeth out their hosts by numbers"; and in Matthew 10: 30, "The very hairs of your head are all numbered." God knows *all* numbers "for his understanding is infinite." [39] Since "ignorance of numbers . . . prevents us from understanding things that are set down in Scripture in a figurative and mystical way," [40] even heathen learning is valuable in teaching "the science of reasoning and of numbers." [41] Augustine is willing to accept the prophecies of the Sybil or Hermes or Orpheus or any of the heathen poets, to aid the faith of the heathen.[42] In regard to number, therefore, Hermes is recognized as a master,[43] and it is recalled that Plato himself represented God as framing the world on numerical principles.[44]

Augustine is everywhere fascinated by the properties of number. A revelatory passage concerns his treatment of the seventh day where he remarks, "much more might be said about the perfection of the number 7, but this book is already too long, and I fear lest I should seem to catch at an opportunity of airing my little smattering of science more childishly than profitably." [45] But even this consideration is not strong enough to keep him from explaining that 7 is composed of the first even and first odd number [46] and is accordingly the symbol of all numbers. Therefore 7 means "perfect completeness."

As a matter of fact, Augustine is one of the most comprehensive sources for information concerning Neo-Pythagorean number theory, and he misses few opportunities to discuss the science. In his commentary on John, he overlooks no single numerical reference, not even the hours of the day or the "25 or 30 furlongs" (John 6: 19).

39. Ps. 147, 5; *Civ. Dei*, XII, 8.
40. *On Christian Doctrine*, II, 16, 25; Dods trans., IX, 52.
41. *Ibid.*, II, 39, 58; Dods trans., IX, 74.
42. *Contra Faustum*, XIII, 1.
43. *Civ. Dei*, VIII, 23.
44. *Ibid.*, XII, 8.
45. *Ibid.*, XI, 31; Dods trans., I, 475.
46. Three and 4 are the first real numbers; See above, pp. 41-42.

Could the truth be aught endangered by a mere estimate. . . ? Let us examine the number 25.[47]

He stands firm on the symbolic intent of scriptural numbers, asking why otherwise the ark should have had precisely those dimensions or why they should have been recorded unless "for the devout study of future generations." [48]

The flood legend was to become increasingly important in Christian theology, since it was regarded as a prototype for the salvation of man by Christianity. In the ark and the flood, that is, man is saved by wood (the Cross) and water (Baptism). Augustine devotes much energy to the interpretation of the entire story, the beginning of which is here reproduced as an example of his striking ingenuity, as well as a comprehensive survey of the method of medieval exegesis in regard to number:

14. Omitting therefore many passages in these Books where Christ may be found, but which require longer explanation and proof, *although the most hidden meanings are the sweetest*, convincing testimony may be obtained from the enumeration of such things as the following: — That Enoch, the 7th from Adam, pleased God, and was translated, as there is to be a 7th day of rest into which all will be translated who, during the 6th day of the world's history, are created anew by the incarnate Word. That Noah, with his family, is saved by water and wood, as the family of Christ is saved by baptism, as representing the suffering of the cross. That this ark is made of beams formed in a square, as the Church is constructed of saints prepared unto every good work: for a square stands firm on any side. That the length is 6 times the breadth and 10 times the height, like a human body [prostrate], to show that Christ appeared in a human body. That the breadth reaches to 50 cubits; as the apostle says, "Our heart is enlarged," (II *Cor.*, VI, 2), that is, with spiritual love, of which he says again, "The love of God is shed abroad in our hearts by the Holy Ghost, which is given unto us" (*Rom.* V, 5). For in the 50th day after his resurrection, Christ sent his Spirit to enlarge the hearts of his disciples. That it

---

47. *On John*, XXV; Dods trans., X, 354.
48. *Contra Faustum*, XII, 38; Dods trans., V, 230.

is 300 cubits long, to make up 6 times 50; as there are 6 periods in the history of this world . . . that it is 30 cubits high, a tenth part of the length; because Christ is one height, who in his 30th year gave his sanction to the doctrine of the gospel, by declaring that He came not to destroy the law, but to fulfill it. Now the 10 commandments are known to be the heart of the law; and so the length of the ark is 10 times 30. Noah himself, too, was the 10th from Adam. . . .

15. . . . That clean and unclean animals are in the ark; as good and bad take part in the sacraments of the Church. That the clean are in 7's, and the unclean in 2's; not because the bad are fewer than the good, but because the good preserve the unity of the Spirit in the bond of peace; and the Spirit is spoken of in Scripture as having a 7-fold operation, as being "the Spirit of wisdom and understanding, of counsel and might, of knowledge and piety, and of the fear of God." (*Isa.* XI, 2, 3,). So also the number 50 which is connected with the advent of the Spirit, is made up of 7 times 7, and 1 over; whence it is said, "Endeavoring the keep the unity of the Spirit in the bond of peace" (*Eph.* IV, 3). The bad, again, are in 2's as being easily divided, from their tendency to schism. That Noah, counting his family, was the 8th; because the hope of our resurrection has appeared in Christ, who rose from the dead on the 8th day, that is, on the day after the 7th, or Sabbath day. This day was the 3rd from His passion; but in the ordinary reckoning of days, it is both the 8th and the 1st.

[Section 16 omitted — concerns division of lower spaces into 2 and 3 chambers.]

17. That the flood came 7 days after Noah entered the ark, as we are baptised in the hope of future rest, which was denoted by the 7th day. . . . That it rained for 40 days and 40 nights; as the sacrament of heavenly baptism washes away all the guilt of the sins against the 10 commandments throughout the 4 quarters of the world, whether that guilt has been contracted in the day of prosperity or in the night of adversity.

18. That Noah was 500 years old when God told him to make the ark, and 600 when he entered the ark; which shows that the ark was made during 100 years, which seem to correspond to the years of the age of the world. So the 6th age is occupied with the construction of the Church by the preaching of the gospel. . . . Again it was the 2nd month of the 600th year when Noah entered the ark,

and in 2 months there are 60 days; so that here, as in every multiple of 6, we have the number denoting the 6th age.[49]
[And so on through Section 21.]

In transcribing this passage I have omitted only a few sentences, chiefly repetitious in character. It will be observed that number is the principal clue to the interpretation of the entire story.

Almost equally ingenious is Augustine's interpretation of the 153 fish. The number is broken up into $50 \times 3 + 3$, all sacred numbers. Or, from another viewpoint, Man in the New Life 7 times refined shall receive his reward in the denarius, so that in reward, 10 and 7 meet in him. Now 153 is the triangular figure of 17![50]

All large numbers, as has been seen, are reduced to their roots for explanation. Strictly speaking, adding numbers sums up their significances into a single unit. Multiplying diffuses a property into a given number of directions or objects. Squaring gives extension. Cubing either produces solidity or, more often, gives height or godliness. The addition of one to any composite number unifies the whole, if a recognized limit is thereby reached. By the same token, the failure of a number to reach a recognized limit implies a defect or deficiency. Thirty-eight, for example, fails to reach the limit of 40, whereas 39 succeeds by adding unity. Therefore the man whom Christ healed was said to be 38 years *in infirmity*.[51]

If the early Christian writers borrowed copiously from the number philosophy of the past, they also added new meanings to the received number symbols and, dropping many of the pagan connotations, surrounded the whole science with a specifically Christian atmosphere. *One* is no longer an abstract "First Cause." It is specifically God, Jehovah, the

49. *Ibid.*, XII; Dods trans., V, 214-19; italics mine.
50. Letter LV, 17, 31; see above, p. 37.
51. John 5: 5; Augustine, *On John*, XVII, 4.

Lord. Similarly the triad is arbitrarily a tri-unity and is also specifically God. By relation to Godhead it becomes the number of perfection [52] and is therefore the essence of all things. The great evidence of Trinity appears in the 3 epochs of a world which is essentially one. These dispensations are labeled "Before the Law" (Adam to Moses), "Under the Law" (Moses to Christ), and "Under Grace" (Christ to the Last Judgment).[53] The list of discovered triplicities in Scripture, in the universe, and in the spiritual life is endless.

Within the Trinity, however, is the duad, whose position, as in Pythagoreanism, indicated diversity, encompassed and harmonized by the triad. Within the Trinity, the dual nature of Christ is the best example of the nature of Christian dualism. For although the opposition of good and evil is recognized, as in Manicheanism, the emphasis is placed on the opposition of spiritual and material. The material, like evil, is opposed to the spiritual, but is subordinate to it. This archetypal duality is signified by the contrasts of earth and heaven, the Old and the New Testaments, the temporal and the spiritual, the active and the contemplative lives, symbolized by Leah and Rachel (in the New Testament by Martha and Mary).[54] The dominance of astrological reasoning is seen in the fixed belief that there must be a congruency between these opposed categories, as between macrocosm and microcosm. Necessarily, that is, trinity implies anti-trinity, or trinity manifested in heaven and earth. Augustine, therefore, posits 3 steps to sin (heart, deed, habit) as a sort of antitype to the 3's of righteousness.[55]

The principal Christian innovation in number science was the identification of this spiritual-temporal duality with the archetypal numbers, 3 and 4. Four, by the known analogues

52. Augustine, *On the Sermon on the Mount*, XIX, 61.
53. Augustine, Epistle LV, 35.
54. Augustine, *Harmony of the Gospels*, V, 18.
55. *On the Sermon on the Mount*, I, 12, 35.

of the 4 winds, the 4 elements, the 4 seasons, and the 4 rivers, is specifically the number of the mundane sphere; and, as the first 3 days of creation foreshadow the Trinity, so the fourth is the "type of man." [56] Mystically, the fact that man is a tetrad is evidenced in the name, *Adam*, whose letters are the 4 winds.[57] For this reason, knowledge of divine things is disseminated throughout the world by the 4 gospels, evangelists or beasts, emblemized by the 4 extremities of the cross,[58] the 4-fold division of Christ's clothing, and the 4 virtues, or forms of love, as Augustine names them.[59] "It is not possible," says Irenaeus, "that the gospels can be either more or fewer than they are." [60]

From the triune principle of God and the quadruple principle of man are produced the universal symbols, 7 and 12. The addition of 3 and 4, spiritual and temporal, produces 7, which is therefore the first number which implies totality.[61] It is the number of the universe and of man, signifying the creature as opposed to the Creator.[62] Seven gifts of the Holy Spirit were derived from Isaiah XI: 1-3.[63] The Lord's Prayer was found to contain 7 petitions.[64] Similarly, the Beatitudes were found to be 7,[65] and by the principle of contraries these septenaries were balanced by the 7 deadly sins.[66] Later, the addition of the 3 theological virtues (Faith, Hope, Charity)

56. Theophilus of Antioch, To *Autolycus*; AN III, 82; also Ambrose, *De fide*, II, Introduction; Augustine, *On John*, IX, 14.

57. Augustine, *On John*, IX, 14; see above, p. 31.

58. The cross was conceived to have 4 or 5 points — 5 if the intersection was included. As the image of 4, it encompassed man and the universe. As an emblem of 5, it coincided with the 5 wounds in providing the salvation of man, with his 5 senses, or of those living under the Old Dispensation of the Pentateuch.

59. *Of the Morals of the Catholic Church*, XV, 25.

60. *Against Heresies*, III, 11, 8.

61. Augustine, *Civ. Dei*, XX, 5.

62. Augustine, *On the Sermon on the Mount*, II, 10, 36; Letter LV, 15, 28.

63. Tertullian, *Against Marcion*, V, 8; Victorinus, *On Creation*.

64. Cyprian, *On the Lord's Prayer*; Tertullian, *On Prayer*, II, 8.

65. Augustine, *On the Sermon on the Mount*, II, 10-11.

66. Tertullian, *Against Marcion*, IV, 9; Augustine, *Harmony of the Gospels*, VI, 13.

to the 4 cardinal virtues produced one of the best-known heptads of Catholicism. The habit of presenting these spiritual entities in precise numerical groupings indicates that a relationship was felt between them, but it remained for Augustine to show the precise connection of the 7 petitions of the Lord's Prayer to the 7 beatitudes, which in turn relate to the 7 gifts of the spirit or to the 7 steps to wisdom.[67] Seven is the number of the Sabbath and Salvation, but it is also the number of sin.[68] Necessarily the churches on earth are 7, forming a likeness of the universe.[69]

Since the universe is constituted in 7, 8 is the number of Immortality.[70] It returns to Unity as the first day of the second week,[71] or in the eighth sentence of the Beatitudes, which repeats the first.[72] It is the number of resurrection and circumcision and the number of those who did not perish in the flood.[73] It is taken as the eighth age of Eternal Salvation, wherefore it is written, "Give a portion to 7, and also to 8." [74]

Ten had long been recognized as the image of unity, but it was Augustinian Pythagoreanism that produced it by adding the Trinity of the Creator to the hebdomad of the created.[75] In Christian usage, its great type is always the 10 Commandments, whose traditional division into 2 groups of 5 was soon to be altered to 3 and 7, in recognition of this doctrine.

The consideration of 3 and 4 as first principles not only accounts scientifically for the meanings of 7, 8, and 10, but also brings into line the great astrological and scriptural num-

67. *On the Sermon on the Mount*, II, 10-11; *Contra Faustum*, XII, 15; *On Christian Doctrine*, II, 7, 9-11.
68. Augustine, *Harmony of the Gospels*, VI, 13.
69. Augustine, Letter LV, 5, 9.
70. Augustine, *Contra Faustum*, XVI, 29.
71. Augustine, Letter LV, 15, 28.
72. Augustine, *On the Sermon on the Mount*, I, 3, 10.
73. Augustine, *Civ. Dei*, XV, 20.
74. Augustine, Letter LV, 13, 23.
75. Augustine, *Against the Epistle of Manichaeus Called Fundamental*, X, 11.

ber 12. For 12, "rightly considered," is merely another form of 7, since both are composed of 3 and 4 and both image forth the universe in 7 planets or 7 days of the week, and 12 signs of the zodiac or 12 hours of the day. Christ chose 12 disciples to indicate himself as the Spiritual Day [76] and to make known His Trinity through the 4 parts of the world.[77] This explanation of the "generation" of the 12 may be found in sculptured representation on medieval cathedrals, where the disciples are generally arranged in 4 groups of 3. The importance of the number is made evident by the choice of another apostle to complete the number when one was lost.[78] Or again, Noah, the tenth generation, had 3 sons, but one fell into sin to preserve the number.[79] The tribe of Levi also made 13 tribes in actuality, but they are always spoken of as 12, thus demonstrating that the idea of the number is more important than the actuality.[80]

The Christianization of number symbolism is especially notable in the treatment of the numbers, 5 and 6. All earlier connotations of 5 are neglected in favor of the 5 senses,[81] which makes the number the symbol of the flesh.[82] It is fitting, therefore, that the Old Law, which lacked final perfection, should be contained in the Pentateuch.[83] The perfection of 6 is similarly limited to earthly perfection,[84] so that both of these numbers are more cognate to the 4 than to the 3.

If a consideration of number was, in a sense, forced upon the early Church Fathers, it was not received unwillingly. Many of them, like Augustine, exhibit a manifest pride in

76. Augustine, On John, XLIX, 8.
77. Ibid., XXVII, 10.
78. Ibid.
79. Augustine, Civ. Dei, XV, 20.
80. Ibid., XX, 5.
81. Lactantius, Divine Institutes, VI, 20; Clement, Stromata, V, 6.
82. Methodius, The Banquet of the 10 Virgins, VI, 3; Augustine, On John, XV, 21.
83. Augustine, On John, XVII, 2.
84. Augustine, Civ. Dei, XI, 30.

their numerical learning, as well as a never-failing delight in discovering new instances of the numerical harmony of all things. It is not unusual in their writings to come upon extended commentaries on number science, commentaries which are not called for by the contexts. It becomes a commonplace also for them to launch into an encomium on a given number, digressing from the theme to point out as many as possible of the meanings or usages of the number in question. Furthermore, numbers are used by the Fathers themselves in a symbolic sense. Augustine classifies the opinions of Vincentius under 11 heads of error,[85] which is a sufficiently suggestive method of treatment, since 11, going beyond or transgressing the 10 of the law, was known to be the number of sin.[86] The Septuagint, as its name implies, is supposed to have been translated by 70 divinely inspired men. Regarding the Council of Nicaea, the number of bishops present is given by Eusebius as 250, by Athanasius as more than 300, by Sozomen as about 320; but by virtue of the newly discovered properties of the number 318, this number becomes the established tradition.[87]

Augustine is lost in admiration at the symbolic division of the 41 books of Varro, the reason for which he carefully elucidates.[88] From such considerations, even the formal arrangement of Christian books pays tribute to the science of number. The *City of God* is carefully organized in 22 books (like the Old Testament and the Hebrew alphabet), 2 groups of 5 devoted to refutation, suggestive perhaps of the 10 prohibitions of the Old Law, and 3 groups of 4, imitative of apostolic evangelization, to positive argument and exposition. Rabanus similarly implies that the sum total of knowledge is contained in the 22 books of his treatise, *De universo*. The

---

85. *On the Soul and Its Origin*, III.
86. *Civ. Dei*, XV, 20.
87. Ambrose, *De fide* I, Prologue and 18; NPN X, 201-2, 320-21.
88. *Civ. Dei*, VI, 3.

encyclopedias of Bartholomew of England, Thomas of Can-
timpré, and Grosseteste are each composed of 19 books, doubtless symbolic of the 12 signs and the 7 planets, and therefore
universal. The famous *Divine Institutes* of Lactantius are
similarly complete as their 7-fold division testifies — complete
and also divine. Other works are classified under 12 headings
or 50 or 100, as in Bonaventura's *Centiloquium*. Following
such models as these, Dante ensures the completeness of his
Divine Comedy by the formal division of the poem into 100
cantos.

VI. MEDIEVAL NUMBER PHILOSOPHY

THE penetration of number consciousness into the Middle Ages was inevitable from the sheer circumstance that there was literally no reservoir of knowledge or inspiration on which this period could draw which was not impregnated with number philosophy. Even the renewed contact with the East, brought about by commerce, the crusades, and the influx of Arabian scholarship from Spain, did not in any way alter the conception of number as the pattern of the cosmos. Eastern additions, such as the principles of Averroism, were Alexandrian in origin and had much in common with Manicheanism and Gnosis. The reintroduction of Aristotle served only to give added, though unnecessary, authority to such fixed numerical groups as the 4 causes, the 4 elements, the 10 categories. As a result of these diversified infiltrations, the only entirely exact statement which can be made concerning medieval number philosophy is that all of the number theories discussed in the preceding chapters, together with several unmentioned variants, may be found in the Middle Ages.

The dominant medieval attitude toward number, however, was the Christian, elaborated from the numerology of Augustine and his predecessors. For this reason the fundamental meanings of the majority of medieval number symbols may be derived from the Augustinian principles elaborated in the preceding chapter. Philosophically, it was explicitly stated or implicitly recognized that number was at least one key, and an important one, to cosmic secrets. As in the writings of Philo and the various Gnostic theories, astrology and Pythagoreanism were combined in an attempt to define the cosmic pattern. From astrology was drawn the hypothesis that all fixed aggregates, defined by the same number, were related (7 planets, 7 days, 7 churches). From astrology also were derived the majority of number symbols whose validity was made unquestionable by their appearance in the pages of Scripture. To Pythagoreanism was owed the ordering of these fixed truths (the relationship of 3 and 1, of 7 and 8), as well as the methods by which numbers might be manipulated in order to disclose profounder secrets than appeared on the surface.

It is probable that no single factor in perpetuating the axiom of cosmic order (and, accordingly, the fixed nature of numerical aggregates) was as important or as widespread as the astrology to which we have traced the roots of nearly all manifestations of number science. From Firmicus Maternus [1] (*ca.* 346) to Roger Bacon [2] (*ca.* 1214 — *ca.* 1294), the principles of astrology remained substantially the same, while its doctrines were diffused through every branch of learning. Theologically, it was admitted, even while denying the effect of the stars on the will and the intellect, that the physical man was influenced by the celestial bodies.[3] Mystically, the sun was the preëminent symbol and type of Divinity,[4] as specifically stated by Albertus Magnus: "In the sun, because it encircles the 'machine' of the world, is signified the power of the Father, the wisdom of the Son, the love of the Holy Spirit." [5] The Phoenix, symbol of Christ in the Old English poem, therefore rises with the sun, 12 times bathes, 12 times sips water from the bubbling spring, and notes the turn of the hours by beating its wings.[6] As a science, astrology flour-

1. *Mathesis*; see above, p. 22.

2. *Opus majus*, II, *passim*.

3. Thomas Aquinas, *Summa Theologica*, I, qu. 5; cf. Bonaventura, *Sentences*, II, dist. 2, pars 2, art. 1.

4. This is the principal thesis of Miss Dunbar's *Symbolism in Medieval Thought*.

5. *De laudibus B. Mariae Virg.*, XII, 5.

6. Cf. lines 28, 69, 106, 108, 144-47.

ished in all degrees, from the prognostications of the quack or the mystification of a Merlin in the seventh book (cap. iv) of Geoffrey's *Historia* to the sober though elementary pedagogy of the seventh book of Gower's *Confessio amantis* and the thoroughly sound scholarship of the Chartres School.[7] But in all versions, from the fantastic to the profound, the essential basis of the Babylonian science remained the same, and the ordering of all things from human life to precious stones,[8] herbs,[9] or metals [10] was held to be patterned in the stars.

The effect of this widespread preoccupation with celestial phenomena may be most clearly seen in *The Kalandar and Compost of Shepherds*. Although not published until 1493,[11] this so-called "first book printed for the people" is a thoroughly medieval document.[12] The tone of the book is set by Chapter II, which follows the prologue of the "author that put this Book in Writing:"

Here beginneth the Master Shepherd.

It is to be understood that there be in the year four quarters that is called Vere, Hiems, Aestas, and Autumnus. These be the four seasons in the year, as Primetime, is the Spring of the year as February, March, and April, these three months.

Then cometh Summer, as May, June, and July; and those three months every herb, grain, and tree is in his kind and in his most strength and fairness even at the highest.

Then cometh Autumn as August, September, and October, that all these fruits waxeth ripe and be gathered and housed. Then cometh November, December, and January, and these three months be in the Winter, the time of little profit.

We Shepherds say that the age of a man is seventy-two year,

7. Cf. Wedel, *Medieval Attitude toward Astrology*, p. 32.

8. Evans, *Magical Jewels of the Middle Ages*; also Kunz, *The Curious Lore of Precious Stones*.

9. Thorndike, *History of Magic and Experimental Science*, II, 259.

10. *Ibid.*, II, 392.

11. Original ed., pub. by Guy Marchant in Paris and translated into English *ca.* 1518. Seventeen English and one Scotch edition were published by 1656.

12. According to Thorndike (*op. cit.*, I, 674), this type of encyclopedia was common as early as the ninth century.

and that we liken but to one whole year. For evermore we take six year for every month, as January or February and so forth: for as the year changeth by the twelve months into twelve sundry manners, so doth a man change himself twelve times in his life, so be that he live to seventy-two, for three times six maketh eighteen, and six times six maketh thirty-six, and then is man at the best and also at the highest, and twelve times six maketh seventy-two, and that is the age of a man.

Thus must ye reckon for every month six year or else it may be understood by the four quarters and seasons of the year.[13] So is divided man into four parts as to youth, strength, wisdom, and age; he to be eighteen year young, eighteen year strong, eighteen year in wisdom, and the fourth eighteen year to go to the full age of seventy-two.

And now to show how man changeth twelve times even as the twelve months do.

This painfully elaborated exposition of the relation of the microcosm to the macrocosm is followed by a regular calendar with saint's days, lunar cycles, and the position of the sun in the zodiac. In succession, then, are given the 7 Dolors of the Blessed Virgin Mary, the trees of vices of sinners, showing the branches of the 7 Deadly Sins, the 7 petitions of the Lord's Prayer, the 12 articles of the Apostles' Creed distributed among the 12 apostles, the 10 Commandments together with the 10 commandments of the devil, the 7 virtues, the 12 signs of the zodiac correlated with the 12 parts of man, the 4 humours, the 7 planets and their domination over the parts of man, the 248 bones of the human body, the 4 elements and the 4 complexions, the 9 moving heavens (and some say 3 others, immobile, crystalline, empyrean), the cycles of the planets, the 4 parts of the zodiac, the 12 signs, degrees, minutes, seconds, and thirds, the 5 zones, the 12 houses of earth and heaven, the rule of the 7 planets over the 7 days of the week, the 4 complexions again (now related to the 4 ele-

13. This is the argument of the December eclogue of Spenser's *Shepheardes Calender*, borrowed from Marot's *Eglogue au Roy*. Marot's shepherd, Robin, also learned the names of the 4 parts of the world and the 4 winds.

ments and the 4 humours), and the 4 keys to Purgatory by
St. Gregory. The fitting conclusion is a poem on the sounding
of the last trump.

Here is a mass of information which is obviously considered both elementary and basic. It is thoroughly numerical.
It is chiefly astrological or theological. Thoroughly typical
is the implied congruency of physical and spiritual truths.

In this synthesis lies at once the simplicity and the complexity of medieval number symbolism. The complexity has
been accounted for in the previous chapters: original number
mystery taking on religious significance, the religious impulse
giving rise to astrology in Babylon, the consequent coloring
of the Old Testament by astrological numbers, the divorce
of official astrology from religion, a renewed confluence in
Pythagoreanism, with a strong numerical bias and an independent number theory. Then, instead of denying or neg-
lecting what had gone before, the Church accepted number
theory in all of its forms, thus preserving and revitalizing
them all. Just as it reduced oriental mysticism and Greek
philosophy to one common denominator, so it coördinated all
previous number sciences and pressed them into the service
of the True Faith.

Medieval number philosophy was therefore truly catholic
and accordingly complex when viewed from without. Within
the Church, however, all discords were resolved and reduced
to the lucid harmony of Ultimate Truth. From the fount of
Revelation this harmony flowed into all channels of medieval
life: Christian, non-Christian, and un-Christian; and the harmony which distinguishes all medieval thinking is attributable to Christianity as the dominating factor in the medieval
equation.

Therefore, although the principle of cosmic order was certainly bolstered by the astrological bias of the Middle Ages,
it was specifically the Church itself that fathered the axio-

matic proposition of a finite and ordered universe so thoroughly coördinated that both spiritual and material truth were included in a single rigid cosmic plan. From a secular viewpoint, the conception was a natural development of the eclectic science and philosophy of the first five centuries. Theologically, its validity was authorized by the constantly repeated scriptural pronouncement that "all things are ordered in measure and number and weight." Stated in terms of Christian dogma, "Nihil in universo est inordinatum." [14] It is hardly possible to construct any philosophical system without premising organization, but seldom have architectonic implications been carried to the extent of exact measurement of such imponderables as the powers of the soul or the duration of the world.

Yet by correlation of the manifold number symbols inherited and discovered (as reflected in the *Kalendar and Compost of Shepherds*), it was thought possible to discover the essential archetypal pattern reproduced in both macrocosm and microcosm, "for as the world is the Image of God, so man is the image of the world." [15] So Isidore names the ounce as a "lawful weight because the number of its scruples measures the hours of the day and night," and the pound as "a kind of perfect weight because it is made up of as many ounces as the year has months." "The Centenarium is a weight of 100 pounds. And this weight the Romans established because of the perfection of the number 100." [16] Albertus Magnus discusses the 3 methods and times of adoration of God, the 3 attributes of God, the 3 dimensions of space, and the 3 dimensions of time.[17] The number 3, he concludes, is therefore in all things and "signifies the trinity of natural phenomena." [18] Aquinas further specifies the relation of the creature to the Creator: The

14. Bonaventura, *Sentences*, II, dist. 6, art. 2, qu. 1.
15. Agrippa, *Occult Philosophy*, II, 36.
16. *Etymologiae*, 16, 26, 19-23.
17. Past, present, future.
18. *De caelo et mundi, ab initio.*

Creator is threefold: Father, Son, and Holy Ghost. The creature is also threefold, and its triplicity is specifically related to the Trinity. As a created substance, it represents cause and principle and shows the Father. According as it has form and species, it represents the Word. According as it has relation of order, it represents the Holy Ghost, since he is love, and order is from the Will of the Creator.[19] Raoul Glaber shows how the 4 gospels are related to the 4 elements, the 4 cardinal virtues, and the 4 rivers of Paradise.[20] Or, reversing the procedure, Aquinas proves that the number 7 signifies universality because the life of man revolves through 7 days, because of the 7 gifts of the Holy Spirit, because faith in the Trinity was announced through the 4 parts of the world, because there are 7 churches.[21]

Relationships between identical number groups were eagerly sought after. Honorius measures the distances between the planets by the intervals of the musical scale, "because man, being 7 (4 = body, 3 = soul) has 7 voices (tones of the scale) and as microcosm reproduces the celestial music."[22] Albertus Magnus points out the relationship between the 7 gifts of the spirit and the 7 words of Christ on the Cross,[23] the 7 sins,[24] the 7 petitions of the Lord's Prayer,[25] and the theological and cardinal virtues.[26] Bonaventura charts the correlation of the 7 petitions with the 7 gifts, beatitudes, virtues, and vices.[27] The arguments concerning the validity of these number symbols operate in either direction: Seven is the number of universality; therefore there are 7 churches since the Church is universal. On the other hand, one proof of the universality of 7 is that there are 7 churches, 7 planets,

19. *Summa Theologica*, I, qu. 45, art. 7.
20. Thorndike, *op. cit.*, I, 674-75.
21. *Expositio II in Apocalypsim*, VIII.
22. *De imagine*, I, 81-82; cp. Erigena, P. L. 122, 718 *et sqq.*
23. *Commentarii in Psal.* LVI, 9.
24. *Sermo XV de tempore.*
25. *Expositio in Matth.* VI, 9.
26. *Sermo XLIII de tempore.*
27. *Expositio in cap. sextum evang. S. Matth., De oratione dominica.*

and so on. It is clear that these fixed aggregates were accepted as dogma — we have seen what their origins were — and that they were made part and parcel of the scripturally authorized truth of the Middle Ages.

The organization of these numerical truths; that is, their relationship to each other and to Godhead, was made possible by the principles of Pythagoreanism. In keeping with the doctrine of the procession of the many from the one, the cosmic plan was conceived of as a graded progression of microcosm and macrocosm, as well as the Intellectual World, from a First Cause in a fashion similar to the progression of the celestial spheres from the Primum Mobile. Some, like Aquinas, allowed infinity to the First Cause,[28] while others, like Bonaventura, retained the Pythagorean tenet that infinity was not consistent, even in Godhead, with "perfection and order."[29] All agreed, however, that the First Mover was One or Unity, and it remained only to find the correlation between One Cause and diversified effects. An inherited *modus operandi* was provided by the philosophical implications of arithmetical progression, in which multiplicity proceeds from unity in an orderly fashion and periodically returns to its source (in the terminals, 10, 100, and so on). Aquinas is expressing a widely applicable theorem when he states, concerning the soul, "Since the soul is one, and the powers are many; and since a number of things that proceed from one must proceed in a certain order; there must be some order among the powers of the soul."[30]

On the mathematical aspects of this order Pythagoras and Hermes Trismegistus, "who was before Pythagoras,"[31] were the recognized authorities. Isolated sayings or doctrines of these men were matters of common knowledge among the educated. Thomas Hoccleve, in a whimsical mood, even in-

28. *Summa Theologica*, I, qu. 7, art. 1.
29. *Sentences*, I, dist. II, qu. 3.
30. *Summa Theologica*, I, qu. 77, art. 4.
31. Albertus Magnus, *De caelo et mundi*, I, 1, 2.

vokes Pythagoras to prove the thoroughly un-Pythagorean proposition that women are superior to men. The conclusion is inevitable, for woman was created from a crooked rib and

> . . . in the writyng and in the scripture
> Of Philosophers, men may see and reede,
> Cercly shap is most perfite figure,
> Bitokenyng, in gemetrie, onhede;
> And crokydnesse a part is, that may lede
> Sumwhat unto cercle or a cumpas:
> What so men seyen, women stonde in gode caas.[32]

There was, in actuality, little need to consult the "Philosophers" for this information, since the source of most medieval Pythagoreanism may be found in any of the standard arithmetics of the time. For all these works appear to derive from the *Introduction to Arithmetic* by Nicomachus (*ca.* 100), who was, as we have seen, a member of the Neo-Pythagorean school.

The *Introduction* opens with a glorification of arithmetic in now-familiar terms, asserting the existence of the science in the mind of God as a design or archetypal pattern for his material creations.[33] Number is therefore the true and eternal essence.[34] There follows a definition of number and a mathematical explanation of the exclusion of 1 and 2 from the decimal system. The major concern of the book is an attempt to systematize or order the rational integers. This is accomplished by classifying numbers as perfect, abundant, and deficient;[35] again by the four distinctions of evenness and oddness;[36] by the prime and relatively prime;[37] and finally

32. *The Regement of Princes*, lines 5125-31.
33. *Introduction*, I, 4, 2.
34. *Ibid.*, I, 6.
35. Also termed *defective* or *diminutive* numbers; see above, p. 37.
36. Even, Odd, Evenly Even (always divisible by 2 until the monad is reached; e.g., 64), Oddly Even (an even number which contains an odd factor; when successively halved it reduces to 3; e.g., 24).
37. A prime is factorable only by itself and 1; *Relatively prime* = two numbers which have no common divisors and will not divide each other; e.g., 21 and 25.

by means of figured numbers.[38] A discussion of ratios closes
the book. Ten diverse ratios are distinguished, "making up
the number 10, which, according to the Pythagorean view,
is the most perfect possible." [39] Nicomachus was introduced
to the Roman world shortly after his death, or possibly before,
by Apuleius of Maudaura, who is said by Cassiodorus [40] and
Isidore of Seville [41] to have been the first to translate the Greek
Introduction into Latin.[42] At any rate, the *Introduction* is
almost literally reproduced in the Arithmetics of Capella
(*De nuptiis*, VII), Boethius, Cassiodorus, Isidore, Bede,
Alcuin, Gerbert, and Hugo of St. Victor. Boethius remained
the standard text in the Church schools throughout the Middle Ages,[43] and Capella's *Textbook of the Seven Arts*, although held suspect during the centuries immediately following its composition, because of the pagan allegory woven
through it, was restored by Erigena (who wrote a commentary on it), and became a highly esteemed text.[44]

Authorized by the writings of Augustine, medieval philosophers and theologians understood the purely mathematical
aspects of number to be of divine origin. Innocent III includes
in a sermon [45] a lecture on diminutive, perfect, and abundant
numbers. Alcuin explains that the second origin of the
human race was occasioned by the deficient number 8, the 8
souls in Noah's ark, wherefore the second origin was not as
perfect as the first, which was accomplished in 6 days.[46] Concerning the latter, Rabanus explains that the senarius is not
perfect because God created the world in 6 days, but rather
that God perfected the world in 6 days because the number

38. See above, p. 37.
39. II, 22, 1.
40. P. L. 70, 1208.
41. P. L. 82, 155.
42. Robbins and Karpinski, *Studies*, p. 124.
43. D. E. Smith, *Rara mathematica*, p. 28.
44. *Ibid.*, p. 66.
45. *Sermo* 3, *De sanctis*; P. L. 217, 459 *et sqq.*
46. P. L. 100, 665.

was perfect.[47] Arithmetic is therefore the key to the pattern
or form of the world; or, in another sense, it is the method
by which the Divine Intellect becomes intelligible *per enig-
matem* to human comprehension.

This conception, borrowed from the Gnostics and implicit
in Pythagoreanism itself, carried with it two corollaries
which were especially fostered by the mystics:

1. The essential numbers of the Divine Plan are all included in the decad, since numbers above 10, with the exception
of primes, are reducible to decadic component parts, and
primes are reckoned as 1. The 12 disciples, that is to say, are
really the 4 × 3 disciples preaching the Trinity throughout
the 4-fold world.[48]

2. All things are essentially *One* with God. But just as 3
is the first number which can be visualized (in the triangle,
the first plane figure) by the human eye, so manifoldness is
more comprehensible to human understanding, which cannot
aspire to the intensity of the One.[49] Bonaventura lists the 12
qualities of God, as opposed to mortals.[50] In these 12, he
propounds, are included the highest nobility of Divine Essence, but these 12 are reduced to 3, Eternity, Knowledge,
Beatitude, and these 3 to 1 Knowledge.[51] The doctrine is
succinctly stated by Aquinas:

The human soul requires many and various operations and powers.
But to angels a smaller variety of powers is sufficient. In God there
is no power or action beyond His own Essence.[52]

47. P. L. 107, 399.

48. Aquinas, *Expositio in Apocalypsim*, IV.

49. "Quanto virtus magis est unita, tanto magis est intensa: sed in patria
virtus charitatis erit potentissima: ergo erit unitissima. Sed quod maxime accedit
ad unitatem, maxime recedit a latitudine: si ergo charitas in patria habit magis
uniri, videtur quod potius ibi habeat arctari quam dilatari" (Bonaventura,
Sentences, dist. XXXI, art. III, qu. 2).

50. Life to our lives, Sense to our senses, Intelligence to our intelligences,
Immortality to our mortality, Power to our impotence, Justice to our injustice,
Beauty to our deformity, Good to evil, Incorruptible to corruptible, Immutable
to mutable, Invisible to visible, Incorporeal to corporeal.

51. *Breviloquium*, I, 1.

52. *Summa Theologica*, I, qu. 77, art. 2.

God is unity, says Alanus de Insulis, because unity regulates all plurality.[53] The purer the essence, therefore, the smaller is the number required to express it. The triple triad is allocated to the angels as being less holy than the Trinity, and the sacred 3 is but the expressive number of Unity. Raymon Lull, in the *Book of the Lover and the Beloved*, says,

In the numbers 1 and 3 the Lover found greater harmony than between any others, because by these numbers every bodily form passed to existence from non-existence. And the greatest harmony of number, the Lover thought, was in the Unity and Trinity of his Beloved.[54]

In Trinity, unity is extended in 3 directions, but essence is not thereby multiplied.[55]

In order to discover the ultimate meanings inherent in significant numbers, various methods were employed. We are indebted to Hugo of St. Victor [56] for an analysis of the nine different ways in which numbers may be meaningful:

1. By order of position:
    Unity = first number = principle of all things
    Binary = second number, first which recedes from unity, signifying sin which deviates from the First Good

Hugo has here selected the two instances where the meaning of a number is rigorously dependent on its place in the decimal system. More loosely, this is the statement of my second corollary: that the numbers may be said to become more imperfect in direct proportion as they recede from unity, and a large number is therefore much more applicable to the creature than to the Creator. In actual practice, however, nearly any large number could be shown to partake of the nature of unity. Seven is a sacred number partly because it is made up of the *first* even number (4) and of the *first*

53. *Regulae Alani de sacra theologia*; P. L. 210, 623.
54. *Op. cit.*, 259.
55. Peter of Poictiers, *Sentences*; P. L. 211, 926; Bacon, *Opus majus*; Burke, I, 245; see above, p. 73.
56. *Exegetica*, XV; P. L. 175, 22-23.

odd (3).[57] This is also true of 12. Ten, 100, and 1,000 are all
a return to unity. Forty is apparently far removed from
unity, but the aliquot parts of 40 add up to 50, which is
unity because it signifies 1 Jubilee.[58] By such astonishing feats
of mathematics and logic, nearly any "rule" set down for the
science of numbers may be abrogated at will.

2. By quality of composition:
   2 can be divided in 2, signifying the corruptible and transitory.
   3, because, by presence of unity in the midst, it cannot be
   divided into 2, is called indissoluble and incorruptible.

The statements here made concerning 2 and 3 apply respectively to all even and all odd numbers. Odd numbers were
universally considered more godlike, more perfect, and (in
magic) more powerful than the even. This was apparently
one of the most widely known of Pythagorean principles.[59]

3. By manner of extension: (relation to other numbers)
   7 beyond 6 = rest after work
   8 beyond 7 = eternity after mutability
   9 before 10 = defect among perfection
   11 beyond 10 = transgression outside of measure

4. By form of disposition: (geometric)
   10 = 1 dimension = rectitude in faith
   100 expands in width = amplitude of charity
   1000 rises in height = height of hope

Less mystically, a number might be considered as linear, super-
ficial, or solid. Geometically, a number might represent a
point, a line, a triangle, a square or other plane figure, or a
solid. By virtue of the concept that unity is the first power
of any number, 1 represented a point, 10 was often loosely
considered as linear, 100 as two-dimensioned and 1,000 as
three-dimensioned, or solid. For this reason 1,000 was called

57. Gregory, *Morals*, I, i; pp. 18-19.
58. Innocent III, *Sermo* XI; P. L. 217, 357 et sqq.
59. "Good luck lies in odd numbers. . . . They say there is divinity in odd
numbers, either in nativity, chance, or death" (*M. W. of W.*, Act V, sc. 1).

the ultimate boundary of number.[60] Squaring a number was understood to give it extension; cubing added the dimension of height. In a special category belong the circular or spherical numbers, 5 and 6. A circular number is one which reproduces itself in its last digit when raised to its powers. When cubed, it was considered to have reached a third or spherical dimension. Nine was also considered as circular, after the introduction of arabic numerals, because, however often multiplied, it continually reproduces itself in the sum of its digits. Ten, which is actually neither perfect nor circular, was nevertheless so considered; perfect because it includes all number and is 1, circular because, like it, the circle includes all plane figures.

5. According to computation of numbers: [decimal system]
   10 = perfection because it signifies the end of computation.

6. By multiplication: [factorization]
   12 = sign of universality because it is composed of 4 x 3, of which 4 is corporeal and 3, spiritual.

This was easily the most popular method of all. So Aquinas discusses the 144,000 of the Apocalypse. The thousand is easily disposed of as signifying perfection. The remaining $144 = 12 \times 12$. One 12 signifies (as always) faith in the Trinity, diffused through the 4 parts of earth. By the other can be understood the doctrine of the 12 apostles or the 12 tribes.[61] Similarly 7,000 signifies universal perfection; perfection by the thousand, universality by the 7.[62] Hugo neglects to mention that this rule applies equally to addition; 7 is also composed of 4 and 3.

7. According to aggregate parts;
   6 is perfect, 12 abundant, etc.

8. According to the number of parts: (number as a group of units)
   2 = 2 unities = love of God

---

60. Thomas Aquinas, *Expositio II in Apocalypsim*, VII.
61. *Expositio II in Apocalypsim*, VII.
62. *Ibid.*, XI.

3 = 3 unities = Trinity
4 = 4 unities = 4 times of year
5 = 5 unities = 5 senses

This classification includes all numerical meanings derived from concrete representations (9 openings of the human body), or from authority (7 churches, 12 apostles, 4 humours).

9. According to exaggeration:
   7 penalties (Leviticus 26: 28) = multiplicity of penalties

Hugo's attempt to organize the principles of medieval number science is itself an indication of the looseness with which these principles were applied. It was never a matter of defining the meaning of a given number by checking it against these rules, but rather of selecting the rule which would provide the traditional or desired meaning. The number 12 was traditionally universal because of the 12 months (rule 8). The fact that its factors (4 × 3) added to 7, another symbol of universality (7 days), made the sixth rule also applicable. Rule 7 (the abundance of 12) was often cited when speaking of the 12 disciples (abundance of grace), but ignored when discussing universality, which is perfect rather than deficient or abundant. The perfection of the universe was demonstrated by the creation of the world in 6 days. The imperfection of 12 or 6 (as an even number, rule 2) was not considered. Similarly, 13 might be a sacred number by rule 6 (the 10 Commandments + faith in the Trinity) and a number of sin by rule 3 (going beyond the 12 apostles). In fact, no medieval writer seems to have been aware of any disparity between the concept of a number's significance as part of the decimal system, or as an astrological index of time, or as representing symbolically a specific physical or spiritual truth. In the last analysis, the meanings of the integers were drawn from old traditions or by direct reference to the use of the number in Scripture. If it happened that mathematical or astrological reasoning gave added justification for the number, so much the better.

Along with arithmetic, therefore, a kindred science now known as arithmology was developed. Arithmology may be loosely defined as the philosophy of the powers and virtues of particular integers. Scattered commentaries of this sort were probably as old as the Pythagoreans, but complete works on the subject appear to originate with the *Theologoumena arithmeticae*, variously attributed to Nicomachus and Iamblichus. The theology of numbers considers individually each member of the decad, stating concisely its mathematical properties, its corresponding deity in the Greek pantheon, its moral attributes, and its reflections in the cosmos.[63]

The outstanding practitioners of arithmology were Capella (*De nuptiis*, II, VII), Isidore (*Liber numerorum*), and Rabanus (*De numero*). Capella repeats substantially the dicta of the *Theologoumena* and likewise limits his discussion to the decad. Rabanus and Isidore repeat the essential Pythagorean attributes of each number, but subjoin the specifically theological applications. Authority is drawn from the early Fathers and ultimately from the Bible itself, so that both of these works might properly bear the full title used by Isidore, *Liber numerorum qui in sanctis scripturis occurrunt*. Some numbers are justified both mathematically and by direct revelation. Others, like the 30, 60, and 100 of the parable of the sower (Matthew 13) are interpreted by direct reference to scriptural source. These, the exegeticist readily deduced, referred to the 3 degrees of Sanctity or Chastity within the Church. To the Virgins or Prelates, accordingly, was allocated the 100; to the Continent or Widows, the 60; to the Conjugal, the 30.[64] Beyond the decad the mathematical pro-

---

63. Robbins and Karpinski, *Studies in Greek Arithmetic*, pp. 101-7.

64. Mathematical justification is offered by Albertus Magnus: 100 = 5 interior + 5 exterior senses, "led through" the 10 Commandments = 100 = virgins. 60 = 6 works of mercy in obedience to the 10 Commandments = widows. 30 = 3 conjugal goods (Institution, Practice, Fruit — good of sacrament, good of faith, good of children) under the 10 Commandments (*Expositio Matt.* 13: 8).

gression becomes highly selective. Isidore does not go beyond 153, but Rabanus, some two centuries later, manages to extend the list to 144,000, the Final Number of the Elect.

Although ambitious in design, both of these works are extremely brief. Isidore gives more references. Rabanus is more elaborate from the mathematical viewpoint. Both collect material from an already well-established tradition and omit as much of that tradition as they record, a circumstance which can be accounted for only by the generally laconic tendency of their encyclopedic works. Prominent among the later authorities on arithmology may be mentioned Cornelius Agrippa, whose *Second Book of Occult Philosophy* is the most elaborate of all the texts, and Petrus Bungus, a priest writing his *Mysticae numerorum significationis liber* for the use of preachers.

Although such works as these indicate the attempted definition of a number science, they do not indicate the popularity which symbolic numbers enjoyed in the Middle Ages. Actually, no branch of medieval thought appears entirely to have escaped the influence of number symbolism. Its philosophical implications affected theology, science, and magic. Its essentially mysterious character caused it to leave its mark on imaginative writing — lightly on popular literature, but heavily on the erudite *Divine Comedy*.

The most extensive and most profound employment of these symbolic numbers was made by the Church. Medieval theology was very largely concerned with an attempt to establish the numerical relationship of the supramundane, ecclesiastical, and temporal worlds. One chain of reasoning led to the establishment of the 9 orders of angels, and it would be difficult to surpass the beauty and justness of this numerical assignment whereby the theological position of the angelic host is precisely defined. For the angelic perfection is simultaneously absolute and relative. The perfect creations of God are entirely perfect. In them is the perfect 3 reflected upon itself, *super se reflexa*.[65] Yet this perfection is secondary to the perfection of God, wherefore the addition of the Unity of Godhead is necessary to complete the Decad. Again, the angelic nature is nearer and more comprehensible to man than absolute Godhead; so also is 9 more "expressive" than Trinity.[66] Again, the angelic host is impaired by the defection of the Fallen Angels. Consequently, one school of thought held that the Fallen Angels composed the 10th order, to be replaced by Man in the Final Perfection. Scriptural justification for this theory may be found in Luke 15: 8-9, the parable of the woman with 10 pieces of silver who loses one and seeks diligently until she finds it.[67] Langland elucidates this conception:

> For Christ, king of kings, knighted ten
> Cherubim and Seraphim, seven such and another
> And gave them mastery and might, in his majesty
>
> .   .   .
>
> Lucifer with legions learned it in heaven.
> He was loveliest to see, after our Lord
> Till he broke obedience through boast of himself
> Then fell he with his fellows, and fiends they became.[68]

"Seven such" are the orders below the first two named. "Another" refers obviously to the order of Lucifer.

Another vein of reflection attempted to fix and allocate the ages of the temporal world.[69] Another was concerned with the 7 stages of contemplation, or other classifications of the spiritual life. Always the abstraction of the Trinity remained a first principle. Roger Bacon is echoing a familiar thought when he says,

65. Bonaventura, *Sentences*, II, dist. 9, qu. 8, ad opps. 2.
66. See above, pp. 99-100.
67. Bonaventura, *Sentences*, II, dist. 9, qu. 7.
68. *Piers the Plowman*, ed. by Nielson, I, 102-12. Version A substitutes "an al the four ordres" for "seven such and another" which in reference to angels means nothing. Cf. Skeat ed., I, 104.
69. See above, pp. 31, 77-78.

For unity multiplied into itself cubically, that is, thrice, as once one taken once, does not multiply essence, but remains the same although it is produced equally in 3 directions. And so by a familiar example theologians designate the blessed Trinity.[70]

Aquinas gives scriptural authority for the 3 dimensions of God (Job 11: 8-9):

He is higher than the heaven, and what wilt thou do? He is deeper than hell and how wilt thou know? The measure of Him is longer than the earth and broader than the sea.[71]

Furthermore, "by His rising on the third day, the perfection of the number 3 is commended, which is the number of everything, as having beginning, middle, and end."[72] Theologians never grew weary of dilating upon the Sublime Mystery of the Trinity, One in Essence but Three in Persons, and the stores of all learning, sacred and profane, were zealously scrutinized to pile up witnesses for the Three-in-One.

To the mystics, number symbolism was of especial importance. Hildegard of Bingen not only utilizes the traditional number symbols in her visions, but adds to them her own numerical discoveries. The denarius, she says, was lost in sinful man, to be recovered by Christ in the multiplication of 10 by 100 (virtue in the salvation of souls), by which 10 through 100 ascends to 1,000, the perfect number of all virtues, sufficient to dispel the 1,000 acts of the devil.[73]

The principal thread of medieval mysticism was spun from the writings of Dionysius the Areopagite. His works, *The Ecclesiastical Hierarchy, The Celestial Hierarchy*, and *On Divine Names*,[74] now generally assigned to the fifth century, were believed to have been written by the Athenian disciple of St. Paul, who was further identified with St. Denis, the

70. *Opus majus*, Burke, I, 245.
71. *Summa Theologica*, I, qu. 3, art. 1, obj. 1.
72. *Ibid.*, III, qu. 53, art. 2.
73. *Scivias*, III, 2; P. L. 197, 585-86.
74. P. G., 3.

patron saint of France. The works were translated into Latin by Erigena [75] in the ninth century, and the commentary of Hugo of St. Victor (*ca.* 1097-1141) on the *Celestial Hierarchy* gave new impetus to their popularity.

The philosophical tradition of the Dionysian writings is that of Gnosticism and Neo-Platonism. A procession of emanations is posited from the Superessential (unknowable, incomprehensible) to essence, to universals, to individuals. [76] It is impossible to know the Superessential until we have become incorruptible and immortal; thus the necessity for symbols. "But now, to the best of our ability, we use symbols appropriate to things Divine, and from these again we elevate ourselves, according to our degree, to the simple and unified truth of the spiritual visions." [77]

As usual, the symbols chosen were numerical. The Superessential ONE bounds both the One existing and every number, but we may nevertheless figure him as UNIT and TRIAD. [78] The First Cause is both Good and Beautiful, and the First Movement is Love, which moved itself to creation. [79] All is essentially Good, since all proceeds from the Monad, which is Good. [80] "Even anger participates in the Good, by the very movement and desire to direct and turn the seeming evils to the seeming good. [81] Evil is therefore a falling away from Good or Unity and may be symbolized as diversity, or the Duad. It is the state of this life, from which we look forward to the time "when our divided diversities have been folded together, in a manner supermundane [and] we are collected into a godlike Unit and divinely imitated union; but also as a Triad, on account of the tri-personal manifestations of the

75. P. L. 122.
76. *Oeuvres de St. Denis*, trans. by Duloc, p. 34.
77. *On Divine Names*, IV.
78. *Ibid.*, XIII, 3.
79. *Ibid.*, IV, 10.
80. *Ibid.*, IV, 21.
81. *Ibid.*, IV, 20.

superessential productiveness from which all paternity in heaven and earth is, and is named." [82] Both the Celestial and Ecclesiastical Hierarchies are constructed on the basis of the Divine Triad. Furthermore, the Beautiful and the Good have neither beginning nor end, wherefore the movement of the angels is circular or spiral.[83]

Having accepted number as the most exact representation of the Unknowable, the mystic is concerned to find evidences of significant numbers throughout the universe. Hugo of St. Victor finds multiple instances of the Trinity everywhere. The Testaments are each divided into 3 parts: law, prophets, and hagiographers of the Old; and evangelists, apostles, and fathers of the New.[84] Three hierarchies are made up of God, Angels, and Man.[85] There are 3 theological virtues,[86] and a triple triplicity of angels imaging the Trinity.[87] The Dionysian distinction between Unity and Diversity is carried out in a list which includes heaven and earth, invisible and visible, angels and man, prelates and subjects, contemplative and active, spirit and flesh, Adam and Eve, perfect and imperfect.[88] Typical also is Hugo's De quinque septenis, which are the 7 vices, 7 petitions, 7 gifts, 7 virtues, and 7 beatitudes.[89]

One of the most prominent heirs to the mystic school of St. Victor was the Calabrian abbot, Joachim of Flora. In him is exampled the faith of the mystic, who in "the silence of harmony" may penetrate into the secrets of the superessential. To him the Apocalypse of John was the book of the secrets of wisdom, and the array of symbolic numbers contained therein gave support and encouragement to his own

82. Ibid., I, 4.
83. Ibid., IV, 8-9.
84. P. L. 175, 15.
85. Ibid., 929-30.
86. P. L. 176, 42 et sqq.
87. Ibid., 85.
88. P. L. 175, 635-39.
89. Ibid., 403.

numerical theorizing. Most startling of his teachings were the prophecies concerning the third age. Since the time of Augustine,[90] it had been customary to apply the conception of three ages to the time-schedule of the Universe.[91] Bernard introduced a new conception by combining the first two ages and postponing the third age to the Last Judgment. He renamed these ages, "Under Adam, In Christ, and With Christ," citing as his authority Hosea 6: 3, "After two days he will revive us, and the third day he will raise us up." [92]

Joachim was one of thousands of sincere and reverent men who felt that the height of earthly perfection had not been reached under the guidance of the then incredibly corrupt Church of Christ. Building upon the theory that the time of Law represented the Rule of the Father, and the Evangelical Law the Reign of the Son, he was able to extend the hope of a third earthly age to come — an Age of Love and Grace under the Holy Spirit.

The Joachite writings became a center about which the widespread spiritual unrest, especially in Italy, rallied. Numerous dates were proposed for the inception of the Third Age, but the most widely accepted (until that date had passed) was Joachim's own theory that Benedict was a forerunner, a John the Baptist, and that the crucial hour would arrive in 1260. This was a sufficiently sound computation, granting the hypothesis that "all things are ordered in measure and number." The time between Adam and Jesus is given by Matthew as 42 generations, divided into 3 periods of 14 each. Counting 30 years to a generation the resulting 1,260 is derived, which is therefore the length of an age.[93] The 30 is authorized by the record of the life of Christ, who began to preach in his thirtieth year, and the 1,260 may itself be found in Revelations

90. Epistle LV, 3, 5.
91. Before the Law, under the Law, under Grace; see above, p. 83.
92. Sermo XIII, 2, De tempore.
93. Concordia, II, tract. 1, cap. 16.

12: 6,[94] which, if correlated with Ezekiel 4: 6, "A day for a year... I have appointed to thee," may be taken as a prophecy.

Most clearly, in such predictions as these, is it patent that in many minds the symbolic implications of number had come to be regarded as realities, indisputable and final. Innocent III piously sought to count the appearances of Christ on earth after the Resurrection. He was able to enumerate 10, but felt that there ought to be 12, a number particularly associated with Christ, who added 2 Commandments to the Decalogue and chose 12 disciples. He therefore states that there *must* have been 2 other appearances not mentioned, possibly to Paul and to his Mother in Glory.[95] The practical exigencies of architecture ordinarily required more than 7 pillars in the structure of a church. "Yet," says Durandus, "are they called 7." [96] In this instance, the number, as an attribute of the pillars, could not be arrived at by counting. The pillars are 7, not by human computation, but by Divine Revelation, for "Wisdom hath builded her house, she hath hewn out her 7 pillars," [97] and in them may be recognized the 7 outpourings of the Holy Ghost.[98] Similarly, Isidore reckons the nations of the earth: 15 from Japhet, 31 from Ham, and 27 from Shem, a total of 73, "or rather," he concludes, "as calculation shows, 72, and as many languages began to exist throughout the earth." [99]

In these and similar pronouncements is demonstrated the conception of number as abstraction, symbol, idea — as part of a philosophical system, rather than as a summation of concrete units. Faith in number was so strong that the specific

94. Rev. 12: 6: "And the woman fled into the wilderness where she hath a place prepared of God, that they should feed her there a thousand two hundred and three score days." This date had been accordingly proposed as the date of the Last Judgment (Aquinas, *Summa Theologica*, III, qu. 77, art. 3).

95. I. Cor. 15; *Sermo V, De sanctis*; P. L. 217, 471.

96. *Rationale*, I, 27.

97. Prov. 9: 1.

98. Durandus, *ibid*.

99. *Etym.*, IX, 2, 2.

date of the Last Judgment was believed to be a predictable certainty. Stronger than that, when the 7 ages of the world had been actually completed without event, there followed no loss of faith in the number 7 as the cosmic period. If the fact did not coincide with the archetypal pattern, it was not the pattern that was at fault. Therefore Albertus Magnus continued to call 8 the Day of Justice,

not, as some have erroneously thought because this, after 7 thousand years, would complete the 7 ages of the world. For it is uncertain, and known only to God when that day will come — Matthew, 24: 36, "Of that day and hour knoweth no man." But it is called 8 for two other reasons, because it follows after this life, which is halved by 4 and 3. For the human body is composed of 4 humours, and varies through the 4 seasons of the year, and it is composed of 4 elements. On the part of the soul, on the other hand, are 3 powers or forces by which the spiritual life of man is ruled. From this it follows that the day of Judgment will be 8. Or better, it is called 8, because it is the consequence of this life which runs the circuit of 7 days.[100]

In the same spirit of absolute faith, Saint Guthlac, at the end of his life, is made to remark, "The meaning of my illness is this, that the spirit must be taken away from this body, for on the eighth day there will be an end of my illness." [101] Guthlac is here uttering a literal prediction, but he is also giving voice to his own inspired vision of Eternal Truth.

One of the most extensive usages of number symbolism may be found in scriptural exegesis, which builds steadily upon the tradition of Philo and Augustine as each expositor repeats his predecessor and occasionally adds an original interpretation. The allegorical tendency produced the custom of considering any given passage in the light of the 4 "intellectual theologies": historical, allegorical, tropological, and ana-

100. *Commentary on Psalm 6*, ed. by Borgnet, XIV, 72.
101. *Vita Sci. Guthlaci*, XX; p. 81 in C. W. Goodwin, *The Anglo-Saxon Version of the Life of St. Guthlac*. The verse rendition in *Codex Exoniensis*, lines 1005 *et sqq.*, is identical in meaning.

gogical. In accordance with this scheme, Innocent III interprets the historical 4 rivers of Paradise. By allegory, the rivers of truth are intended, flowing from Christ through the 4 evangelists, or from Moses through the 4 major prophets. Morally, the rivers represent the 4 cardinal virtues. The anagogical interpretation points to the 4 blessings which irrigate Paradise: clarity, impassivity, knowledge, delectation.[102]

So, too [says Isidore], other numbers appear in the Holy Scriptures whose natures none but experts in this art can wisely declare the meaning of. It is granted to us, too, to depend in some part upon the science of numbers, since we learn the hours by means of it, reckon the course of months, and learn the time of the returning year. Through number, indeed, we are instructed in order not to be confounded. Take number from all things and all things perish. Take calculation from the world and all is enveloped in dark ignorance, nor can he who does not know the way to reckon be distinguished from the rest of the animals.[103]

In many instances, numerical interpretation of the Scriptures produced results not very far removed from the original intention of the writer. On the other hand, the current belief that no word or number in Scripture was superfluous [104] gave rise to the most intricate and tortured revelations of enigma, where no enigma existed. When Bonaventura wrote his *Commentary on Luke*, he encountered the sentence, "Two of them that same day walked to a village called Emmaus which was from Jerusalem about three score furlongs." [105] It would be difficult to surpass the ingenuity of his reduction of 60 furlongs to 7,050 paces or $7\frac{1}{2}$ miles, indicating that they were sure of sepulcher but doubtful of resurrection, sure of 7 but doubtful of 8! It required a similar type of ingenuity to find 7 petitions in the Lord's Prayer; 7 beatitudes and 7 virtues in

102. P. L. 217, 327-30, and again in 605-8.
103. *Etym.*, III, 4, 3.
104. Bonaventura, *Illuminationes in ecclesiae hexameron, Sermo* I.
105. Luke 24: 13.

Luke 6; 7 gifts of the Holy Spirit in Isaiah 11: 2-3; and a
host of other scattered scriptural 7's, such as the 7 journeys of
Christ or the 7 outpourings of his blood, the 7 sacraments, the
7 parts of theology, the 7 dolors of the Virgin, the 7 words
of Christ on the cross.

The zest for numerical allegory is carried over to the
medieval sermon, which often consists of little more than an
extensive interpretation of a scriptural passage. So Honorius
of Autun, in the most popular handbook of sermons in the
Middle Ages, uses the two laws of love of Matthew 22: 37-39,
to explain the favorite division of the Ten Commandments
into two tables of 3 and 7. The first table contains 3 precepts,
because it pertains to the love of God in heart, mind, and
soul. The other, of 7, concerns the love of neighbor. It is
7-fold, to signify the 3-fold soul added to the 4-fold body.[106]
Similarly, the elucidation of the 2 miracles of the loaves and
fishes provided a favorite sermon topic.

Since these symbolic numbers were an important part of
the Eternal Pattern, since they were intrinsic in the form
and structure of Church Triumphant, it was a necessary consequence that they should be recognized in the construction
of the offices and monuments of the Church on earth. The
"frozen eloquence" of cathedral architecture is therefore to a
great extent the eloquence of number, by which the very sum
of pillars, gates, or windows is held to be meaningful.[107] The
altar steps are always 3 or some multiple. The baptismal font
is octagonal because 8 is the number of salvation.

At the consecration of a cathedral, the central door of the
royal portal is sprinkled thrice with holy water, 12 candles
are lighted, and triple thanks offered to Heaven. Three sol-
emn knockings prelude the opening of the door, whereupon

    106. *Ecclesiae*; P. L. 172, 873.

    107. Cf. Durandus, *Rationale divinorum officiorum*; Sicardus, *Mitrale*; Hon-
orius, *Gemma animae*; Bayley, *The Lost Language of Symbolism*, II; Hulme, *The
History, Principles and Practice of Symbolism in Christian Art*, pp. 10-16.

the 4 extremities of the cruciform structure are triply
sprinkled, as are 7 altars. Twelve priests, the Day of Christ,
then carry crosses through the 4 parts of the Church.[108]

All the offices of the Church are arranged in accordance
with number symbolism. The mass itself is composed of 7
parts, or offices. The full episcopal procession is led by 7
acolytes, indicating the 7 gifts of the spirit. Then follow
the pontiff, 7 subdeacons (7 columns of wisdom), 7 deacons
(from apostolic tradition), 12 priors (the apostles), and 3
acolytes with incense (the magi). The sign of the cross
"which redeems the fourfold world" is always made thrice to
express faith in the Trinity, and 6 orders of the cross are made
to indicate this perishable world. The first order includes 3
crosses for the triple division (Adam to Noah, to Abraham,
to Moses) of the Time before Law. The second order sym-
bolizes the Time under the Law by 5 crosses for the Pentateuch. In the third order, the Time of Grace, the bread is
blessed. In the fourth order, 5 crosses signify the 5 wounds.
The Trinity is accepted in the fifth order by 3 crosses. The
sixth order betokens the 5-fold passion by 5 crosses. In the
entire canon, 23 signs of the cross are made, 10 for Law in
the Old Testament, and 13, indicating the addition of faith
in the Trinity, 10 + 3, in the New. The sign is made with 3
fingers, which, multiplied by 23, brings the total to 69. Later,
with the *Pax Domini*, 3 more signs are made over the chalice
to complete the 72 of the languages of the world. "Sic
tragicus noster pugnam Christi populo Christiano in theatro
Ecclesiae gestibus suis repraesentat." [109]

Here is an exposition which, in its numerical subtlety, goes
far beyond the intention of the creators of the office in
question. For that reason, it is thoroughly typical of the
constant growth and elaboration of number symbolism and
the determination to find numerical significance everywhere,

108. Sicardus, *Mitrale*; P. L. 213, 28-34.
109. Honorius, *Gemma animae*; P. L. 172, 543-70.

and to coördinate all things — the Trinity, the Commandments, the gifts of the Spirit, the languages of the world — under the absolutism of a dogmatic numerology from which there was no appeal. To solidify the 15 of the 15 steps of the temple, there were educed the 15 "Psalms of Degrees" (Pss. 120-34), which rise from virtue to virtue. The feasts of the Church (*Septuagesima, Quinquagesima, Pentecost*), the canonical hours, the arrangements of the chants, the penances imposed, the very episcopal garments were all found to be elaborately symbolical of the "times" of the world and innumerable spiritual and material goods.

To a lesser degree the philosophy of number left its mark on the sciences and pseudosciences of the Middle Ages. Roger Bacon was assured that to the secrets of Nature "the gate and key is Mathematics, which the saints discovered at the beginning of the world . . . and which has always been used by all the saints and sages more than all the sciences." [110] As summarized in Thorndike, his reasoning runs:

Grammar and logic must employ music, a branch of mathematics, in prosody and persuasive periods. The categories of time, place, and quantity require mathematical knowledge for their comprehension. Mathematics must underlie other subjects because it is by nature the most elementary and the easiest to learn and the first discovered. Moreover, all our sense knowledge is received in space, in time, and quantitatively also the certitude of mathematics makes it desirable that other studies avail themselves of its aid.[111]

In point of fact, the amount of "mathematics" and especially of the kind of mystical mathematics which we are considering, depended largely on the individual "scientist." Thorndike has discovered a few examples of science almost free of number mysticism, but in the main all the sciences inherited the fixed numerical truths, such as the 4 elements, and all of them sought to bolster their own efficacy by the

---

110. *Opus majus*, IV, dist. i, cap. 1; Burke, I, 116.
111. Thorndike, *History of Magic*, II, 648.

aid of astrology and numerology. According to Bacon, "if a doctor is ignorant of 'astronomy,' his medical treatment will be dependent upon 'chance and fortune.' " [112] The physics of Grosseteste holds that "the supreme body" is composed of form, matter, composition, and compound. Form is represented by the number 1, matter by 2, and composition by 3. The compound itself is represented by 4. By invoking the tetraktys (1 + 2 + 3 + 4 = 10), it is clear that "every whole and perfect thing is ten." [113]

The sciences of the Middle Ages were so largely hypothetical and so little scientific that the assistance of the power thought to reside in numbers was not to be scorned.[114] In alchemy, the very symbol of chemical change was the dragon or salamander devouring its tail, thus forming a circle and bearing the mystical motto of 3 words and 7 letters, "εν τό πάν" — all is one, illustrated in the unity of 3 and 7, whose sum in turn reverts to the unity of the decad.[115] In addition, there were the 4 mutations of matter, the 7 colors of the planets,[116] the fifth element or quintessence,[117] the 3 chief stages and 10 processes,[118] and innumerable magic 7's. Thomas Vaughan, who, by the seventeenth century, had added to the essentials of alchemy and astrology considerable cabalistic lore, with a liberal admixture of Neo-Platonism, is nevertheless true to the principle of Ultimate Unity when he says,

Know then that every Element is threefold, this triplicity being the expresse image of their author, and a seall He hath laid upon his Creature. . . . Every compound whatsoever is three in one and one in three. . . . Now he that knows these three perfectly with their severall gradations, or annexed links — he is an absolute compleat magician. . . . In the second place you are to learn that every

112. *Ibid.*, II, 670.
113. *Ibid.*, II, 444.
114. Numerical "spells" and charms often aided scientific experiments.
115. C. A. Brown, "The Poem of Theophrastus," p. 204.
116. *Ibid.*, p. 199.
117. Waite, *Lives of the Alchemystical Philosophers*, p. 39.
118. *Ibid.*, p. 42.

Element is twofold. This duplicity or confusion is that *Binarius.*
. . . This is it in which the creature prevaricates and falls from
his first Harmonicall Unity. You must therefore subtract the Duad,
and then the magician's Triad may be reduced "by the Tetrad into
the extreme simplicity of Unity" and, by consequence, "into a
metaphysical union with the Supreme Monad." [119]

The medico was also much concerned with numerical science. Quite apart from his concern for the balancing of the 4
humors, he was very apt to combine numerical charms with
his pharmacy,[120] or to prescribe pills in odd numbers as being
certainly more efficacious than the even.[121] Montaigne, in-
dulging himself in a tirade against his principal foes, the
doctors, remarks, "I omit to speake of the odde number of
their pilles."[122]

Determining the fate of the patient from the day of the moon
upon which his illness was incurred enters also into certain spheres
of life and death which were much employed in the early middle
ages. . . . In these the number of the day of the moon is combined
with a second number obtained by a numerical evaluation of the
letters forming the patient's name. . . . Having calculated the value
of a person's name by adding together the Greek numerals represented by its component letters, and having further added in the
day of the moon, one divides the sum by some given divisor and
looks for the quotient in the compartments [in the Sphere of
Fortune].[123]

Even in astrology itself the casting of the horoscope involved various more or less complicated maneuvers, including
multiplication and division by astrological numbers. According to Henry of Avranches, "astrologers 'reveal the secrets of
things' by their art affecting numbers, by numbers affecting
the procession of the stars, and by the stars moving the uni-

119. *Anthroposophia Theomagica*, in *Magical Writings*, ed. by Waite, pp. 19-20.
120. Thorndike, *History of Magic*, I, 82, 91, 93, 583, 592, 676, 725, 756;
II, 143, 275, 323-24, 330, 481-85.
121. *Ibid.*, IV, 229.
122. Florio trans. Vol. II, Essay XXXVII, "Of the Resemblance between Children and Fathers."
123. Thorndike, *op. cit.*, I, 682-83.

verse." [124] It was even considered possible to discover the sign of any individual by means of arithmancy, which was itself a method of divination utilizing a highly involved combination of Pythagoreanism, gematria, and simple mathematics, which I will not attempt to describe.[125]

In reality, the principles of all the sciences were fundamentally very much the same, for medieval science was ordinarily part science and part magic, and it is often difficult to tell where one ends and the other begins. From a medieval standpoint, science might be defined as a knowledge of cosmic secrets, and magic as the use of this knowledge to control or to predict the operations of nature. "Cosmic Secrets" in this sense include all the gradations of the cosmos, from the Intellectual to the Infernal world; the former to be implored, the latter to be coerced.

Circumstances conspired to make the Chaldaeo-Babylonian-Assyrian East the most fertile source of European magic. The eastern magi were reputably possessed of occult powers beyond the ordinary, not to mention their compilations of astrological, alchemical, mathematical, scientific, and pseudo-scientific information, generally unknown in the West. It is also a sufficiently demonstrated fact that the gods of old religions become the devils of the new. The Gnostic gods, gathered from the overflowing deific abundance of the East, provided very nearly too many Infernal Powers for the Church of Christ to cope with.

From the East, therefore, are derived, wholly or in part, many of the most potent numbers of the magic arts — in particular, the number 7. The welter of Chaldean magic revolved largely about the propitiation of the 7 malevolent gods or phantoms.[126] The Babylonian Pleiades, the Egyptian

124. *Ibid.*, II, 309.
125. This science is fully explained and illustrated in the *Secretum secretorum*; Gaster, *Studies and Texts*, II, 742 *et sqq.*
126. Lenormant, *Chaldean Magic*, p. 17.

Hathors, became in this way the 7 devils of the Middle Ages, germane in origin to, but quite distinct from, the 7 deadly sins. It was the 7 devils, not the 7 sins, who taught Pietro d'Abano the 7 arts.[127] To cope with the 7 demons, who were capable of working any harm from headache to impotence or death, it was deemed advisable to tie them up by 7 knots in a handkerchief, scarf, or girdle.[128] The practice became well-nigh universal.[129] Pliny's *Natural History* takes cognizance of this belief,[130] and it will be found in such accessible medieval textbooks of magic as *The Sword of Moses*[131] and the *Picatrix*.[132]

But if diabolical numbers could ensnare diabolical powers, so could sacred numbers, a truth demonstrated by two diverse processes of reasoning. One of these, fostered by Manicheanism and Averroism, saw hell as an exact inversion of heaven. The other theory held that the devil was subordinate to God and might therefore be coerced by divine symbols. Accordingly, it is observed in the *Malleus maleficarum* that

the following procedure is practiced against hailstorms and tempests. Three of the hailstones are thrown into the fire with an invocation of the Most Holy Trinity, and the Lord's Prayer and the Angelic Salutation are repeated twice or 3 times, together with the Gospel of St. John, "In the beginning was the Word." And the sign of the Cross is made in every direction toward each quarter of the world. Finally, "the Word was made Flesh" is repeated 3 times, and 3 times, "By the words of this Gospel may this tempest be dispersed." And suddenly, if the tempest is due to witchcraft, it will

127. Grillot de Givry, *Witchcraft, Magic, and Alchemy*, p. 120; Thorndike, *op. cit.*, II, 889.

128. Thompson, *Semitic Magic, Its Origin and Development*, pp. xxvii, 33-34, 123, 165, 169, 170, 172, 188. See also Farbridge, *Studies in Biblical and Semitic Symbolism*, p. 124; Rogers, *The Religion of Babylonia and Assyria*, p. 153.

129. Cf. Müller, *Mythology of All Races*, XII, 142, 199, 421; Frazer, *The Golden Bough*, 3d ed., I, 326; III, 13, 303, 306-7, 308; Conway, *Demonology and Devil-Lore*, p. 258.

130. *Op. cit.*, XXVIII, 27.

131. Gaster, *Studies and Texts*, III, 91.

132. Thorndike, *op. cit.*, II, 819.

cease. . . . But he must commit to the Divine Will the effect which is hoped for.[133]

Magic formulas were therefore repeated 3 times, in honor of the Trinity or anti-Trinity. Many demons were depicted as 3-headed. Spenser's magic was entirely orthodox:

> Then taking thrise three haires from off her head
> Them trebly breaded in a threefold lace,
> And round the pots mouth, bound the thread,
> And after having whispered a space
> Certaine sad words, with hollow voice and bace,
> She to the virgin said, thrise said she it;
> Come daughter come, come; spit upon my face,
> Spit thrise upon me, thrise upon me spit;
> Th'uneven number for this businesse is most fit.[134]

The Christian cross itself was as potent a magic as any, and magic circles were often described by a circular arrangement of x's. John Evelyn saw such a figure on the arm of a servant maid.[135] Even the Pythagorean or astrological efficacy of a number could be bolstered by theological implications, the pentacle itself being strengthened by reference to the cross or the 5 wounds of Jesus.

Thus there is seldom but one basis for the potency of any given magical operation. The magic circle ("nothing can be done without a circle") has both an astrological (as the zodiac) and Pythagorean significance (geometric symbol of 10). The cross brings with it powers which antedate Christianity. The number 7 has not only diabolical but Pythagorean powers, and belongs, furthermore, in the category of the odd numbers which were always held to be more powerful than the even. The "aged nurse" of the *Faerie Queene* well knew that

> Th'uneven number for this businesse is most fit.

133. Part II, qu. 2, cap. 7.
134. *Faerie Queene*, III, ii, 50.
135. *Diary*, Aug. 5, 1670.

To the layman, all astrological numbers were doubtless considered as magical. The author of *Les Faits merveilleux de Virgille* was probably quite satisfactorily mysterious when he caused his hero to create a palace with 4 corners, within which could be heard what was being said in the 4 quarters of Rome.[136] Another castle in Rome was distinguished by a gate made with 24 iron flayles, 12 men on each side smiting with the flayles.[137] When the magician became old, he directed his man to kill him, cut him into small pieces, quarter his head, and salt him in a barrel for 9 days, whereupon he would revive as a young man.[138]

Actually, the most "potent" numbers in magic appear to have been 3, 4, 5, 7, and 9. The *Black Book of Solomon* prescribes that the magic circle should be 9 feet in diameter, within which 4 pentacles must be drawn.[139] Agrippa also suggests the figure of the cross, because it "hath a great correspondency with the most potent numbers 5, 7, and 9" and "is also the rightest figure of all, containing 4 right angles." [140]

Each of these numbers is here used with eastern, Gnostic, Christian, astrological, or Pythagorean definition. The quaternary is employed partly for its astrological significance, partly for its Pythagoreon "rightness," and partly because the ineffable mystery of the Tetragrammaton is thereby invoked.[141] The number 9, composed only of the all-powerful 3, carries with it a host of attributes. Its antiquity goes back to the great Egyptian Ennead. It recalls, from the Pythagorean viewpoint, the *Enneads* of Plotinus. It invokes the

136. Thoms, *Early English Prose Romances*, p. 221.
137. *Ibid.*, p. 233.
138. *Ibid.*, p. 234.
139. Grillot de Givry, *op. cit.*, p. 104.
140. *Occult Philosophy*, II, 23. Agrippa is of the sixteenth century, and influenced by the cabala, but, as here appears, agrees with medieval magicians on the potent numbers, which were older than either the cabala or medieval magic.
141. Grillot de Givry, *op. cit.*, p. 104; see above, p. 67.

favor of the triple triad of the angels and at the same time enlists the power of the devil, who was thought to be represented in the Old Testament by King Og, who was 9 cubits high.[142] With the introduction of Arabic numerals, there was added to the number the mathematical virtue of incorruptibility. Like the salamander, it may change its shape, but, however often multiplied, it always reproduces itself.[143] The most famous testimony to the cogency of this incomparable symbol comes from the weird sisters of *Macbeth*:

> The weird sisters, hand in hand,
> Posters of the sea and land,
> Thus do go about, about:
> Thrice to thine and thrice to mine
> And thrice again, to make up nine.
> Peace! the charm's wound up.[144]

The magic properties of 5 probably derive ultimately from Persian religion, where it was of prime importance. In the East, cruciform emblems were considered as 5 "pointed," the intersection of the arms forming a fifth definite point, which the Rigveda includes by referring to the 4 directions and "here." [145] Consequently, 5 became in the East a holy number, which filtered westward in magic, Zoroastrianism, Manicheanism and other fragments of eastern learning. In Egypt, 5 per-

142. Rabanus, *De universo*, XVIII, 3; P. L. 111, 491.

143. It is on the unique behavior of this integer that the "rule of nines" depends. "A number divided by 9 will leave the same remainder as the sum of its digits divided by 9. The rule known as 'casting out the nines' for testing the accuracy of multiplication is founded on this property. The rule may be thus explained: Let two numbers be represented by 9a + b and 9c + d and their product by P; then

$$P = 81\ ac + 9\ bc + 9ad + bd$$

Hence P/9 has the same remainder as bd/9; and therefore the *sum of the digits* of P, when divided by 9 gives the same remainder as the *sum of the digits of bd*, when divided by 9. If on trial this should not be the case, the multiplication must have been incorrectly performed. In practice b and d are readily found from the sum of the digits of the two numbers to be multiplied together" (Hall and Knight, *Higher Algebra*, 4th ed., London, 1927, p. 63). See above, p. 102.

144. Act I, scene 3.

145. Levy-Bruhl, *Les Fonctions mentales*, p. 249; Keith, *Mythology of All Races*, VI, 16; Hopkins, *The Holy Numbers of the Rig-Veda*, p. 147.

fect circles were the symbol for "daylight and splendour." [146]
The magic power of 5 received the testimony of Plutarch in
the *Ei at Delphi*, where he explains that the 5 points of the E
and the fact that this letter is the fifth in the Egyptian,
Phoenician, Greek, and Latin alphabets, together with its
position on the Oracle, gave the number 5 a great power over
all things. It is also, like 9, incorruptible, by virtue of its
recurrence in multiplication. [147]

The cross, because of its broad signification, was habitually
used in magic as the figured representation of the number, but
a far more accurate symbol was "Solomon's Seal," the pentacle, pentangle, or 5-pointed star. The properties of this
figure coincide perfectly with the attributes of the number
5, for, like the lover's knot, it is endless and thus corresponds
to the "circular" property of the number. [148]

Unlike the cross, however, the pentacle appears to have
been almost exclusively of magical significance. [149] Its appearance on the shield of Gawain [150] is therefore much more in
keeping with the magic of the Green Knight than with the
Christian and chivalrous connotations assigned to it. [151] It
appears as though the Gawain poet had deliberately amassed
as many Christian pentads as possible, to account for the
legendary ensign of the Christian hero. Had the author been
primarily interested in these moral and spiritual pentads,
there is no conceivable reason for his not choosing that other
and more fitting 5-pointed emblem, the cross, rather than
such a notorious magical symbol. Nor can it be said that the

146. Bayley, *The Lost Language of Symbolism*, p. 267.
147. *De E apud Delphos*, IV.
148. See above, p. 102.
149. I have never found it used otherwise.
150. *Gawain and the Green Knight*, II, 6.
151. It is admitted to be the seal of Solomon, but is said to betoken abstract
truth, rather than his traditional magical powers. It shows Gawain faithful in
5 things, and each of them in 5 ways. He was faultless in his 5 wits, he never
failed in his 5 fingers, his faith was in the 5 wounds and the 5 joys of the Virgin,
he was distinguished in 5 virtues (II, 6-7).

Christian attributes were added to strengthen the purely occult powers of the pentacle, for the primary significance of the pentacle is not even alluded to. The by-no-means-novel conclusion is that *Gawain* is another example of the Christianization of a secular legend. The original story would therefore take on more the theme of magician versus magician than that of Christian Knight versus fairy trickery.[152]

Divination and the Black Arts took numerous forms on which it is not necessary to dwell further, unless it be to remark that all of them utilized the magic properties of numbers in their rituals and that one of them, arithmancy, relied entirely on the mysteries of the decimal system.

It is clear that number science had quite thoroughly penetrated the worlds of learning and religion in the Middle Ages. To the uneducated and the relatively uneducated, number mysteries and the common numerical groupings must have been accepted as simple fact, or else held in the suspicion with which the common man ordinarily regards learning.[153] When John Skelton writes, "by that Lord that is one, two, and three," [154] he is not so much stating a doctrine as repeating a commonplace. When, in the same poem, *Drede* describes the "subtle persons in our ship," it is no more extraordinary to find that they number "four and three" than that Dunbar should have added to the macabre literature of the period

152. This aspect of the story does not conflict with the pagan ritualistic interpretation offered by Miss Weston. She identifies the pentangle as one of the 4 suits of Tarot (*From Ritual to Romance*, p. 74) then, as now, one of the instruments of the Black Art.

153. So Langland:
> "Bote astronomye is hard thing and cruel to knowe,
> *Gemetrie and gemensye* is gynful of speche
> That worcheth with theose threo thriveth he late,
> Fore sorcerye is the sovereyn bok that to science longeth.
>
>   .   .   .
>
> Alle theose sciences siker, I my-selven
> Have i-founded hum furst folk to deceyve."
>   Piers Plowman (A version), XI, 152-55, 160-61; italics mine.

154. *The Bouge of Court.*

The Dance of the Seven Deadly Sins. As a result of this same heritage, we still speak instinctively of the 4 winds and the 5 senses as if the ordinals were inseparable from the nouns. In the Middle Ages, the list of such numerical compounds was enormous. From Hippocrates to Shakespeare, readers never wearied of the 7 ages. In the interlude, *Mankind*, the euphemism of *Now-a-days*, "Remember my broken head in the worship of the 5 vowels" (wounds), runs side by side with the un-numerical euphemism, "by Cock's body;" an oath by "Christ's cross" is matched by "the Holy Trinity."

Beyond such naïve repetitions and the use of "magic" numbers in charms, the common man could not be expected to go. Metaphysical profundity varied then, as always, with the individual, and even in the profound mind of a Dante number philosophy is regarded as anything but simple:

> Tu credi che a me tuo pensier mei
> da quel ch' è primo, così come raia
> da l' un, se si conosce, il cinque e 'l sei.[155]

Se si conosce! It is not to be supposed, therefore, that even all authors who employed symbolic numbers were guilty either of "science" or of philosophic meditation on the infallibility of the Divine Plan. The description of the Celestial City in *The Pearl* is interlarded with symbolic numbers. This does not mean that either author or reader necessarily had any conception of their import, since they were admittedly directly transcribed from the *Apocalypse*,[156] and were probably intended to be equally mysterious. Less frank, but equally obvious in its scriptural indebtedness, is the famous letter of Prester John to the Christian Princes. His description of his Indian Kingdom, with its 72 tributary kings and provinces, includes such prodigies as 40-ell-high giants, 12 maneating warriors, a sort of fountain of youth 3 days' journey

155. *Paradiso*, XV, 55-57.
156. Stanza 83.

from Paradise, a mirror guarded by 3,000 men, 7 serving kings.[157] It is logical to suppose that the superstitious regard which has always attended number must have been uncommonly strong in an age when charms, philters, potions, spells, and incantations abounded, many of them confused numerically as well as verbally with priestly pronouncements and dispensed in much the same manner as pardons and holy relics.

Consequently, although symbolic numbers are profusely scattered through the pages of nearly all medieval writings, it is necessary to distinguish, especially in secular and unscientific literature, between the philosophical or scientific use of number, the symbolic, the imitative, and the merely naïve preference for certain commonly used numbers.

Concerning the last, no more elaborate explanation need be sought than the very human predilection for repeating the commonplace. The modern still exhibits a well-marked habit of approximating an amount as 3, 5, 7, 10, or easily handled multiples of 5 and 10, rather than 4, for example, or 6.[158] In a numerically minded age, this habit was accentuated, so that into whatever region of medieval Europe Christianity and learning had penetrated, the epics, the chronicles, the *chansons de geste*, the romances were colored by numbers derived from those sources.

As always, multiples of 5 and 10 were the principal round numbers. The use of 15, 40, and 120 was more habitual then than now by virtue of liturgical and scientific usage.[159] But vying in popularity with the decimal limits were the astrological numbers, 4, 7, and 12 (always including multiples) used in precisely the same fashion, as when Roland brags that

157. Baring Gould, *Curious Myths of the Middle Ages*, pp. 37 et sqq.

158. Fred C. Kelly, "Number Prejudices" *Reader's Digest*, Aug., 1936, p. 98.

159. The 15 psalms of Degrees (120-34), see above, p. 116, 15 as one-half of the astrological 30; the 40 days, Lent; the 120 as one-third of the zodiacal circle = 3 x 40.

he will smite 700 blows, or mayhap a thousand.[160] The phrase, "a twelvemonth," was at least as common as "a year." A peculiarity arising from the habitual usage of other than decimal limits is the occasional appearance of such unusual round numbers as 24 (also astrological) and 48.[161] Similarly, the constant employment of the "score" made 60 and 120 as recognizable round numbers as 50 and 100. The ubiquitous triad, now not only "statistical" [162] but reinforced by all the enormous weight of theological connotations, was easily the favorite number of the Middle Ages. Without unduly laboring the obvious, one may recall the 3 caskets of the Merchant of Venice,[163] and the 3 phrases of Fryer Bacon's head repeating the 3 dimensions of time.[164] Three times, in the Chanson de Roland, Oliver begs Roland to sound the horn. When finally persuaded, Roland blows 3 blasts. At the third blast, the emperor turns.

Because of the constant appearance of symbolic numbers as merely convenient limits, it is necessary to depend almost entirely on the context to provide the clue that symbolism is actually being intended. This is especially true in the case of what I have termed imitative symbolism: the use of familiar integers, not as specific symbols but as "atmosphere," to supply a tone of seriousness, mystery, or sanctity by their general connotations. In the Chronicle of the Cid, 12, 24, or 40 individuals always take part in councils or oath-makings. The council is certainly more serious, the oath more binding, when sanctified by the memory of the 12 apostles, the 24 elders, or the Lenten period. Similarly Tristram's birth on the third day of travail [165] might suggest without precisely

160. Line 1078, Butler trans.

161. Forty-eight is merely a multiple of 12, as in Tristram's promise to fell the 48 trees of the giant, in Thomas of Britain, The Romance of Tristram and Ysolt, LXXV.

162. See above, pp. 5-6.

163. Derived from the Gesta Romanorum.

164. The Famous Historie of Fryer Bacon, in Early English Prose Romances.

165. Thomas of Britain, XV.

symbolizing, the sorrowful death of Our Lord. On the other hand, the fact that Tristram learned the 7 arts; then 7 kinds of music,[166] and shortly thereafter purchased 7 birds [167] need only be attributed to the narrator's, as well as the listener's, delight in the number of seas, planets, days of the week, wise men, and so on. The same formula, which might be designated as part of the poetic diction of the time, accounts for the 7 Sleepers of Ephesus, the 7 Wise Masters, Tannhäuser's 7 years at Venusburg, St. George's 7 years of torture.

In this twilight zone of symbolism, it is extremely hazardous to attempt or even look for an interpretation of such a widely significant number as 7. To each of the above heptads may be allocated some specific meaning or application of the integer, but it would not be logical to suppose that any but a very general connection was made by the teller or the hearer of the story. Particularly elusive are the astrological 12 and 24, which become round numbers wherever the calendar is important, are heavily endowed with Christian connotations, and at the same time retain their original astrological implications. John Rhys [168] has identified the 24 damsels of the castle of *The Lady of the Fountain* [169] with the hours of the day. This I believe to be a sound interpretation, but only because of the strong case made out by Loomis for the derivation of the story from a solar myth.[170] Groupings of 12 are so common, even among rather primitive tribes, that it is difficult to prove any special origin for the 12 peers of France. In view of the Indo-European 12-month year, together with the 12 days by which their solar year exceeded the lunar,[171] the "dozen" would be at least a convenient round number

166. *Ibid.*, XVII.
167. *Ibid.*, XVIII.
168. *Lectures on the Origin and Growth of Religion as Illustrated by Celtic Heathendom*, p. 354.
169. *The Mabinogion*, trans. by Guest.
170. Loomis, *Celtic Myth and Arthurian Romance*, especially cap. vi.
171. Webster, *Rest Days*, p. 276.

and at most a sacred number, ordained by the celestial movements or by the tradition of the 12 apostles.[172]

On the other hand, the coincidence of the dozen, the 12 months, and the 12 apostles made the correlation between them inevitable in Christianized countries. It is in the *Pelérinage de Charlemagne à Constantinople*, an early twelfth-century composition, that the relationship between the peers and the apostles is specifically made. A Jew, who has seen Charles and the Peers, reports to the Patriarch:

> Alez, sire, al muster pur les funz aprester.
> O vendreit me frai baptizer e lever.
> Duze cuntes vi ore en cel muster entrer,
> O veoc euls le trezime. Unc ne vi si formet.
> Par le men escientre! ça est meimes Deus.
> Il e li duze apostle vus venent visiter.[173]

The famous "unlucky 13" and especially the "13 at table" is, I believe, somehow connected with this tradition. Ernst Böklen has attempted to prove the prevalence of the superstition as early as Homeric times, but his evidence is drawn from his own discovery of instances where a misfortune is said to have occurred to one of 13 individuals.[174] I cannot believe this type of evidence to be valid, since the number is never asserted to be the cause of the misfortune nor is it

---

172. On the same basis, the weakest link in Loomis' chain of resemblances between Arthur's war with Lucius and with Lot is his statement, "In the final battle with Lucius much is made of the division of his army into twelve battalions, each with its senatorial or royal commander, while in the army of Lot there are twelve kings" (*Celtic Myth and Arthurian Romance*, p. 348). For in the first place, in the relaying of a secular tradition, the numbers involved do not necessarily remain the same; consider the number of knights of the Round Table (Lewis F. Mott, "The Round Table," PMLA XX, 231-64). In the second place, the dozen is too common a choice for counselors, companions, or leaders to make any particular 12 in any way remarkable. The many possible sources of the 12 connected with Arthur and Charlemagne have been examined by Laura Hibbard Loomis: MP XXV, 331-54; MLR XXVI, 408-26; XLIV, 511-19; PMLA XLI, 771-78. This last article holds that the peers were specifically created on the model of the 12 apostles.

173. Lines 134-39.

174. *Die unglückszahl Dreizehn und ihre mythische Bedeutung.*

ever directly labeled as "unlucky" in any discussion of significant numbers or elsewhere. The first specific mention of the unlucky 13 which I have been able to find occurs in Montaigne:

> And me seemeth I may well be excused if I rather except an odd number than an even . . . if I had rather make a twelfth or fourteenth at a table, then a thirteenth. . . . All such fond conceits, now in credit about us, deserve at least to be listned unto.[175]

The fact that the number was associated with Epiphany [176] by the Church, and appears not to have been considered other than holy by any of the medieval number theorists leads to the inference that the unlucky 13 was a popular superstition entirely disconnected from the "science of numbers." Petrus Bungus is the first arithmologist to recognize any evil inherent in the number. He records that the Jews murmured 13 times against God in the exodus from Egypt, that the thirteenth psalm concerns wickedness and corruption, that the circumcision of Israel occurred in the thirteenth year, thus not reaching the satisfaction of the law and the evangelists, which are figured by 10 and 4. As 11 is a number of transgression, because it goes beyond the 10 Commandments, so 13 goes beyond the 12 apostles. Therefore, *hic numerus Judaeorum taxat impietatem.*[177] The previous absence of any such explanation in the arithmologies gives the impression that popular belief had forced upon the priest this painful and rather unconvincing interpretation of the Commandments + the Trinity. Montaigne's intimation that the superstition was widely in vogue would tend to push its origin back at least to the Middle Ages. To find a 13 which might popularly achieve baleful connotations is so easy that I should rather assign the super-

---

175. Florio trans., Book III, Essay VIII, "Of the Art of Conferring."

176. *Legenda aurea,* Epiphany. The 3 kings came to see the Christ at the age of 13 days. In a method of divination cited by Thorndike (*op. cit.,* I, 679), the Lord's Day is assigned the number 13. See above, p. 115.

177. *Mysticae numerorum,* 31-32.

stition to a confluence of factors, rather than to a single source.

With nearly every traditional 12, a 13 is somehow associated. Earliest in time is the intercalated thirteenth month, which Böklen asserts was regarded as discordant and unlucky.[178] Webster agrees that such was sometimes the case.[179] There is a slender chance that a tradition, even as uncertain as this, might have been orally transmitted to the Middle Ages. There is a much better chance that the omnipresent 13 of the lunar and menstruation cycle made the number fearsome, or at least unpopular.

At the same time, the number may have become popularly associated with the diabolical arts. In Faust's *Miraculous Art and Book of Marvels, or the Black Raven*, 13 are said to compose the Infernal Hierarchy.[180] This must be the same astrological 13, since the Raven is the thirteenth symbol in the intercalary month year, as well as the effigy for the moon.[181] Simultaneously, cabalistic lore may have introduced the 13 Conformations of the Holy Beard, also astrological in origin and magical in common belief. In Britain, 13 became associated with witchcraft. Whether for the same reason or because the inclusion of a leader with any group of 12 makes a thirteenth, as seems to have been the case in Druidic ceremony, a witches' koven was ordinarily composed of 13, or a multiple.[182]

It will be noted, however, that the specific superstition mentioned by Montaigne is that of 13 at table. Here the connection is indisputably with the Last Supper. One wonders how much the legend of the Siege Perilous had to do with drawing attention to the thirteenth unlucky chair. True enough, the Siege Perilous was sanctified, but it was also

178. *Die unglückszahl Dreizehn*, pp. 8-9.
179. *Rest Days*, p. 276.
180. Conway, *Demonology*, p. 229.
181. Böklen, *op. cit.*, pp. 8-9.
182. Murray, *The Witch-Cult in Western Europe*, pp. 16, 50, 191.

Perilous and distinctly unlucky for the wrong person — "wherein never knight sat that he met not death thereby." [183] This is something more than a guess, because, although the thirteenth chair is ordinarily reserved for the leader — Charlemagne in the *Pelerinage* [184] and the All-Father in the temple of the Gods at Gladsheim[185] — Boron's *Joseph* assigns the vacant seat to Judas, and the Modena *Perceval* to "Nostre Sire" in one place but to Judas in another.[186] It is also possible that "Nostre Sire" might have been the author's intention but that the copyist and public opinion altered it to Judas.

These are the kinds of number symbolism — atmospheric, traditional, superstitious — which are most common in the secular literature of the Middle Ages. Direct symbolism is rare and, since it is nearly always explained, one would assume that it was considered too complex for popular consumption. In the *Trump of Death* from the *Gesta Romanorum*, a king puts his brother in a deep pit on a chair with 4 decayed feet. A sword is hung over his head and 4 men with swords surround him. Then, causing music to be brought and food, he asks his brother the cause of his sorrow. After the obvious reply, the king explains that his brother's sorrow is like his own. The frail chair is his throne. His body is supported by the 4 elements. The pit is hell. The sword of Divine Justice hangs above. In front is the sword of Death; behind, of sin; at the right is the Devil; at the left are the worms to gnaw the body after death.[187] An explanation in this case is actually required, but should hardly be necessary in the following:

And then he [King Ban] plucked 3 blades of grass in the Name of the Holy Trinity.[188]
The two edges [of the sword] signify that the knight should be

---

183. *Le Livre de Lancelot del Lac*, XXXIX.
184. Line 118.
185. MacCulloch, *Mythology of All Races*, III, 327.
186. Weston, *The Legend of Sir Perceval*, II, 132.
187. Morley, *Medieval Tales*, pp. 155-57.
188. *Le Livre de Lancelot del Lac*, III.

the servant of our Lord and of His People.[189] [The active and the contemplative lives bound up with the 2 commandments of Christ, love God and neighbor, form the most commonplace duad of the Middle Ages.]

Again, in the *Lay of the Ash Tree* of Marie de France, the Lady who was shamed for bearing twins placed one at the foot of an ash tree *near an abbey, petitioning God for Grace.* "It was a fair tree, thick and leafy, and was divided into four strong branches." The "four strong branches," together with the context, strongly indicate that the ash tree is meant to symbolize the cruciformed church.[190]

It is also true that the prevalence of symbolic numbers, used merely as round numbers, makes it difficult to be certain of symbolic intent without an accompanying clue. In the following, for example, it would seem that the reiterated 7 was certainly a reference to the 7 of repentence or the 7 stages of contemplation:

When Arthur, that renowned King of England . . . had by twelve severall set battailys, conquered the third part of the earth, and being wearyed with the exploytes of martiall adventures, in his old dayes betook himselfe to a quiet course of life, turning his warlike habiliaments to divine bookes of celestiall meditations; that as the one had made him famous in this world, so might the other make him blessed in the world to come. Seven yeares continued quiet thoughts in his brest; 7 yeares never heard hee the sound of delight-full drummes; nor in 7 yeares beheld he his thrice worthy Knights of the Round Table.[191]

Yet even here, there is no guarantee that a symbol rather than a highly popular aggregate is being used. In *Joannes Turpini historia de vita Caroli Magni et Rolandi*, the comparison of Roland, wounded in 5 places,[192] to Christ, and the assumption of Divine Protection given to Charlemagne, when

189. *Ibid.*, X, trans. by Paton.
190. Mason trans., p. 74, in his *French Medieval Romances.*
191. *The Second Part of the Famous History of Tom a Lincolne,* I; p. 655, in Thom's *Early English Prose Romances.*
192. *Op. cit.*, XXII.

the sun stood still for 3 days while the pursuit of the pagans endured,[193] would be somewhat hazardous to make, if in the same book the mystery of the 3 in 1 had not been elucidated and if that book had not borne the name of Turpin.[194]

Such are the rather faint and popularized echoes of a tradition which was more at ease on higher planes of learning. In all of these instances, the number is a symbol only in a secondary sense. The 5 wounds of Charlemagne connote specifically the 5 wounds of Christ, without touching the deeper question of the meaning of the number 5. For, strictly speaking, number symbolism belongs more to metaphysics than to trope or allegory. It is the language of Eternal Verities; not of concrete realities. As such, it has little part in the poetic aim of "intensification and clarification of experience," unless the poet writes for the limited audience of those who "well understand." Unlike the more objective medieval symbols (the Pelican = Christ), the abstraction of number was itself shrouded in mystery, to which only a complete metaphysical erudition could provide the key. For this reason, such numerical references as occur in popular literature or, with the exception of Dante, in the literature of the vulgar tongue, are but dim echoes of the notation of science, philosophy, and theology.

193. *Ibid.*, XXVI.
194. Morley, *Medieval Tales*, pp. 11-53.

VII. THE BEAUTY OF ORDER:
DANTE[1]

IN CONTRAST to the uncertain and often "atmospheric" number symbolism employed by other medieval writers of the vulgar tongue is Dante's sharp and studied usage of significant numbers. As a scientist, philosopher, theologian, mystic, and poet, he necessarily belongs to the small company of those who "well understand." For this reason, the modern reader of Dante must have at the least some slight acquaintance with the nature of medieval learning and, even more important, must be prepared to alter his mental attitudes.

Medieval mysticism and medieval allegory are foreign to the modern mind. When the modern thinks of mysticism at all, he is apt to think of it in terms of Vachel Lindsay or of Walt Whitman. The visions of the medieval mystics were, however, neither extravagant nor undisciplined. On the contrary, the vision of the true mystic was a revelation of order, and the depth of his penetration was in direct proportion to his comprehension of the precise coördination of all things in a Universal Harmony. Allegory, likewise, is not only foreign but often repugnant to the modern mind. It is therefore pleasant to discount the subtlety of the *Divine Comedy*, to call it unimportant or even nonexistent. In the Middle Ages, however, allegory was the natural mode of expression, even in secular writings, especially when such writings assumed a didactic tone. In religious writings, as we have seen in the last two chapters, attempts to find ever-deeper and more subtle interpretations of Scripture were often carried

1. Quotations from the *Divine Comedy* are drawn from the *Testo Critici della Societa Dantesca Italiana*; translation by Jefferson Butler Fletcher. For all other works of Dante, I have used Edward Moore's *Tutte le opere* (4th ed.), with translations supplied by the Temple Classics, in order that the same line references might be used for both the Italian text and the translation.

to fantastic lengths, from a modern point of view. Medieval Church literature is largely composed of such commentaries and of sermons similarly devoted to explanation of the historical, allegorical, moral, and anagogical meanings of favorite scriptural passages. The *Divine Comedy* is both didactic and religious. In his letter to Can Grande, Dante specifically states that his work is a complex net-work of meanings and explains that its interpretation must be based on the fourfold scheme of scriptural exegesis.[2] Dante's extraordinary love of allegory is amply demonstrated in the *Convivio,* where each ode is followed by an exposition which seems so entirely out of proportion to the ode itself that it would hardly receive a hearing if it had been proposed by any commentator other than the poet himself. The evidence of the *Vita nuova, Convivio,* and *De monarchia* would imply allegorical subtlety in the *Comedy,* but implication becomes certainty in view of the letter to Can Grande and the complementary fact that Dante twice in the *Comedy* itself calls the reader's attention to truths hidden below the surface of his verse.[3] To discover these inner meanings was not considered a bore, but the keenest pleasure, for as Augustine said, "the most hidden meanings are the sweetest."[4]

Simply because of this deliberate subtlety, interpretations of Dante are bound to be as diverse and often as wide of the mark as medieval interpretations of Scripture. The soundness of such exegesis depends on coördinating such interpretation with the express beliefs, mental habits, and purposes of both Dante and his generation. It depends as well on the clarification of each segment of the poem, as part of the pattern of the whole. In all humility and with full admission of my own

2. Epistle X, par. 7.
3. *Inf.,* IX, 61-63; *Purg.,* VIII, 19-21. Cf. also the testimony of Guido da Pisa and Fraziolo Bamboglioli, early readers, who found the *Comedy* "most subtle" (Flamini, *Introduction to the Study of the Divine Comedy,* p. 21).
4. See above, p. 80.

inadequacy as a student of Dante, I offer the following commentary as a suggestive method, rather than a final statement, of at least one "gate and key" to the Dantesque vision of the universe.

Our first acquaintance with Dante comes through the *Vita nuova*. Here we are given to understand that, whatever his past had been, Dante was made one of the number of those who had embraced the "New Life." The "New Life," which is the Christian Life,[5] comes not by study but only through "revelation," specifically granted to Dante through Beatrice, who, in her earthly perfection, bore the impress of the Divine Stamp. Here we see Dante the incipient mystic, convinced of the order of all things, though not yet capable of full comprehension of that order. The reality of the Divine Plan was revealed to him by the constant recurrence of the number 9 in his relationship with Beatrice.[6]

Of all the number symbols of the Middle Ages, few were so specifically meaningful as the number 9, which is always, first and foremost, the angelic number. No contemporary reader could have missed this graceful indication of the mold in which Beatrice was cast. Yet for Dante the number itself has a greater reality than its concrete angelic association. His well-known explanation is resolved to the simple fact that "this number was her very self."[7] Now it is well known that God is 1, but that he is expressed in 3 persons. Human understanding cannot readily comprehend essence, which is Unity. Therefore 3 is more comprehensible than 1, and similarly 9, whose sole root is 3, whose source is 1, is even more capable of human realization.[8] Beatrice, says Dante, "is a miracle."[9] A miracle, we learn from the *De monarchia*, "is

5. Augustine, Letter LV, 17, 31; see above, p. 82.
6. Grandgent has suggested a plausible practical reason for Dante's usage of this number imagery (*The Ladies of Dante's Lyrics*, pp. 107-45).
7. *Vita nuova*, XXX, 26-27.
8. See above, pp. 99-100.
9. *Vita nuova*, XXX, 39.

the immediate operation of the first agent, without the co-operation of second agents." [10] The reason for miracles is also specifically explained as the visible representation of invisible things. [11] To put it baldly, Beatrice and 9 are both earthly mirrors of the First Cause, and her nature is directly cognate to the angelic. She is, as J. B. Fletcher puts it, "Like the blessed Virgin — an immaculate conception." [12]

It is incidentally tempting to wonder whether there was not a secondary reason for Dante's fondness of this number. In view of Dante's apocalyptic tendency and his knowledge of astrology, it is pertinent to consider the place of the number in astrology. The ninth house alone is singled out for special comment by Roger Bacon, who summarizes the work of his predecessors as follows:

Whence the 9th house, as they say, is that of peregrinations and journeys of faith and deity and religion, and the house of the worship of God, of wisdom, of books, letters, and the accounts of ambassadors and reports and dreams. Therefore rightly, as they say, is the house assigned to Jupiter, who is significant with regard to the blessings of the other life, because for those blessings there are needed faith and religion and the worship of God and the study of wisdom, and a multitude of books and letters, as is evident from the sacred law; and a large number of ambassadors such as prophets and apostles and preachers making suitable reports regarding the noble state of that life and having frequent revelations in dreams and ecstasies and visions concerning this life. [13]

Although there is no indication that the ninth house figured in the horoscopes of either Beatrice or Dante, it is not unlikely

10. II, 4, 15-17.

11. *Ibid.*, 73-75.

12. "Allegory of the Vita Nuova," MP XI, 5. It is significant that Can Grande della Scala, the most probable candidate for the title of DVX, *Veltro*, is first introduced to Dante in the *Comedy* as being then 9 years old (*Par.*, XVII, 79-81). Thus Dante meets both his spiritual deliverer (Beatrice) and, figuratively, his proposed saviour of the Empire at the age of 9. We have seen how significant this circumstance was considered in the case of Beatrice. Why not, then, in the case of the great Lombard? Cf. J. B. Fletcher, "The Crux of Dante's Comedy," *Romanic Review*, XVI, 1-41, especially p. 21.

13. *Opus majus*, I, 277-78.

that this astrological 9 increased Dante's veneration for the number. Beatrice had been for him an "ambassador" of heaven, and through love of her Dante had been granted frequent revelations in dreams and ecstasies and visions.[14] It was such a vision [15] that determined him to write no more until he might say of Beatrice "what hath never been written of any woman," of Beatrice who was incidental in originating his own great "journey of faith and deity and religion." For although he had been instructed concerning the spiritual harmony of the circle,[16] he was at that time still so far from attaining that harmony that he was capable of yielding to the mundane temptations of the *Donna pietosa* or other *pargoletta*.

The second stage of Dante's development is his defection from Beatrice as he seeks consolation in Philosophy. The wrong which he committed was not the search for knowledge, but the worship of knowledge as an end in itself, independent of revelation. Like Ulysses, he sought truth by a way not good. He had not yet learned to be content with the *quia*,[17] nor to await Beatrice

> ch' è opra di fede.[18]
> for matter 'tis of faith.

How much of this period is represented in the *Convivio*, which is a narration after the event, it is impossible to say. How far he strayed from the path of Salvation can only be surmised by the pointed question of Cavalcanti,

> "Se per questo cieco
> carcere vai per altezza d' ingegno,
> mio figlio ov' è? perchè non è ei teco?" [19]

---

14. *Vita nuova*, III, XII, XXIII, XXIV, XL, XLIII.

15. *Ibid.*, XLIII.

16. *Ibid.*, XII. The circle is the symbol of unity and completeness. It is the geometrical representation of 1 and 10. See above, p. 102.

17. *Purg.*, III, 37. "In scholastic logic a demonstration *a priori*, from cause to effect, was called *propter quid*, and a demonstration *a posteriori*, from effect to cause, was called *quia*" (Grandgent, ed. note).

18. *Ibid.*, XVIII, 48.

19. *Inf.*, X, 58-60.

"If so thou goest free
Through this blind prison by loftiness of wit,
My son — where then is he? Why not with thee?"

a question which savours strongly of a type of learning not theological. Cavalcanti apparently still believes that the underworld may be conquered through "altezza d' ingegno," and intimates that Dante and Guido had been companions in the study of one or more branches of the esoteric knowledge which was always filtering in via Spain from the East and which, regardless of its content, was generally regarded in Christian Europe as "magic" and "heresy." [20] This impression is intensified, as I have remarked elsewhere,[21] by the beast-catching cord which Dante wears, until he gives it up to Virgil,[22] since both the description of the cord and its properties coincide with the girdle which was traditionally part of the costume of the magician. If Dante had dabbled in magic of any sort, he might easily have been initiated in the complex numerology which generally accompanied it.

It is, at any rate, certain that he returns from his excursion into the Speculative Life with an unshaken conviction of the order of the universe. Conscious as he is of the dualism of body and soul,[23] matter and spirit,[24] action and contemplation,[25] he nevertheless subordinates matter to spirit, conceiving of the microcosm and the macrocosm as mirrors, more or less perfect, of the Intellectual world, since "it is of the intention of God that every created thing should present the divine likeness in so far as its proper nature is capable of receiving it." [26] He thus subscribes to the concepts of Dominican

20. This confusion is amply demonstrated throughout Henry Charles Lea's *A History of the Inquisition of the Middle Ages,* and particularly in Dante's reference to the Latin translator of Averroes as a magician (*Inf.,* XX, 116-17).

21. "Geryon and the Knotted Cord," MLN LI, 445-49.

22. *Inf.,* XVI, 106-14.

23. *Convivio,* I, 1, 16-26.

24. *Ibid.,* III, 2, 23-34.

25. *Ibid.,* II, 5, 66-80.

26. *De monarchia,* I, 8, 6-9.

Realism as expounded by Albertus and Thomas Aquinas, showing that "particular nature is obedient to universal nature when it gives a man 32 teeth neither more nor less." [27] This is "the foresight of universal nature which ordains particular nature to her perfection." [28] If particular nature is not as perfect as the universal, it is because of the ancient duality of matter and form, in which matter is essentially imperfect: "Every substantial form proceeds from its own first cause which is God, as it is written in the *Book of Causes*; and they derive their diversity not from it, for it is most simple, but from the secondary causes or from the material upon which it descends." [29]

To Pythagoreanism he owes the method by which the particular proceeds from the universal:

> Tu credi che a me tuo pensier mei
> da quel ch' è primo, cosi come raia
> da l' un, se si conosce, il cinque e 'l sei. [30]

> Thou deemest that to me thy thought must flow
> From Primal Thought, as out of unity,
> Well studied, five and six are seen to grow.

Veneration of Pythagoras was common enough in the Middle Ages, and Dante's own reverence is clear from his eight references to Pythagoras, [31] one of which names Pythagoras as the first philosopher and places him "almost at the beginning of the foundation of Rome." [32] The combination of priority and proximity to the foundation of Rome was in Dante's mind tantamount to divine approval.

The extent of Dante's Pythagoreanism is clearly indicated throughout his prose works. In the *Convivio*, he likens arithmetic to the heaven of the Sun —

27. *Convivio*, I, 7, 53-58.
28. *Ibid.*, IV, 26, 18-20.
29. *Ibid.*, III, 2, 24-39.
30. *Par.* XV, 55-57.
31. Cf. Toynbee, "Dante's References to Pythagoras," *Dante Studies and Researches*, pp. 87-96.
32. *Convivio*, III, 11, 23-24.

for by its light all the sciences are lightened; for in the consideration of them there is always a numerical process. . . . And as for
the speculations of natural science they are chiefly concerned with
the principles of natural things, which are three, to wit material,
privation, and form; in which we see that there is not only number
collectively, but there is also number in each one severally, if we
consider subtly. Wherefore Pythagoras, as Aristotle says in the first
of the *Metaphysics*, laid down "even" and "odd" as the principles
of natural things, considering all things to be number.[33]

In the same passage he calls geometry "white," [34] and explains
in the *De vulgari eloquentia* that colors partake of the nature
of number, being measured by white as numbers are measured
by unity —

. . . and the simplest quantity, which is unity, is more perceptible
in an odd than in an even number; and the simplest color, which
is white, is more perceptible in orange than in green.[35]

His exposition of the miracle of Beatrice as the triple 3 is also
his explanation of the angelic orders,[36] which is the conventional theological reasoning of the time.[37] In speaking of the
starry heavens, he is led to a "subtle consideration" of the
numbers 2, 20, and 1,000.[38] His argument for a unified
Empire is based in part on a Pythagorean principle:

Whence it comes about that "being one" is seen to be the root of
"being good" and "being many" the root of "being bad." Wherefore
Pythagoras . . . places "unity" on the side of good, and "plurality"
on the side of evil.[39]

Even in metrics, Dante's preference for the line of an odd
number of syllables is substantiated by philosophical truth:

As for the line of an even number of syllables, we use them but
rarely, because of their rudeness; for they retain the nature of their
numbers, which are subject to the odd numbers as matter to form.[40]

33. *Ibid.*, II, 14, 128-48.
34. *Ibid.*, II, 14, 220-21.
35. *Ibid.*, I, 16, 12-57.
36. *Ibid.*, II, 6, 39-94.
37. Cf. Bonaventura, *Sentences*, II, dist. 9, qu. 7.
38. *Convivio*, II, 15, 23-43.
39. *De monarchia*, I, 15, 16-18; see above, pp. 39-41.
40. *De vulgari eloquentia*, II, 5, 63-8; see above, pp. 39-41.

Dante's procession of emanations begins, therefore, with the One which is God. Unity, however, expands into the ideal Form of Trinity, and the 3 dimensions of God, Power, Wisdom, Love, are further expanded in the 9 orders of angels.[41] For the Power of the Father is contemplated by the 3 orders of the first hierarchy, the Wisdom of the Son by the second hierarchy, the Love of the Holy Spirit by the third. "And inasmuch as each person of the Divine Trinity may be considered in a 3-fold manner, there are in each hierarchy 3 orders diversely contemplating."

The angels, or intelligences, in turn, are the movers of the heavens,[42] which accordingly correspond to the 9 angelic orders, the tenth, or Empyrean, proclaiming "the very oneness and stability of God." [43] Finally, it is the movement of the heavens, the cause of substantial generation,[44] "which disposes things here below diversely to receive the several informing powers." [45] This determining influence is most patent in the effect of the heavens on the 4 seasons, which, in turn, correspond to the 4 ages of life, composed of the 4 humours. There are also 4 parts of the Church day.[46] The intellectual life of man is similarly correlated by Dante, in his discovery of the similarity of the sciences to the heavens, "especially in connection with their order and their number." [47] In all parts of this cosmic scheme may be seen the beauty of order, for "men call that thing beautiful the parts whereof duly correspond." [48]

For Dante, the Universe possesses this Ultimate Beauty in every way, running its predestined course of the 6 ages pre-

41. *Convivio*, II, 6, 39-94.
42. *Ibid.*, II, 5.
43. *Ibid.*, II, 6, 101-2.
44. *Ibid.*, II, 14, 26-30.
45. *Ibid.*, IV, 2, 48-52.
46. *Ibid.*, IV, 23-24.
47. *Ibid.*, II, 14, 8-9.
48. *Ibid.*, I, 5, 92-94.

figured in Creation [49] to the supernal goal, which will be attained when the final number of the elect has been reached.[50] Then man, as the tenth piece of silver, will replace the fallen angels.[51]

> Le cose tutte quante
> hanno ordine tra loro, e questo è forma
> che l' universo a Dio fa simigliante.[52]

> All things howe'er diverse
> Have order among themselves: this principle 'tis
> That likeneth unto God the universe.

Perhaps Dante fancied himself as subject to the Universal Pattern, when, at the apex of his life,[53] he is saved by gratuitous grace to follow the pattern of Christ, beginning his journey on Good Friday [54] at the age of 35, just as Christ, *quasi* 35,[55] was translated from the life of the flesh to the eternity of the Spirit. Like Christ, Dante descends to hell at sunset,[56] remains in hell a night and a day and a night, and rises on the morning of the third day.[57]

The *Divine Comedy* is literally the account of Dante's journey, through which he is granted the vision of "the glory of the First Mover" and "how it reglows in all parts of the universe, yet so as to be in some part more and in another less." [58] In the first book of *De monarchia*,[59] Dante posits a strict relationship of the part to the whole. We may be assured from this and from his other utterances on the subject that Dante would conceive of his vision as a vast unit, com-

49. "We are already in the final age of the world, and are verily awaiting the consummation of the celestial movement" (*ibid.*, II, 15, 115-18).
50. *Par.*, XXV, 124.
51. *Convivio*, II, 6, 95-99.
52. *Par.*, I, 103-5.
53. *Convivio*, IV, 23.
54. *Inf.*, XXI, 112-14.
55. *Convivio*, IV, 23.
56. *Inf.*, II, 1-3.
57. *Purg.*, I, 13-18.
58. Epistle X, 20, 349-52; *Par.*, I, 1-3.
59. *Op. cit.*, VI.

posed of many related parts, as perfectly related as the poet's individual nature should permit, in his reconstruction of the Divine Order. It shall be our task, then, "to discover a two-fold order in [the *Comedy*], to wit the order of the parts with reference to each other, and their order with reference to some unity which is itself not a part . . ., the order of the parts with reference to that unity is the superior order, as being the end of the other." [60]

Beginning, as Dante would have us begin, with the superior order, we may find the key to much of his meaning by placing ourselves at Dante's own starting point, the first and ultimate fact of the Three-in-One. For 1 is the Alpha and Omega of all things. As 1, it is beginning. As 10, 100, or 1000, it is end. As Trinity, it is both beginning and end, including the dimensions of matter and the dimensions of time (past, present, future) within the unity of the Spirit. Dante's vision of the Trinity gives both its meaning and its method:

> Ne la profonda e chiara sussistenza
> de l' alto lume parvermi tre giri
> di tre colori e d' una contenenza.[61]

> Within the deep and luminous extension
> Of the High Light three circles showed themselves,
> Of three fold color and of one dimension.

The 3 circles (each answering to 1 and 10) [62] represent, by the 3 colors and the 1 magnitude, the 3 "dimensions" of God. The procession of the 3 Persons is also indicated:

> e l'un da l' altro come iri da iri
> parea reflesso, e 'l terzo parea foco
> che quinci e quindi igualmente si spiri.[63]

> One by the other, as Iris by Iris wreathed,
> Appeared reflected, and the third seemed fire
> Which equally the one and other breathed.

60. *De monarchia*, I, 6, 8-14.
61. *Par.*, XXXIII, 115-17.
62. See above, p. 102.
63. *Par.*, XXXIII, 118-20.

The Father as First Cause, Origin, Creator [64] is reflected by His own emanation, which is Light, represented by the Son. In the Trinity, the Father is the principle of the 1 and the Son is the principle of the 2, the God-man, Divine and human, representing the procession of Intelligence (or Form) and matter from the First Cause:

> Forma e matera, congiunte e purette,
> usciro ad esser che non avia fallo,
> come d' arco tricordo tre saette.[65]

> Matter and form, mixed, and in purity,
> Came into being that had no defect,
> As from a bow three-corded arrows three.

Thus even the Trinity is informed with the essence of humanity:

> dentro da sè, del suo colore stesso,
> mi parve pinta de la nostra effige.[66]

> Within itself, with color of its own
> Was painted with our image, as it seemed.

or, stated more clearly —

> ma tre persone in divina natura,
> ed in una persona esse e l' umana.[67]

> But the three Persons in the Godhead one,
> And the one Person who is Man and God.

The method by which Unity is recovered from diversity is, as we have seen, the addition of the 1 and the 2.[68] Therefore the Third Person, the Holy Spirit, is "breathed equally from one and from the other."

The most obvious expression of the 3 in 1 is in the external form of the *Divine Comedy*, 1 poem including 3 canticles. The verse form is *terza rima*, whereby 3 lines share a single

64. Cf. *Inf.*, VII, 30-3; *Par.*, X, 1-3.
65. *Par.*, XXIX, 22-24.
66. *Ibid.*, XXXIII, 130-31.
67. *Ibid.*, XIII, 26-27.
68. *Ibid.*, see above, pp. 41-42.

rhyme.[69] The unity of the whole is further assured by its division into 100 cantos.

Given the problem of dividing 100 into 3 equal parts, the expected solution would be $33 + 33 + 33 = 99$, to which the addition of 1 would cement the whole in the bond of unity.[70] There is some indication that Dante had something of this idea in mind, since the first canto of the *Inferno* is segregated from the remainder by the postponement of the invocation to Canto II, whereas the invocations to the other canticles occur in the opening canto of each. The events of *Inferno* I are also, in a sense, discrete from the remainder of the *Comedy*, in that they indicate Dante's situation before the journey was undertaken.

> A te convien tenere *altro* viaggio.[71]
> Thou must betake thee by *another* path

says Virgil. Actually no progress, unless intellectual, is made in the second canto, but technically the journey must be understood to begin as we take leave of Canto I with the closing line:

> *Allor* si mosse, e io li tenni retro.[72]
> *Then* moved he onward, and I went behind.

But militating against this method of dividing the poem would be the unfortunate result of 4 parts instead of 3. It appears, therefore, that Dante was attempting to ride two horses at the same time. He keeps to 3 actual divisions of 34, 33, 33 cantos, numbers eloquent of the life of Christ, who died in his thirty-fourth year, at the age of 33. At the same

69. H. D. Austin adds, "He [Dante] was surely grateful that for his meter there had already been evolved the noble verse called hendecasyllabic because the majority of Italian words are rhythmically 'feminine,' but the one invariable rule of stress in which is that the last ictus must always fall on the *tenth* syllable" ("Number and Geometrical Design in the Divine Comedy," *The Personalist*, XVI, 310-30. See especially p. 311).

70. See above, pp. 81-82.

71. *Inf.*, I, 91.

72. *Ibid.*, I, 136.

time, he hints that *Inferno* I is the extra or unifying canto.

Professor Fletcher has suggested to me a rather special significance of this numerical pattern. Both Beatrice and the *Comedy* have their basis in the number 3. Beatrice is conceived by Dante as a miracle. God may achieve his ends by miracles. So the *Divine Comedy*, a *poema sacra*, would bring men back to Christ's great "plan" of redemption, the plan outlined in *De monarchia*. And if the sanctity of the "miracle" is attested by being rooted in 3, the completeness of the plan is foreshadowed in the 100 cantos, product of the complete number 10, self-multiplied. Simultaneously, within the structure of the *Comedy*, the ultimate effect of the miracle of Beatrice is attained, and the 9 becomes a 10.

Considerably more important is the structure of the spiritual world into which the poet leads us. Here also is the Trinity manifest in the triad of Heaven, Purgatory, and Hell.

Of these, Heaven receives necessarily the most perfect impress of Divinity. Here, therefore, will be found the perfect pattern, as set forth in the *Convivio*: the Trinity informing severally the 3 hierarchies, each divided into 3 orders, the decad being completed by the First Principle. Here are the 9 moving spheres and the Empyrean, each in turn endowing man with attributes equally divine, but none the less graded by their relative distance from the First Cause; from the perfect contemplation of the angels to the almost earthly inconstancy of those in the circle of the moon.

> Li altri giron per varie differenze
> le distinzion che dentro da sè hanno
> dispongono a lor fini e lor semenze.
> Questi organi del mondo così vanno,
> come tu vedi omai, di grado in grado,
> che di su prendono e di sotto fanno.
> Riguarda bene omai sì com' io vado
> per questo loco al vero che disiri,
> sì che poi sappi sol tener lo guado.

Lo moto e la virtù de' santi giri,
come dal fabbro l' arte del martello,
da' beati motor convien che spiri;
e'l ciel cui tanti lumi fanno bello,
de la mente profonda che lui volve
prende l' image e fassene suggello.
E come l' alma dentro a vostra polve
per differenti membra e conformate
a diverse potenze si risolve,
così l' intelligenza sua bontate
multiplacata per le stelle spiega,
girando sè sovra sua unitate.[73]

The other spheres, by various difference,
The powers distinctive they themselves possess
To their begettings and their ends dispense.
These organs of the universe thus go,
As thou by now mayest see, from grade to grade,
Receiving from above to give below.
Mark well how in this issue I proceed
Unto the truth thou seekest, that henceforth
Thou of thyself canst keep the ford at need.
The virtue and motion of the spheres of heaven
Must needs by blessed movers be inspired,
As by the smith the hammer's blow is given;
And from the deep Mind causing it to wheel
That heaven which so many lights make fair
Its image takes, and makes thereof a seal.
And even as doth the soul within your dust
Itself through members differing diffuse,
And unto faculties diverse adjust,
So the Intelligence there setteth free
Its goodness multiplied among the stars,
Circling itself on its own unity.

"Its unity" is figured by the very fact of the circular revolution. So revolving images and emblems of Trinity are common throughout the ascent: the lights in the Sun, who circle
3 times about Dante and Beatrice,[74] the 3 circles in the same

73. *Par.*, II, 118-38.
74. *Ibid.*, X, 76-77.

heaven, the second thrice singing of the One and Two and Three,[75] the 3 disciples joining in circling dance in the Starry Heaven.[76] These, together with constant references to the Trinity, diffuse the atmosphere of Supreme Perfection throughout the entire Realm.

Hell is also rigidly constructed according to Divine Plan and resembles Heaven for two reasons. In the first place, this realm was created by God, as the inscription on the gate of Hell testifies. In the second place, it is the exact opposite, the antitype of Heaven. Therefore, just as 7 virtues are opposed by 7 vices, so the 9 spheres of Heaven must have their counterparts in the 9 circles of Hell, to be completed by the tenth category of the "trimmers" at the brim of the abyss. Whether by intent or by chance, the Origin of all movement and all action is well balanced by the epitome of inaction in those who lived for self and emanated nothing.[77]

> Questi sciaurati, che mai non fur vivi [78]
>
> These wretches who never had been indeed
> Alive

endure as their just punishment the eternal goading of hornets and wasps into an activity that accomplishes nothing.

By reason of the absolute opposition of Hell to Heaven, the many representations of the Trinity in Paradise are echoed in the subterranean vaults of the Inferno. Lucifer is 3-headed; so is Cerberus. Geryon is triple in nature. In Lucifer's 3 mouths are clamped 3 archtraitors, Brutus, Cassius, Judas. There are 3 furies, 3 centaurs, 3 giants, 3 rivers flowing into the frozen lake of Cocytus,[79] 3 popes mentioned in the eighth circle, 3 signal lights before the city of Dis.

75. Ibid., XII, 28.
76. Ibid., XXV, 106-8.
77. Inf., III, 34-42.
78. Ibid., III, 64.
79. Actually one continuous stream.

The unique quality of these infernal triads is in their distortion, by which they appear as perverted images or even parodies of the triplicities of Paradise. In the same way, the opening of Canto XXXIV is an ironic premonition of the pageant of the Church. Tricephalic Lucifer is an anti-Trinity in himself, and his 6 wings, sending 3 winds, make him an antitype of the seraphim. The black cherubim of the eighth infernal circle correspond to the white cherubim of the eighth sphere of Paradise. The circling dance of the 3 heavenly lights, Peter, James, and John, is parodied by the 3 who wheel, heads backwards, in the third round of the seventh circle.[80] Even the infernal crucifixion of Caiaphas, cross-fixed in the ground with only 3 stakes, is a parody of Trinity, borrowed from a cruciform mockery of the Cathari.[81]

Concerning the dimensions of Hell, only the faintest hint is given: the ninth *bolgia* is said to be 22 miles in circumference, and the tenth is 11 miles around and not less than one-half mile across.[82] Although it is not possible to reconstruct the architectural design of Hell from such meagre specifications, it is possible to assume that the infernal dimensions are made up of fractions (used to designate the devils in ancient Babylon,[83] and good numerical reasoning in any case) or of multiples of 11, the number of sin since the time of Augustine.

At the very bottom of Hell are those farthest removed from the spiritual life. All of the inhabitants of Hell have "lost the true good of the mind," but Dante's especial repugnance to treachery is indicated by his representation of the traitors as having lost the mind itself. Accordingly, they are delineated as images of unregenerate nature, such as Dante had in mind when he wrote, "And we see many men so vile

80. *Ibid.*, XVI.
81. *Ibid.*, XXIII, 109; Lea, *A History of the Inquisition*, I, 103.
82. *Inf.*, XXIX, 9; XXX, 86-87.
83. Farbridge, *Studies*, p. 87; Lenormant, *Chaldean Magic*, p. 25.

and of such base condition as scarce to seem other than beasts."[84] The 5 senses, indicative of the sensitive power without the rational, are to be found isolated in brute beasts alone.[85] In this class belong the traitors who are described by animal epithets throughout, and the giants may be said to be exaggerated images of the 5 senses, proud against spiritual rule. Nimrod utters 5 words in a line shortened to call attention to the number.[86] Ephialtes is uncovered to the fifth turn of the chain which binds him.[87] Antaeus issues from the cavern full 5 ells.[88]

The realm of Purgatory is entirely distinct in that it is temporary rather than eternal. Although it exists for the purpose of spiritual regeneration, its summit is the Earthly rather than the Heavenly Paradise. It is reared upon the crust of this corruptible earth and does not reach to

quel ciel c' ha minor li cerchi sui.[89]

the sphere
Which has the smallest circles for its own.

Purgatory, unlike Heaven and Hell, will have no place after the Last Judgment[90] and partakes, therefore, of the relative and temporal imperfection of earth. The steps of the mount, it is true, are disposed according to a Trinitarian principle, representing excessive, defective, and perverted love. But in Purgatory the souls still retain the images of their bodies, and the ascent of the terraced slope numerically recalls the transit of man through the 7 ages of the world, to be rewarded by the Eternal Glory of the eighth age, prefigured in the Earthly Para-

84. *Convivio*, III, 7, 80-83.
85. *Ibid.*, III, 2, 109-12; cf. Philo, above, pp. 48-49.
86. *Inf.*, XXXI, 67.
87. *Ibid.*, XXXI, 90.
88. *Ibid.*, 113. Shortly before this, Dante had seen, in the eighth circle, 5 Florentine thieves (XXVI, 4). The Papacy was to be slain as a thief (*Purg.*, XXXIII, 43-44).
89. *Inf.*, II, 78.
90. *Purg.*, XXVII, 127.

dise. Seven, figured in the planets and in the days of the week, is the number of the earth, as it is the number of the spiritual life of the microcosm. In Purgatory, therefore, the 7 *peccata* are effaced from the poet's forehead, for as man falls through 7, so he rises through 7.[91] So the vice of each ledge is opposed by a virtue and a beatitude, a scheme used by Bonaventura, though with different results.[92] Similarly, earthly man reaches at last the regeneration of the 8, number of baptism.[93] It was, in a sense, fortuitous that the Decad of Purgatory could not be completed by the 1, but by the lesser and corruptible 2, in the Late-Repentant and the Excommunicate in the Antepurgatory.

Over the gates of Hell are inscribed the 3 attributes of Divinity: Power, Wisdom, Love. In the *Convivio*,[94] Dante expressly relates this triad to the members of the Trinity, assigning Power to the Father, Wisdom to the Son, and Love to the Holy Spirit. It is, of couse, true that all functions of the Trinity are operative in all the three realms. Yet it is tempting to suggest that this triad also is discretely represented in the 3 parts of the Spiritual World.

Nowhere, certainly, is the Power of the Father more graphically felt than in the Inferno, where Christ is never named, there where the Old Testament saints were forced to dwell

> fin ch' al Verbo di Dio di scender piacque.[95]
>
> Till pleased the Word of God to condescend.

The justice of Purgatory, then, may be understood as an expression of the Wisdom of the Son. Functionally, it corresponds to the Word in making possible the salvation of man. Temporally, its institution was connected with the Church of Christ. Before Christ, no soul had climbed the

91. Prov. 24: 16; cf. Albertus, *Sermo*, X, 2, *De tempore.*
92. *Expositio in cap. VI evang. S. Matt., De oratione Dominica.*
93. See above, p. 114.
94. *Convivio*, II, 6, 61-70.
95. *Par.*, VII, 30.

mount, but with the annunciation to Mary came the decree, long awaited,

> ch' aperse il ciel del suo lungo divieto.[96]

> [that] Reopened Heaven after the long ban.

Purgatory, like Hell and Heaven, is informed with Love, but for the most complete fulfillment of "the fire of the Holy Spirit which is Love," [97] we must await Paradise. The entire canticle is suffused with the effluence of Love from the first canto's

> amor che 'l ciel governi [98]

> Love which rulest heaven

to the concluding

> amor che move il sole e l' altre stelle.[99]

> Love that moves the sun and every star.

This somewhat tenuous distinction, which may be felt rather than precisely argued, recurs in Bernard's definition of the 3 days: "After two days he will revive us, and the third day he will raise us up." [100] So Dante must pass through Lethe to forget the sins represented in Hell, and through Eunoe before he can partake of the Wisdom of the Son and his dispensation, as it had been represented to him in the pageant of the Church. Then, on the third "day" he is raised up, having been made in the preceding two "days"

> puro e disposto a salire a le stelle.[101]

> Pure and disposed to mount up to the stars.

These "days" were specified as the Days of Wrath, Grace, and Glory,[102] almost precise epithets for the three realms of the *Comedy*. Again, it was the Old Testament Creator who most

96. *Purg.*, X, 36.
97. Rabanus, *Allegoriae in sacram scripturam*; P. L. 112, 966.
98. *Par.*, I, 74.
99. *Ibid.*, XXXIII, 145.
100. Hos. 6: 3; see above, p. 110.
101. *Purg.*, XXXIII, 145.
102. Albertus Magnus, *Sermo XVI, De tempore*.

fully exemplified the God of Wrath, Christ who was the manifest Grace of God, and the Holy Spirit, descending upon the apostles in tongues of flame, which evidenced the Divine Glory.

Bernard had denominated the 3 days as "Before Christ, Under Christ, and With Christ." If we conceive of the time "Before Christ" in the sense of "without Christ," these 3 days are an entirely possible definition for the 3 realms, as has already been indicated. Furthermore, if we borrow a common enough diurnal analogy to this gradual approach to glory, calling the first age Night, the second Dawn, the third Noon (symbols used by Joachim), we may add another link to our chain of "correlations."

The journey from Hell to Paradise, recounted to "remove those living in this life from the state of misery and lead them to the state of felicity," is accomplished in 3 stages, from the darkness of the Inferno to the eternal light of Heaven, following thereby the course of Augustine, the progress of whose life was from bad to good, and from good to better, and from better to best.[103] Between night and day, Purgatory, the state of Grace, might be said to be the dawn. Throughout the journey, there are, of course, constant revolutions of day and night. Yet in view of the full and continued day of the *Paradiso*, it seems worth while to scrutinize the peculiarity that Hell is the only region where Dante travels at night; at night by virtue of the darkness, as well as by earthly reckoning.

At night, Dante is in the forest,[104] the "state of misery." A complete day elapses before, on the next *evening*, he reaches the gate of Hell.[105] At midnight, he sees the city of Dis.[106] At nightfall of the second day, he reaches the bottom of the world and the Emperor of the realm.

103. *Convivio*, I, 2, 105-8.
104. *Inf.*, I, 21.
105. *Ibid.*, III, 1.
106. *Ibid.*, VIII, 98-99.

When we look for mentions of dawn, we find only one in the *Inferno*, and this occurs in this life when Dante is at the foot of the hill which is apparently out of the forest.[107] It is again dawn as Dante comes through the earth to the shore of the island of Purgatory.[108] At dawn, he reaches the gate of Purgatory,[109] as contrasted with evening at the gates of Hell. At dawn, he reaches the Earthly Paradise,[110] having been forced to spend the preceding night on the rocky approach.

He does not ascend to the Eternal Paradise until noon,[111] where he continues to exist in full day. According to Albertus Magnus, day in astronomy begins at noon.[112] Furthermore, as Gardner has pointed out, "Noon has a special significance for the mystics, as representing celestial desire or divine illumination, or eternity." [113]

107. *Ibid.*, I, 13-18.
108. *Ibid.*, XXIX, 139; *Purg.*, I, 19-21, 107, 115; II, 1-9.
109. *Purg.*, IX, 13-14.
110. *Ibid.*, XXVII, 109-12, 133; XXVIII, 16.
111. *Par.*, I, 43-45. Cf. Orr, *Dante and the Early Astronomers.*
112. *Summa Theologica*, II, tract. 11, qu. 51, mem. 3.
113. *Dante and the Mystics*, p. 300. " 'Man,' writes Aquinas, 'has three kinds of knowledge of divine things. The first of these is according as man, by the natural light of reason, ascends through creatures into the knowledge of God; the second is in so far as the divine truth, exceeding human understanding, descends to us by way of revelation, not however as though demonstrated to our sight, but as set forth in words to be believed; the third is according as the human mind is elevated to the perfect intuition of the things that are revealed.' (*Summa contra Gentiles*, IV, 1.) We have something analogous to these three kinds of knowledge in the *Divina Comedia*: Dante is led by the natural light of reason in Vergil through the *Inferno* and the *Purgatorio*, thus ascending to the knowledge of God through creatures; [actually Vergil accompanies — he does not lead Dante through Purgatory] the divine truth descends to him in the Earthly Paradise by way of revelation in Beatrice, and is set forth in the allegorical pageants; then, in the *Paradiso*, his mind is uplifted by stages to the perfect intuition of the things revealed. Thus, too, Bonaventura writes of the soul's ascent to God: — This is the *three days' journey into the wilderness* (*that we may sacrifice to the Lord our God*, Exod., III, 18) this is the threefold illumination of one day, whereof the first is as evening, the second as morning, the third as noon; this represents the threefold existence of things, to wit, in matter, in intelligence, and in eternal act; as it is said: '*Let there be*, he *made*, and *it was so* (Gen., I); this likewise represents the threefold substance in Christ, who is our ladder: to wit, bodily, spiritual, and divine.' (*Itinerarium*, I, 3)" — Gardner, *Ibid.*, pp. 298-99.

If Hell is the reverse image of Heaven, we should expect to find a negative triad opposed to the 3 positive attributes of Divinity. The opposites to Power, Wisdom, Love are specified by Aquinas as Impotence, Ignorance, Malice.[114] Lowermost in the pit of Hell, opposed to the highest point of Heaven, stands the image of anti-Trinity, 3-faced: red, black, and "pale" (between yellow and white). The orthodox interpretation of the meaning of these faces is inescapable: the red representing malice, the worst, and in the center; [115] the black, ignorance; and the pale, impotence.[116]

If the 3 traitors hanging from the mouths are to fit into this scheme, we must assume that Dante meant Judas, who is punished most severely, to represent malice. Then Brutus, in view of Dante's admiration for Cato, who thought it "more fitting to die than to look upon the face of a tyrant," [117] may have been conceived to have sinned through ignorance. He was led to treachery by Cassius, who was impotent, in that he did not act without the aid of Brutus and later killed himself upon hearing the false report of Brutus' death.[118]

Reade's study of the *Inferno* is sufficient warning to those who seek a precise order in the "moral system" of the "dark prison." He points out, however, that malice and impotence

114. *Summa Theologica*, II-II, qu. XIV, art. 1. Cf. Reade, *The Moral System of Dante's Inferno*, pp. 305-17.

115. Hell, which knew not the light of Christ, is illumined by the red fire of malice.

116. Medieval iconography does not contribute much toward the symbolism of these colors. According to Durandus, black, red, and white (medieval white cloth was actually pale) cloths were hung over the altars at Easter, indicating respectively the time Before Law, Under Law, and Under Grace (*Rationale*, I, 3, 41). That there was some other traditional meaning for these colors appears possible, in view of a legend that Christ entered a field and found 3 worms, one black, one white, and one red, and killed them (recounted by Thomas Ebendorfer of Haselbach, 1387-1464; see Thorndike, *History of Magic*, IV, 295).

117. *De monarchia*, II, 5, 168-70.

118. If this analogy holds, Dante's gratuitous description of Cassius as *si membruto* is effective sarcasm (*Inf.*, XXXIV, 67).

may justly be considered as causes; the first, of sins punished in Dis; the second, of the incontinence of the second through the fifth circles,[119] with the morally baffling sin of heresy between them.[120] Ignorance, he points out, is not a cause of sin,[121] nor is there punishment in Limbo, where are those who, in invincible ignorance,

> le tre sante
> virtù non si vestiro, e sanza vizio
> conobber l' altre e sequir tutte quante.[122]

> although unclad
> With the three holy virtues, without vice
> The others knew, and followed as they bade.

Very nearly as fundamental as the Trinity itself, in the Middle Ages, were the 3 virtues by which salvation was attained, Faith, Hope, and Love. The virtue of Love was so universally associated with the Holy Spirit that these two denominations of the Third Person were interchangeable.[123] Since all things are ordered in measure and number, Faith and Hope were necessarily identified in their proper order with Father and Son,[124] that the 3 highest virtues might take the archetypal form of the One, Two, and Three. This identification is presented in Dante's final vision of the 3 circles:

> Ne la profonda e chiara sussistenza
> de l' alto lume parvermi tre giri
> di tre colori e d' una contenenza.[125]

> Within the deep and luminous extension
> Of the High Light three circles showed themselves,
> Of threefold color and of one dimension.

The colors are not given, but one wonders what they could

119. Reade, *op. cit.*, pp. 316, *et seq.*
120. *Ibid.*, pp. 367-81.
121. *Ibid.*, p. 379.
122. *Purg.*, VII, 34-36.
123. Cf. *Par.*, VII, 30-33.
124. Cf. Busnelli *Il Concetto e l'ordine del paradiso Dantesco*, I, 263-64.
125. *Par.*, XXXIII, 118-20.

have been if not the best-known colors of the Middle Ages, the white, green, and red of the virtues, as they are represented in the pageant of the Church.[126]

If the 3 Persons may be represented by the colors of the 3 virtues, so too may the 3 virtues take on the image of Trinity. Shortly before Dante's final vision, the Theological Virtues had been represented by Peter (Faith), James (Hope), and John (Love).[127] After Dante's examination on Faith and Hope, the 3 join in circling dance in premonition of the later image of Trinity.[128] The song which accompanies their dance is made "del suon del trino spiro" — "by the sound of the trinal breath." [129] The "breath," be it noted, is trinal, not triple; and the comparison of emanation to breathing is Dante's favorite expression in connection with Trinity.[130]

The procession of the 3 Persons is also similar to the procession of the 3 virtues. Dante, following Aquinas,[131] tells us in the *Convivio* that Faith precedes Hope, which precedes Love.[132] In the same sense, the Father is the Creator, the *prima virtù*.[133] Commenting on Augustine's statement that the Father is the Principle of the Whole Deity,[134] Aquinas says, "As the Father is the one whence another proceeds, it follows that the Father is the Principle." [135] He continues:

The Son proceeds by way of the intellect as Word, and the Holy Ghost by way of the will as Love. Now love must proceed from a word. For we do not love anything unless we apprehend it by a

---

126. *Purg.*, XXIX, 121-26; cf. J. B. Fletcher, "The Allegory of the 'Vita Nuova,'" pp. 6-7; Busnelli, *op. cit.*, I, 260-64.

127. *Par.* XXV.

128. *Ibid.*, XXV, 108.

129. *Ibid.*, XXV, 132.

130. Cf. *Par.*, XXIII, 120; *Par.*, X, 1-3.

131. "Absolutely speaking, faith precedes hope. . . . In order of generation hope precedes love. . . . Love flows from hope." *Summa Theologica*, II-II, qu. 17, art. 7-8.

132. *Convivio*, III, 14, 133-36.

133. *Par.*, XXVI, 84.

134. *De trinitate*, III.

135. *Summa Theologica*, I, qu. 23, art. 1.

mental conception. Hence also in this way it is manifest that the Holy Ghost proceeds from the Son.

It is also recognizable that, although the members of the Trinity are actually coeternal, there is a definite sense (intensified perhaps by Joachim's doctrine of the 3 ages, ruled respectively by the Father, Son, and Holy Ghost) of the priority of the Father to the Son in the temporal manifestations of the 3 Persons to man. So Adam was created by the First Power [136] and walked with the Father. In the newborn ages, Faith alone sufficed.[137] Faith, says Dante with Paul, is the evidence of things unseen, wherefore Adam fell, since, like Lucifer, "he would not wait for light." [138]

Light was given to man with the advent of the Word. Thus Dante refers to Christ in the *Convivio* as "the light which lightens us in the darkness." [139] The Son, not revealed until the sixth age of the world, became the mediator between the Father and sinful man. He is indeed the Hope of the world.[140] It might not otherwise be significant that Dante first sees the twofold beast reflected in the *green* eyes of Beatrice.[141] The third emanation, Love, or the Holy Spirit, descended upon the apostles at Pentecost *after* the appearance of the Son.

The sense of the temporal procession of the virtues is implied in the pageant of the Church Militant. The 24 patriarchs of the Old Testament wear the white lilies of Faith.[142] Following them, the 4 evangelists surrounding the chariot and the Griffon of Christ are crowned with the green of Hope.[143] At the end of the procession are the 7 New

136. *Par.*, XXVI, 83.

137. *Ibid.*, XXXII, 76-78.

138. *Ibid.*, XIX, 48; cf. *Purg.*, XXIX, 25-27.

139. *Convivio*, II, 6, 16-17.

140. John 1: 17: "For the law was given by Moses, but grace and truth came by Jesus Christ." Heb. 7: 19: "For the law made nothing perfect, but the bringing in of a better hope did; by which we draw nigh unto God." Aquinas, *Summa Theologica*, II-I, qu. XLI, art. 5.

141. *Purg.*, XXXI, 121.

142. *Ibid.*, XXIX, 82-84.

143. *Ibid.*, 91-93.

Testament figures whose garlands are of the red of Love.[144]

So far, we have dealt almost exclusively with Dante's conception of fixed and eternal truths, most of which were discussed by medieval theologians. We may look for no such external assistance in attempting to fix the function of the 3 ladies, Mary, Lucia, and Beatrice. Mary is the earthly Mother of Christ. Beatrice is the earthly mirror of Heavenly Beatitude. Lucia seems most probably identifiable as Ste. Lucia of Syracuse, though Dante has given no certain clue. It is at least true, however, that her appearance with Mary and Beatrice indicates that she too represents some earthly woman in apotheosis. Taking our cue from Beatrice, we may assume that all 3 partake of the nature of miracles, the earthly representations of heavenly truth. As such, being 3, they should somehow coincide with the design of the One and Two and Three.

It is not difficult to see in Mary the One. She is the Mother of Christ, as the Creator is the Father. In the dual nature of Christ, hers is the earthly part, and her maternity corresponds to the Creative Power of the Father. In the *Comedy* also, it is she who originates the quest for the salvation of Dante. In the same way, just as the order of the virtues is from Faith to Hope to Love, Mary calls Lucia, who delegates Beatrice.[145]

Lucia, etymologically *light*, is the intercessor, like the Son bringing Hope. By very virtue of being *light*, she is functionally comparable to the Son and Wisdom,[146] and her sphere is definitely that Purgatory established through the intercession of Christ. In the *Purgatorio*, Hope is apparently felt to be similar to light:

144. *Ibid.*, 145-48.

145. *Inf.*, II, 97-102.

146. It is interesting to note, in this connection, that twice in the *Inferno* Dante speaks of *light* where *word* is implied: "il sol [il verbo?] tace" (I, 61); and "Io venni in luogo d'ogni luce muto" (V, 28). Christ is the Word of the Father and the "Light of the World."

di retro a quel condotto
che speranza mi dava e facea lume [147]

that guidance following
Which gave me hope, and was for me a light.

Beatrice, finally, is easily recognized as love. When she appears to Dante in the Earthly Paradise, although clothed with the white veil of faith and the green mantle of hope, her essential color is the "living flame" of love.[148] In the *Comedy*, hers is the "activity of charity." [149] True love and Beatrice are identified throughout the *Vita nuova*. That this is the same Beatrice is made irrefutable in *Inferno* II:

Disse: Beatrice, loda di Dio vera,
chè non soccorri quei che t' amò tanto
ch' uscì per te de la volgare schiera? [150]

Beatrice, she said, thou praise of God in truth,
Why aid'st not him who in his love for thee
Turned from the vulgar many in his youth?

A few lines before this, Beatrice has told Virgil,

amor mi mosse, che mi fa parlare.[151]

Love moved me, and compels me to speak so.

In the *Convivio*, another related expression of Trinity, "the way, the truth and the light," (n. b., not the *life*, John 14: 6) [152] clarifies further the functions of the 3 ladies. Mary is the truth, which "suffereth no error." Lucia is the light, "which lighteneth us in the darkness of earthly ignorance," as Lucia also appears in the ante-Purgatory to carry the sleeping Dante to the entrance to Purgatory, there to reveal to his eyes the entrance to the arduous route to the Earthly Paradise.[153] Beatrice is the way "in which we advance unimpeded to the blessedness of immortality." This truth is

147. *Purg.*, IV, 29-30.
148. *Ibid.*, XXX, 31-33.
149. *Convivio*, III, 14, 136.
150. Lines 103-5.
151. *Inf.*, II, 72.
152. *Convivio*, II, 9, 114-20.
153. *Purg.*, IX, 55-63.

demonstrated in Dante's unimpeded progress with Beatrice in the *Paradiso*.[154]

In the foregoing commentary on the most prominent triads of the *Divine Comedy*, I have tried to convey my own sense of the intricate interrelationships of all these expressions of the *fact* of Trinity. Most of the relationships which I have pointed out have been derived, directly or indirectly, from the works of previous commentators on Dante, who have often disagreed among themselves, and yet, in my sense, have all been partially right and partially wrong at the same time. Some, for example, have identified the 3 ladies with Power, Wisdom, and Love; others with Faith, Hope, and Love. I believe both of these correlations to be true and neither of them exhaustive. For ultimate precision, it seems to me that the members of all of these triads must, rather, be conceived of as expressions of the One, Two, and Three. By listing them in that order, this general correspondency may, perhaps, be seen more clearly than I have been able to express it in isolated instances:

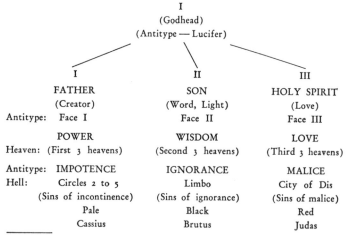

	I (Godhead) (Antitype — Lucifer)	
	I	II	III
	FATHER	SON	HOLY SPIRIT
	(Creator)	(Word, Light)	(Love)
Antitype:	Face I	Face II	Face III
	POWER	WISDOM	LOVE
Heaven:	(First 3 heavens)	(Second 3 heavens)	(Third 3 heavens)
Antitype:	IMPOTENCE	IGNORANCE	MALICE
Hell:	Circles 2 to 5	Limbo	City of Dis
	(Sins of incontinence)	(Sins of ignorance)	(Sins of malice)
	Pale	Black	Red
	Cassius	Brutus	Judas

---

154. For a full discussion of this phase of the Trinity, cf. J. B. Fletcher, "The Three Blessed Ladies," in *Symbolism of the Divine Comedy*, pp. 114-209; also H. Flanders Dunbar, *Symbolism in Medieval Thought*, p. 168.

HELL	PURGATORY	HEAVEN
Day of Wrath	Day of Grace	Day of Glory
Bad to good	Good to better	Better to best
Before Christ	Under Christ	With Christ
FAITH	HOPE	LOVE
White	Green	Red
MARY	LUCIA	BEATRICE
The Truth	The Light	The Way

It is one of the great medieval paradoxes that the Unity of Trinity cannot be effected without the inclusion of the imperfect duad,[155] specifically embodied in the Second Person:

> ma tre persone in divina natura,
> ed in una persona esse e l'umana.[156]

> But the three Persons in the Godhead one,
> And the one Person who is Man and God.

The duality of the Second Person is the image whose conformity to the circle was the ultimate mystery which Dante sought to comprehend.[157] But, however difficult of comprehension, there was no doubt that the image (dual, imperfect) *did* conform to the circle (perfect spirituality); no doubt that corruptible mortality *did* mingle (in the God-man)

155. This is true, both theologically and numerically; see above, pp. 41-42.
156. *Par.*, XIII, 26-27.
157. *Ibid.*, XXXIII, 137-38. For the meaning of *image*, cf. Aquinas, *Summa Theologica*, I, qu. 34, art. 1. The history of medieval Christology indicates an unceasing attempt to eliminate this paradox. The perfection of Godhead could not tolerate so much as a hint of imperfection in one of its Persons. On the other hand, the doctrine of Reconciliation demanded that the Son partake of the imperfection of man: "in quantum homo, in tantum mediator." Theologians solved the problem satisfactorily only by ignoring it, so that "in the doctrine of the person of Christ the *homo* is almost entirely eliminated, and then in the doctrine of the work of Christ this *homo* takes the commanding place" (Harnack, *History of Dogma*, VI, 190 n.). Aquinas held that the God-man union is real, not in the Divine nature, but in the human nature only. But even with the full context, this appears merely to substitute one paradox for another, and Dante, at least, does not appear to believe that human intellect has solved, or can solve, the problem (*Par.*, XXXIII, 137-42). Cf. Harnack, *op. cit.*, VI, 188-94; H. R. Mackintosh, *The Doctrine of the Person of Jesus Christ*, pp. 223-29. A somewhat different, but just as difficult problem, is involved in the question of the filiation of the unincarnate Christ, subordinate by virtue of sonship and yet, as God, equal to God (cf. *Purg.*, III, 34-36).

with the incorruptibility of the Trinity. For, by exalting the God-man as the archetype of cosmic dualism the Middle Ages avoided the Manichean implications inherent in the more obvious antithesis of two antagonistic principles, good and evil.

It is therefore a first principle with Dante that all perfection rests upon the harmonic operation of matter and form. These 2 antithetical principles were conceived to be active throughout the entire cosmos, and the manifestations of their opposition were much more strictly organized in the Middle Ages than were the expressions of Trinity itself. If we would put ourselves in the spirit of Dante's dualism, it were helpful to chart these duads as we have already seen them in the scheme of Hugo of St. Victor.[158] Of each pair, one member is always superior to the other, since the one is always relatively perfect, incorruptible, and the other imperfect, corruptible. We have then:

RELATIVELY { PERFECT SPIRITUAL	RELATIVELY { IMPERFECT MATERIAL
Heaven	Earth
Invisible	Visible
Angels	Men
Prelate	Subject
Contemplative	Active
Figured in the Old Testament by:	
Rachel	Leah
Figured in the New Testament by:	
Mary	Martha
Spirit	Flesh
Adam	Eve

In this list is illustrated the commonplace medieval notion of the distinction between the perfection of spirit and the imperfection of matter. This same distinction may be seen in Bonaventura's contrast of Divine and Mortal qualities.[159] In his compilation of duads are included such mortal attributes

158. See above, p. 109.
159. See above, p. 99, note 50.

as deformity, evil, corruptibility, and mutability, as opposed to Beauty, Good, Incorruptibility, and Immutability.

That Dante adopts this distinction (as how should he not?) may be clearly seen in the pages of his didactic treatises, as we have already observed. In the *Convivio* he constantly infers, or makes, a distinction between the active and the contemplative lives,[160] matter and spirit,[161] body and soul.[162] As he approaches his favorite contention of the necessity for dual rule over Rome, he naturally identifies the active life with the civil life, for "human nature, as it here exists, hath not only one blessedness but two, to wit that of the civil life and that of the contemplative life."[163] A traditional illustration of this distinction had been drawn from the macrocosmic duality of sun and moon, 2 lights, not 1.[164] Unfortunately for Dante's thesis, Innocent III had used this same image to argue the subordination of the State to the Church, since the one luminary draws its light from the other.[165] To this argument Dante replies rather lamely: (1) that the sun and moon do not represent Church and Empire, since Church and Empire were created as remedies against sin, whereas the sun and moon were created before the Fall and even before the creation of man; (2) that even if the analogy held, the State might draw its *light* from the Church without receiving its authority from the Church, since the moon draws light from the sun, but exists independently.[166] Dante is willing to agree that the Church is superior to the State, the contemplative life to the active, and the divinity of Christ to his humanity. Superiority, however, does not mean autocracy; on the contrary, the members of each duad are con-

160. *Convivio*, II, 5, 66-70; IV, 17, 85-89; 22, 103-16.
161. *Ibid.*, II, 15, 95-102.
162. *Ibid.*, I, 1, 16-18; III, 14, 1-4; IV, 21, 8-10.
163. *Ibid.*, II, 5, 66-70; *De monarchia*, III, 16.
164. An analogy implied in the conclusion of Epistle V.
165. P. L. 216, 998; 214, 378.
166. *De monarchia*, III, 4.

ceived to be antithetical, related by their mutual antagonism. The members of a duad do not achieve harmony by merging into each other, but by being subject to the One from which the 2 proceeds.[167] The *image* in Dante's vision does not lose its identity as *image*, but merges with the circle. It is obvious, nevertheless, that Dante feared the inferences of the sun-moon analogy and, much as he might protest, felt the force of Innocent's argument. He therefore changes the analogy to 2 suns:

> Soleva Roma, che 'l buon feo,
> due soli aver, che l' una e l' altra strada
> facean vedere, e del mondo e di Deo.[168]

> Rome, when she turned the world to good, used then
> To have two Suns, which one and other way —
> God's way and the world's way — made clear for men.

Dante's insistent preachments and representations of duality were doubtless inspired by the realization that every dual pattern in the universe was, by inference, an additional argument for the twin rule of Church and State. For each particular duad is to be understood as merely an individual expression of the Universal Duality, as it is seen in Dante's vision of Godhead, where image and form are bound together. It is also true that just as any duad, even the Archetypal Duad, is imperfect in relation to Unity (or Trinity), so the perfect member of any duad may be imperfect in relation to a higher reality. The civil life is earthly, imperfect, active, in comparison to the contemplative, spiritual perfection of the Church. But the Church Militant, the Church on earth, is imperfect, active, in relation to the Church Triumphant in Heaven. In the *Convivio*, Dante calls the cardinal virtues active, in comparison to the speculative virtues,[169] but in *De monarchia* the cardinal and intellectual virtues are lumped

167. *Ibid.*, III, 16, especially 120 *et sqq.*
168. *Purg.*, XVI, 106-8.
169. *Convivio*, IV, 22, 201-6.

together as active, in comparison to the theological virtues, which are contemplative.[170]

The sense of the congruence of all dualities is perhaps best seen in the medieval symbols of *right* and *left*, whose ultimate definition is resolved to the fact that right is superior and left is inferior, a conception inherited from the most ancient times. In Genesis Abram went to the right and Lot to the left.[171] Christ also had ordained that the sheep would stand at his right hand and the goats at his left.[172] In conformity with this tradition, Dionysius makes the right Godly and the left Diabolic.[173] According to Rabanus, the left indicates the present life, depravity, reprobate angels, and reprobate men.[174]

Dante's adoption of this usage is most notable in his contrasting journeys through Hell and Purgatory. In Hell his course is to the left. When he and Virgil are halted before Dis, an angel comes to the rescue, moving his left hand before him.[175] In Purgatory, approaching always nearer to Divinity, his steps are always to the right. In the pageant of the Church in the Earthly Paradise, the 4 cardinal virtues are on the left-hand side of the car, and the 3 "whose is profounder sight" are on the right.[176] Here the duad of action and contemplation is substituted for the duad of good and evil, but it is still a duad and therefore the same symbolism may be employed. The car of the Church rests on a left and a right wheel, the meaning clarified when the 2 wheels reappear in the Heaven of the Sun, the one containing Bonaventura, who put behind "the lefthand care," [177] which appears here to imply the active life, choice of the Domini-

170. *De monarchia*, III, 16, 53-63.
171. Gen. 13: 9.
172. Matt. 25: 33.
173. *Eccles. Hierarch.*, II, 1-7.
174. *Allegoriae in sacram scripturam*; P. L. 112, 1055.
175. *Inf.*, IX, 83.
176. *Purg.*, XXIX, 121-32.
177. *Par.*, XII, 127; cf. lines 106-11.

cans.[178] The Old Man of Crete, who looks at Rome as if it were his mirror, rests on 2 feet.[179] If these feet can be interpreted as Church and State, the clay foot (right) must symbolize the Church. In these instances, evil, the cardinal virtues, the active life, and the Empire are all identified as *left*, when opposed to goodness, the theological virtues, the contemplative life, and the Church. To this group of dualities might be added the Old and the New Testaments: the Old, left, relatively imperfect; and the New, right, relatively perfect. For, according to Aquinas, the Old Law was given to men imperfect, having not yet received Spiritual Grace. It consisted of temporal promises. The New Law was entirely spiritual.[180] In the interpretation of the miracle of the loaves and fishes, the 5 loaves were commonly referred to the category of the left, being identified with good works, the 5 senses, the active life, the Jews, the Old Testament, the Old Law.[181] This is the pattern to which the many duads of the *Comedy* are keyed.

One of the most inclusive and, to Dante, one of the most important duads was that of the 2 lives, the active and the contemplative; the active concerned primarily with love of neighbor and the contemplative with love of God. Since Dante believes the harmonious operation of these two lives (exampled in Church and State) to be necessary to human felicity, it suits his didactic purpose not only to scatter direct

178. This interpretation of the "left-hand care" rests upon Bonaventura's identification of these 2 wheels of the car as Dominican and Franciscan (*Par.*, XII, 31-111). That these are the same 2 wheels is implied by the extensive references to Dominic and Francis, made by Thomas and Bonaventura, respective spokesmen for the membership of the 2 wheels in the heaven of the sun (cf. Gardner, *Dante and the Mystics*, pp. 225-35). The right and the left sides of the car are distinguished by the splitting of the virtues, as active (on the left) and contemplative (on the right). Here the reference to the "left-hand care" appears to belong to the same general pattern.

179. *Inf.*, XIV, 103-11.

180. *Summa Theologica*, II-I, qu. 106-7.

181. Cf. Albertus Magnus, *Sermones de tempore*, XXVII and LXXVIII; Innocent III, *Sermo* XXVII.

preachments to that effect throughout the *Comedy*, but also to describe his encounters with varied representations of action and contemplation on his journey through the three realms. On this journey, in fact, he has 2 guides, Virgil and Beatrice. Of the two, the significance of Beatrice is obviously Heavenly, Churchly. In antithesis, Virgil, champion of Rome, may easily be said to represent State. Or, in the more ordinary interpretation, Beatrice, as Revelation, belongs with the theological virtues, contemplative, on the right side of the car in the pageant in Eden; and Virgil, as Reason, takes his place with the cardinal, active virtues.

Virgil's assigned habitation in Limbo is the Noble Castle, which may be regarded as a spiritual representation of pagan Rome. Dante was insistent upon the divinely ordained greatness of ancient Rome. But he also insisted that good government could not exist without a clear distinction between material and spiritual welfare. In the Noble Castle, therefore, this distinction is maintained, the active or civil life being represented by such as Caesar, Brutus, Camilla,[182] and the speculative life (which would be the nearest pagan approximation of the contemplative) typified by Socrates, Plato, and Aristotle.[183]

Purgatory is even more thoroughly informed with this dualism. We have already remarked the resemblance of this realm to the earthly life of man, who is a "kind of mean between corruptible and incorruptible things."[184] Here Virgil and Beatrice all but meet. Here mortality mingles with immortality and 7 "virtues" are opposed by 7 vices.[185] In this very 7 is the image of man, composed, as he is, of the 4 of the body and the 3 of the soul. The 4 of the active, speculative, or temporal life is represented by the 4 cardinal virtues. The

182. *Inf.*, IV, 121-29.
183. *Ibid.*, IV, 130-44.
184. *De monarchia*, III, 16, 30-33.
185. Pride-Humility, Envy-Love, Wrath-Meekness, Sloth-Zeal, Avarice-Poverty, Gluttony-Temperance, Lust-Chastity.

3 theological virtues preside over the spiritual, or contemplative life. In Purgatory, Dante is active during the day, and just before dawn, before the activity of daylight, he is lost in dreams. Three stars, therefore, shine at night as the lights of contemplation, the 3 who deeper gaze, while the 4 stars which illuminated the face of Cato at dawn remain above the horizon during the day.[186]

On the first ledge of Purgatory, three "examples" are given of Humility in the persons of Trajan, Mary, and David. In these three figures may be seen again the temporal-spiritual, active-contemplative duality: Trajan, Gentile, emperor, represents the active, or temporal, life.[187] David, Jew, ancestor of Christ and Church, singer of the Holy Spirit,[188] exemplifies the spiritual life. This relationship is emphasized in the *Convivio*, where the 2 lines of descent are drawn from Aeneas and David (held by Dante to have been contemporaries), the line of Aeneas to Rome and State (active); the line of David to Christ and Church (contemplative).[189] In Mary, mother of the God-man, is the link between the 2. In her earthly life, she represents the earthly nativity of Christ. As Queen of Heaven, she is a fit symbol for the spiritual life. Similarly, Mary is both active and contemplative, as says Albertus Magnus, "like the angels." [190] The succeeding ledges of Purgatory follow the same general scheme in giving examples of the virtues; Roman virtue being illustrated by Orestes, Pisistratus, Caesar, Fabricius, Roman women, Diana [191] (of the type of the inhabitants of Limbo),

186. *Purg.*, I, 37; VIII, 88-93.
187. Cf. *De monarchia*, III, 16, 79-82.
188. *Par.*, XX, 38; *De monarchia*, III, 4, 84-87.
189. *Convivio*, IV, 5, 1-50.
190. *De laudibus B. Mariae Virg.*, IV, 35.
191. Pisistratus, Orestes and Diana can hardly be counted as Roman citizens. They are Roman only in the sense that Aristotle and Plato are Roman; i.e., they were contributors to pagan Roman culture, which produced the perfection of the civil life in the Roman Empire (a perfection which Dante wishes to see restored), in the same sense that David and Daniel, Jews, were forerunners and spiritual members of Dante's Church.

and chuchly virtue by Christ, St. Stephen, St. Nicholas, and Daniel (spiritual inhabitants of Paradise).

When Dante has passed through the experiences of the seventh ledge, he dreams of Leah and Rachel, Old Testament types of action and contemplation. Dante is then *crowned* (state) and *mitred* (church). Upon reaching the Earthly Paradise, the dream is actualized in the figures of Matilda and Beatrice. The description of Matilda, singing and gathering flowers,[192] leaves no doubt of her symbolic identity with Leah, who is similarly occupied.[193] Matilda may therefore be said to represent the earthly, active element, in its perfection in the Garden of Eden. Beatrice, descending from Heaven, is the very spirit of God as it was infused into man in that Garden and later reinfused into the world in the person of Christ. Therefore, at the rising of the sun, the Light, clad in the 3 theological virtues, she comes to the acclaim, *Benedictus qui venis*.[194] Here is the image of earthly action and contemplation in its most perfect form. As Dante's progress is from Matilda to Beatrice, from Lethe (forgetfulness of evil) to Eunoe (knowledge of good), from the 4 stars to the 3 stars, so in Eden he moves from the dance of the 4 cardinal virtues (active) to the more complete spirituality of the 3 theological virtues.[195]

In their entirety, both Earthly Paradise and the Church Militant are active, in comparison to the Heavenly Paradise and the Church Triumphant. Yet even the symbolic extension of the Heavenly Paradise through the 9 spheres, which one might expect to be all contemplation, contains the cross of Mars as well as the ladder of Contemplation, the eagle of Empire as well as the trinal circles of Divinity. For the Final Perfection will not be complete until the glorified body is rejoined to the soul:

192. *Purg.*, XXVIII, 40-42.
193. *Ibid.*, XXVII, 97-99.
194. *Ibid.*, XXX, 19-33.
195. *Ibid.*, XXXI, 103-11.

Come la carne gloriosa e santa
fia rivestita, la nostra persona
più grata fia per esser tutta quanta.[196]

When with the flesh, holy and glorious,
We shall have been reclothed, our persons then,
Being entire, will more advantage us.

The angels themselves perform two functions: contemplation of God and the movement of the heavens — they are both active and contemplative.[197] By the same token, a similar duality must figure in the Celestial Rose of Church Triumphant. The entire image of Church Triumphant centers, as of course it should, about the ministry of Christ. The Rose of Christ therefore partakes of the nature of the duality of the Second Person.

The most obvious division of the Rose is described by Bernard in the segregation of the Old Testament from the New. In one half of the Rose are seated those who believed in Christ to come; in the other, those who worshiped Christ come.[198] On the topmost row, apparently at the dividing lines between the 2 groups, are seated Mary and John the Baptist, diametrically opposite each other. In the "examples" of Purgatory, Mary acted as a kind of mean between opposing types and here she fulfills the same function seconded by John the Baptist, who also acts as a link between the ages, being both prophet and follower. Between Mary and John on the Old Testament side are named the figures of Adam, Moses, and Anna; on the New Testament side, Peter, John (the Divine), and Lucia. Beneath Mary, row by row, are ranged Eve (row 2), Rachel with Beatrice beside her (3), Sara (4), Rebecca (5), Judith (6), and Ruth (7). The juncture of the Old Testament Rachel and the "New Testament" Beatrice implies that the dividing line runs between them.

196. Par., XIV, 43-45; cf. Aquinas, Summa contra Gentiles, 84.
197. Convivio, II, 6, 1-3.
198. Par., XXXII, 19-36.

Consequently, we may visualize the group about Mary as follows:

John	Peter	Mary	Adam	Moses
		Eve		
	Beatrice	Rachel		
		Sara		
		Rebecca		
		Judith		
		Ruth [199]		

On the opposite side of the Rose, the figures surrounding John fall into a similar pattern:

Anna	John	Lucia
	Francis	
	Benedict	
	Augustine	

Emphasis on this side is placed on the New Testament figures, in contrast to the Old Testament figures under Mary, a distinction which draws immediate attention to Beatrice seated beside Rachel. The fact that Leah and Rachel, as types of action and contemplation, were always joined together, and that Leah is here replaced by Beatrice, distinguishes another duality in the Rose and provides, as well, the most precise definition of the function of Beatrice. Beatrice has already been defined as the symbol of Love and the Holy Spirit. Here the conjunction of Beatrice and Rachel calls attention to the fact that Beatrice is not the only representative of Love. Two are the precepts of Love: Love of

199. The more usual disposition of these figures is to place the line from Eve to Ruth directly beneath Mary (cf. Porena, *Commento grafico alla Divina Commedia*, pp. 60-62 and Fig. 32). This, however, makes Mary definitely Old Testament and, on the opposite side, distinguishes John, the forerunner of Christ, as definitely New Testament. How such a distinction might be argued is not clear, especially in the implication that Mary, Queen of Heaven, is inferior to John, as the Old Testament was always considered less enlightened than the New. The neighboring figures, Adam, human originator of the Old Testament period, and Peter, human originator of Church, also imply that Mary (as in Purgatory) is a link, rather than a member of either group.

God and Love of neighbor.[200] In the same sense, Rachel and Beatrice exemplify respectively sanctifying grace, whereby man is led to God, and gratuitous grace, by which man leads his fellow to God.[201] Or, as Dante puts it, Charity seeks God and man.[202]

The complication of this part of the imagery of the *Comedy* results from Dante's conception of Beatrice, miracle, as the earthly symbol of Ultimate Perfection. When acting as spokesman for Church Militant, therefore, even though her intrinsic color is the red of Love, she must assume temporarily the white and green of Faith and Hope, as well as the company of the cardinal virtues. Her technical place in the Eternal Pattern may be specifically defined as the "activity of Charity," by which man leads his fellow to God, in contrast to Rachel, who never turns from her fixed contemplation whereby man is led to God.[203] As Leah distinguishes herself from her sister,

> lei lo vedere, e me l' ovrare appaga.[204]
>
> Her seeing, and me doing, satisfies.

The point is that Beatrice "*does.*" In the *Comedy* as in the *Vita nuova*, hers is the active, guiding hand of Dante. At the beginning of the *Comedy*, she leaves her station beside Rachel,[205] acts for Dante's salvation, and returns to the immobile Rachel only when her mission has been completed. She appears to Dante in the *Earthly* Paradise, on the *left* side of the car,[206] attended by the 4 cardinal virtues, who were preordained to be her handmaids.[207] Thus, before her birth, her position in the Archetypal Design had been fixed. Opposed to Beatrice on the third round of the Rose is the con-

200. Aquinas, *Summa Theologica*, II-II, qu. 44, art. 2.
201. *Ibid.*, II-I, qu. 11, art. 1.
202. *De monarchia*, I, 11, 103-4.
203. Cf. *Purg.*, XXVII, 103-5.
204. *Ibid.*, XXVII, 108.
205. *Inf.*, II, 101-2.
206. *Purg.*, XXX, 61, 100-1.
207. *Ibid.*, XXXI, 107-8.

templative Benedict, brightest of the pearls of love in the heaven of contemplation,[208] and who had been named by Joachim as the forerunner of the age of Love. When Dante, at the vision of the Rose, thought to see Beatrice, he saw instead the contemplative Bernard: Beatrice and Rachel, Beatrice and Benedict, Beatrice and Bernard.

Dante, who is led only by degrees to the vision of the Divine Order, sees Beatrice first through earthly eyes. In her actual life, she functions most completely as gratuitous grace, fulfilling her preordained active mission. Simultaneously, she is to Dante the essence of that contemplation from which he is later to swerve. Beatrice is contemplative with respect to this life, but with respect to Heaven she is active; contemplative with respect to Matilda in the Earthly Paradise, active with respect to Rachel in the Heavenly. In this capacity, she transmits heavenly contemplation to mortal activity (the prelative life), carrying Rachel within her eyes, as Dante is instructed by the active virtues:

> Merrenti a li occhi suoi; ma nel giocondo
> lume ch' è dentro aguzzeranno i tuoi
> le tre di là, che miran più profondo.[209]

> To us is given
> To lead thee to her eyes [active manifestation] but for the *light*
> *Within them* rapturous, shall sharpen thine
> That yonder three, whose is profounder sight.

So Dante, moving from the cardinal to the theological virtues, from Purgatory to Heaven, is transferred eventually from Beatrice to Bernard, to bring his desire to its ultimate goal.[210] It is Bernard who guides Dante's vision through the intricacies of the Rose, where the "inner light" of Beatrice is seen beside her in the image of Rachel, and Dante is finally sufficiently elevated to distinguish between them.

Thus two dominant dualities are presented in the vision of

208. *Par.*, XXII, 28-32.
209. *Purg.*, XXXI, 109-11.
210. *Par.*, XXXI, 67.

the Rose: Old Testament and New Testament, Action and Contemplation, the latter being adumbrated by the presence of representatives of State and Church; Henry, earthly king, *agosta*,[211] and Mary, heavenly queen, *Regina*,[212] *Augusta*.[213] In the combined numerical arrangement of the two opposed clusters of figures, there is also an intimation of a similar duality. The named figures of the topmost row total 8, the number of baptism and regeneration; the named members of the lower circles number 10, as if in image of the Decalogue or Old Law, crowned or fulfilled by the New Law, the regeneration of Christ. This may be nothing more than numerical coincidence, but the probability of its being intentional is heightened by the division of the 10 into 7 and 3, the habitual partition of the 10 Commandments.[214]

The highest duality, the duality of the spiritual life, has its symbolic representations in those parts of the *Comedy* where the Church of Christ is dominant. Thus it is imaged in the pageant of Church Militant, in the Rose of Church Triumphant, and, between the two, in the circles of the image in the Sun, symbol of the Light of Christ. There the two named circles (which are all that concern us at the moment) are each composed of 12 lights, a circumstance which at the outset suggests the commonest double 12 of the Middle Ages, the 12 patriarchs or tribes of Israel and the 12 apostles. As Gardner has defined these circles,[215] they represent the orders of Francis and Dominic,

> L' un fu tutto serafico in ardore;
> l' altro per sapienza in terra fue
> di cherubica luce uno splendore.[216]

One was, in ardor, of the Seraphim;

---

211. *Ibid.*, XXX, 136.
212. *Ibid.*, XXXIII, 34.
213. *Ibid.*, XXXII, 119.
214. See above, p. 114.
215. *Dante and the Mystics*, pp. 225-35.
216. *Par.*, XI, 37-39.

The other by his wisdom upon earth
A splendor of the light of Cherubim.

The one, Seraphic, including Bonaventura, who "put behind
the left-hand care," [217] is envisaged as contemplative in nature,
nearest to Church Triumphant and Rachel. The other,
Cherubic, represents the active teaching function of Church
Militant, "wisdom upon earth," Beatrice.

Within the figure of these circles is the constant implication of Dante that this duality, omnipresent in the Spiritual
World, is the pattern which the corporeal world should
follow. Here the correlation of Church and State with contemplation and action is clarified by the inclusion of two
Old Testament figures. They are entirely distinct from the
others, if only for this reason. In the active, Cherubic circle
is Solomon, specifically denominated as the height of *kingly*
wisdom.[218] In the contemplative, Seraphic circle is Nathan
the prophet, the voice of God to this same king.

The most striking image of the Church-State duality appears in the sixth heaven, the heaven of Jupiter and the
Eagle. Dante is the sixth of the singers of the Eagle.[219] The
sixth age is the age of earthly perfection, which many contemporary prophecies, such as the condemned *Postil on the
Apocalypse*, attributed to Pierre Olivi,[220] had contended was
still in prospect. In Canto XIX we are told that in this heaven
of all heavens Divine Justice makes its mirror.[221]

Here the "glowing flames of the Holy Spirit" [222] form
themselves into the prophetic admonition, "*Diligite justi-
tiam qui judicatis terram*," staying fixed in the last M. We
already know, from the didactic utterances liberally sprin-

217. *Ibid.*, XII, 128.
218. *Ibid.*, XIII, 104.
219. *Inf.*, IV, 102; cf. J. B. Fletcher, "Dante's School of the Eagle," *Romanic Review*, XXII, 191-209.
220. Lea, *History of the Inquisition*, III, 49.
221. Lines 28-29.
222. *Lucenti incendi de lo Spirito Santo, Par.*, XIX, 100-1.

kled through the pages of the *Comedy, Convivio,* and *De monarchia,* what justice this is to be. The letter *M,* suggesting the heraldic form of the Eagle, may denote Mary, Monarchy, or the number 1,000, which is the ultimate boundary of number and a symbol of perfection.[223] In the two wings, downstrokes of the M, are also figured the 2 horns of the bishop's mitre, Old and New Testaments.[224] Dante further informs the reader that the letters of the entire phrase number 35. Although it is remotely possible that this is purely gratuitous and pointless information, it is hardly probable that a numerical symbol is not implied. It is true that 35 is both the apex of life and Dante's assumed age at the time of the journey, but the connection between these truths and the truth of the Eagle is certainly not obvious. There is, fortunately, another possibility; for the figures in the Divine Pageant, representing the books of the Old and the New Testaments, also number 35. By this numerical identity, the Justice of the Eagle is related to the Justice of Eden, and the Eagle of Monarchy has its proper counterpart in the pageant of Church Militant.

The justice of the Eagle will include, like the justice of the Rose, a harmony of all earthly dualities. Not only will it include, like Church Militant, the Old and the New Testaments, but also the 2 felicities of man, action and contemplation, or, more specifically, the civil life and the spiritual life, State and Church. For in the eye of the eagle the 2 lines of descent from David and Aeneas, the lines of the Church of Christ and the Roman Empire, are indicated. The pupil of the eye, the inner light, is David, "*il cantor de lo Spirito Santo.*" [225] The arch of the eyelid is made up of 5 figures from the civil life. Four of them are kings and the fifth, Ripheus,

223. See above, pp. 42, 44, 101-2.
224. Durandus, *Rationale,* III, 13, 2; Elworthy, *Horns of Honor,* p. 76.
225. *Par.,* XX, 38.

is a Trojan warrior who loved Justice and, as a Trojan, was among the ancestors of Rome.

Here again may be seen Dante's belief in action and contemplation, State and Church, Old and New Testaments, as variants of the archetypal Duality. For if the union of the 2 councils, Old and New, and the union of the 2 lives, active and contemplative, informs Church Militant and Church Triumphant, it here also creates the

> segno
> che fè i Romani al mondo reverendi.[226]

> sign
> Which made the Romans by the world revered.

In the sixth sphere is the Eagle of Empire, but rising from the seventh to the regeneration of the eighth is the ladder of contemplation. If Can Grande was indeed the *veltro* on whom Dante based his hope, it was for Dante additional proof of his election that these twin images of action and contemplation were figured on the crest of that Lombard

> che 'n su la scala porta il santo uccello.[227]

> Who on the Ladder bears the sacred Bird.

In Purgatory, the figure of Beatrice (Church) at the top of the Mount is complemented by that of the Roman Cato (State) at the foot, and the Paradise of the Church has its forerunner in the pagan Paradise of Limbo, whose 7 walls recall the 7-hilled city of Rome, ruled over by 7 kings.[228]

In presenting the Church-State relationship as an integral part of the divinely ordained plan, Dante shows that his belief in the Eternal Pattern is as practical as it is philosophical. He has shown that the only *right* government of mundane affairs is a twin government of independent Church and independent State. But his certainty of the existence of a

226. *Ibid.*, XIX, 101-2.
227. *Ibid.*, XVII, 73.
228. *Convivio*, IV, 5, 88-96.

Divine Plan enables him to take the next step and to predict with confidence that:

1. This state of earthly perfection, signalized by the dual rule of Church and State, is certainly in prospect.[229]

2. This perfection will be in conformity with the Supernal Pattern.[230]

3. It will be soon.[231]

For if a Divine Pattern is being followed, and the end is near, it is in conformity with numerical logic to assume that the temporal world will see 3 Golden Ages (the perfect 3), with 2 periods of imperfection between (the imperfect 2). The theory obviously involves two cycles, in each of which a state of perfection is followed by a period of backsliding to be, in turn, redeemed by a return to perfection.[232] It is my belief that these two complete cycles are precisely represented in the *Divine Comedy*.

The first cycle is suggested by the 3 steps to Purgatory. The first is of white marble, typifying the innocence of the garden of Eden, the Golden Age.[233] The second, dark and cracked, images the "grievous times" which followed the coming of the serpent into the garden, times represented in the Rose by Moses. The third is the red of redemption, brought about by the passion of Christ.[234] The advent of Christ led to the founding of the Church, and the reign of Christ is distinguished in the 2 suns of Rome, both of which shone brightly in that happy time of redemption. For the world "was never quiet on every side except under divus Augustus, the monarch, when there was perfect monarchy," [235] as well as perfect Church represented by Christ in person.

229. *De monarchia*, II, 12, 21-23; III, 3; *Purg.*, XXXIII, 37-51.
230. *De monarchia*, III, 2, 29-32.
231. *Convivio*, II, 15, 115-18; *Purg.*, XXXIII, 49; *Par.*, XXX, 132-33.
232. Cf. J. B. Fletcher, "Dante's School of the Eagle," pp. 202 *et sqq.*
233. *Purg.*, XXII, 148.
234. *Ibid.*, IX, 76-102.
235. *De monarchia*, I, 16, 6-12.

Paul has called that most happy state the "fullness of time." Verily the time and all temporal things were full, for no ministry to our felicity was then vacant of its minister.[236]

But this second perfection was, at the same time, a mirror of the original perfection. It was a "return from exile," [237] because the world had swerved meanwhile from the way of truth and from its proper life. Consequently, the pageant of the Church occurs in the Paradise of Adam. The actual return to original perfection is rehearsed before Dante's eyes as the Church returns against the course of the sun, or backwards in time, and joins the cross of Christ to the now-barren tree of Adam, which thereupon renews itself. Thus the first cycle is completed [238] and

> Si si conserva il seme d' ogni giusto.[239]
>
> Thus is preserved the seed of all the just.

It is entirely fitting that the steps to the realm of the Son should memorialize the stages which led to the advent of the Son and the institution of Purgatory.

A transition is marked by the slumber of Dante, and his awakening is compared to the transfiguration, during which the 3 disciples were granted a vision of future glory. He awakens to see Beatrice as the new guardian of the chariot. To Dante, she presents the history of the second

236. *Ibid.*, 17-22.
237. *Par.*, VII, 31-39.
238. Dante himself has also completed such a cycle in his early devotion to Beatrice, defection, and return to salvation. Professor Fletcher has pointed out that in turning *left* to return to the tree, Dante is repeating symbolically his own journey of spiritual regeneration through Hell and Purgatory. For in the Inferno he is in the Northern Hemisphere and in turning always to the left he goes against the course of the sun, or backwards in the course of time. In Purgatory, he is in the Southern Hemisphere and consequently must turn right to continue his symbolic journey backwards through time. For "Virgil explains in effect that, since the Sun's course is confined within the tropics, it circles to the south of an observer in the north temperate zone, to the north of one at the antipodes. Consequently, an observer in the Northern Hemisphere following its course will turn from left to right; one in the Southern Hemisphere from right to left" ("Left and Right Turns in the Divine Comedy," *Romanic Review*, XXII, 236-37).
239. *Purg.*, XXXII, 48.

"cracked and calcined" period, figured in the Rose by John the evangelist

> che vide tutti i tempi gravi,
> pria che morisse, de la bella sposa
> che s' acquisto con la lancia e coi chiavi.[240]

> that saw, ere his own days were done,
> The grievous times on which the fair bride fell
> Who with the spear and with the nails was won.

In this period, the car of the Church is successively shaken, and the splitting of the Empire by Constantine is said to repeat the rending of the tree of Adam. Finally the car is represented as completely disfigured by the sprouting of 7 horns. These are related to the 7 virtues by their positions: 4 at the corners — cardinal, and 3 on the pole or cross — theological. Whatever the precise meaning of these 7 sproutings may be, it is at least safe to assume that by them Dante implies that in his own defective age all the virtues of the Christian Era, cardinal and theological, have become deformed. It is fitting that the theological "vices" should be represented by double horns, since they belong to the age of the God-man, perfection of State and Church, and, as has been suggested, offend both God and neighbor, or militate against both contemplation and action.

But such deformity is not to endure forever, for Beatrice prophesies the advent of a second restoration and, presumably, a third appearance of the Golden Age. Dante passes through Eunoe to become

> come piante novelle
> rinovellate di novella fronda [241]

> Like a new tree renewed with foliage new

to see the seed again restored in Paradise. There St. Thomas bolsters Dante's hope:

240. *Par.*, XXXII, 127-29.
241. *Purg.*, XXXIII, 143-44.

ch' i' ho veduto tutto il verno prima
lo prun mostrarsi rigido e feroce,
poscia portar la rosa in su la cima.[242]

For I have seen amid the wintry snows
The briar show itself all stiff and wild,
And bear thereafter on its top the rose.

This cyclical theory of Dante's is philosophically justified by pure numerical reasoning. The Origin is 1, which is perfect. Two, or the second period, departs from the perfection of unity, to be restored by the 3 which is 1. The third period, that is, necessarily returns to the original perfection. Dante, in his self-confessed progress from Beatrice to the *Donna Pietosa* and back to Beatrice, himself exemplifies this cycle. Furthermore, since this is the pattern of the All, succeeding periods can only repeat the first cycle. By the same numerical logic, it is also true that the number of such cycles is limited. There is every reason to believe that Dante considered the forthcoming salvation as the last epoch of earthly perfection, since the perfect 3 of Heaven, which is all, would then have had its earthly counterpart in 3 perfect ages. At the same time, the imperfection of the archetypal 2 would have been realized in the 2 intermediary periods.

Professor Fletcher has kindly called my attention to a confirmation of the conception of 3 spiritual paradises in Bonaventura, who says:

There are 3 paradises, 3 inhabitants, 3 woods of life: First, the terrestrial, whose first inhabitant was Adam; Second, that of the faithful, the Church of the Saints; Third, the celestial; that is to say, Church Triumphant, which God inhabits. In the first is the wood of life, the tree material; in the second, the humanity of the Saviour; in the third, the entire Trinity.[243]

All 3 of these spiritual paradises are to be envisioned by Dante. He has at this point seen the tree of Adam and the

242. *Par.*, XIII, 133-35.
243. *Expos. in Psal.*, I, 3.

tree of Christ. He has in prospect the revelation of Church Triumphant in the Rose.

At the same time, earthly things are but the mirror of heavenly things. James is later to explain to Dante the reason, or at least one reason, for his heavenly directed journey through the three realms:

> sì che, veduto il ver di questa corte,
> la spene, che là giù bene innamora,
> in te ed in altrui di ciò conforte.[244]

> So that, the truth beholding of this court,
> Unto the hope which moves to righteous love
> Thou mayst in thee and others bring support.

The hope of Dante was, of course, the hope of heaven, but it was also and emphatically the hope of earthly perfection. Accordingly, the admonition and prophecies of Beatrice refer not to the heavenly perfection, but to the fulfillment of the Divine Plan on earth.

In the cycle of the 3 perfect ages, there is also the same sense of progression (as seen in Bonaventura) that obtains among the theological virtues and among the members of the Trinity. The perfection of Eden, the first age, was marred by the inadequacy of Adam, creation of the Father. For the sin of Adam restitution was made by the advent of the Son and the institution of the Church. But even in this "Fullness of Time," there was still a lurking imperfection in that State and Church (in Christ) were not in conscious harmony. Hence persecution followed. The third and ultimate perfection, however, will see Church and State in harmony and performing their discrete and proper functions.

The coincidence of the first Golden Age with the Creation by the Father, and the second with the Salvation by the Son, leaves at least the impression that the coming restoration will be effected, as the Spirituals believed, by the Holy Spirit.

244. *Par.*, XXV, 43-45.

Under the Father the Empire originated. The advent of the Son instituted the Church. Will not then the coming peace and love in the harmony of Church and State be effected by the Third Member of the Trinity, as Ladder and Eagle complement each other in the burning flames of Love, as Father and Son together breathe forth the Holy Spirit? The virtue of Love, delegated to the Holy Spirit, was ordinarily considered as the culminating and final perfection. In harmony with this conception, Albertus Magnus names charity as the virtue of the last age.[245] He refers to the spiritual regeneration but, if earth mirrors heaven, love might well be the "virtue" of the earthly regeneration anticipated by Dante.

Before examining more precisely the probability of such implications in the Comedy, it will be advisable to inquire into the possible relationship of Dante and the most famous exponent of the third age, Joachim of Flora. Immediately noteworthy is the high position assigned to Joachim in the *Comedy*. In the temperate judgment of Aquinas, Joachim "foretold some things that were true and in others was deceived." [246] Dante's own regard for him may be educed from his placing him at the very side of Bonaventura and describing him through Bonaventura's lips as

> di spirito profetico dotato.[247]
> Filled with the spirit of high prophecy.

This statement, furthermore, is made at the conclusion of Bonaventura's discourse, and as if introducing the third circle (of the Holy Spirit).

There is, indeed, a kinship between the poet and the prophet, by virtue of their common mystic exaltation and their common faith in Primal Love, which is emphasized by both in their writings. This bond was further strengthened by a similarity in their motives, by which both were made

245. *Sermo* XVI, *De tempore*.
246. *Summa Theologica*, III, qu. 77, art. 2.
247. *Par.*, XII, 141.

part of a wave of reaction against the barefaced corruption of the temporal Church. The triple time schedule of Joachim may, therefore, have provided the hint for Dante's cyclical theory and something of his definition of the 3 Ages. According to Joachim, the first age endured from Adam to Christ, representing Power and inspiring fear. The people then lived according to the flesh, unable to attain to the liberty of the spirit. The second age was the age of Christ, between flesh and spirit, characterized by Wisdom, in liberty by comparison with the past, but not in comparison with the future. The third age is the final perfection of peace, love, and the enjoyment of perfect liberty under the Holy Ghost.[248] The Old Testament was the guide to the first age, the New Testament to the second, but "the Eternal Gospel" of the third will be written in the hearts of men, "for the letter killeth and the spirit quickeneth." [249]

Henry W. Wells has shown how this conception of the cumulative progression of the 3 Persons (each adding new qualities and culminating in the Third) motivates the 3 stages of life elaborated in the *Vita* of *Piers Plowman*.[250] The pilgrim expresses surprise on learning that there are 3 stages of life instead of 2. The definition of these stages, as well as their relationship to the Members of the Trinity, is summarized by Wells as follows:

248. Gardner, *Dante and the Mystics*, pp. 189-90.

249. Gebhart, *Mystics and Heretics in Italy*, p. 86. It is made quite evident in the writings of Joachim that the notorious Eternal Gospel was not to be a written document. Yet such a book, variously attributed to Jean of Parma or Joachim, was certainly condemned or suppressed by the Commission at Anagni in July, 1255 (Lea, *History of the Inquisition*, III, 22). A volume of the Joachite writings may have been issued under such a title, as Lea believes; or, as Rousselot holds, it may have been invented for the specific purpose of embarrassing the Dominicans and the Franciscans who were supposedly named therein as the temporal vicars of the third age (cf. *Roman de la Rose*, 12442-12634). The Spiritual Franciscans had adopted the Joachite doctrines wholeheartedly (Lea, *op. cit.*, III, 13).

250. "The Construction of 'Piers Plowman,'" PMLA XLIV, 123-40.

DO-WELL	DO-BET	DO-BEST
The Active Life of intellectual studies and priestly duties; *Activa Vita*;	The Contemplative Life; discussion of faithful hermits;	The Active Life expressed in the corporate Church, or Unitas; especially the rule of the Bishop;
Self-rule; the Ten Commandments and the Seven Sins; allegorical figures and contempoary allusions;	Self-obliteration; the three contemplative or Christian Virtues; many scriptural figures;	The care of souls; the four Active or Moral Virtues; allegorical figures and contemporary allusions again;
The protection of the Father	The protection of the Son	The protection of the Holy Spirit

How thoroughly Dante agreed with Joachim's theory is difficult to say. Papini is sufficiently convinced of Dante's affinity with Joachim to suggest, more ingeniously than plausibly, that by the *veltro* is intended the Holy Spirit. The key to the enigma he finds in 6 letters of the Eternal Gospel itself: V ang E L e T e R n O.[251]

It is certain that Dante agreed with Joachim and the Spirituals in many of their contentions.[252] His faith, like theirs, was placed in the Mendicant orders as supports for the tottering structure of the Church.[253] His doctrine of love was in entire accord with the preaching of the Spirituals, whose third age was to be informed with this spirit. He, too, longed for a reign of peace and love on earth. He, too, regarded the papal chair as vacant,[254] and the contemporary incumbent, together with the Church under his jurisdiction, as the whore of Babylon. In view of these coincidences, it is also more than likely that it was indeed Celestine V who "made the great refusal." [255] In a broader sense, it is also true that Hell, Purgatory, Heaven, and the progress through them, present a

251. *Dante vivo*, p. 284.
252. Cf. De Salvio, *Dante and Heresy.*
253. *Par.*, XII, 38.
254. *Ibid.*, XXVII, 10.
255. *Inf.*, III, 59.

pictorial analogy to Joachim's conception of the 3 ages, even to the partial liberation of Purgatory (*In exitu Israel de Aegypto*)[256] and the full liberty attained at the summit (Dante crowned and mitred).[257]

On the other hand, Dante had in mind his own objective, the discrete automony of Church and State, as the definition of the third age. It is also obvious to any reader of the *Comedy* that its author could not conceive of any such positive separation of the members of the Trinity as Joachim suggests. It seems more likely that Dante tempered this well-known theory to suit his own didactic as well as poetic ends. Stated as simply as possible, a definition of Dante's 3 ages would be as follows:

The First Age: Man created by the Father. A Golden Age in Eden, followed by the defection of Eve and punishment by the God of Wrath. Hell receives its first human tenants. A tentative search for Light: origin of monarchy to guide the civil life, the cardinal virtues discovered. Infusion of the Holy Spirit into the Jews. Birth of David, precursor of Christ. Father, Son, and Holy Spirit are all present in every age, but the dominant character of the age proceeds from the Power of the Father. The dominant virtue is the Faith of the Jews. The contribution of the age is the perfection of the civil life, as represented in the Noble Castle, the Empire "which had its full virtue when the Church did not exist."[258]

The Second Age: Marked by the advent of the Son, Light, Hope. Momentary perfection of Church and State. Institution of Purgatory. Revelation of the theological virtues. Inevitable defection, marked by the crumbling of the Empire and corruption of the Church. The distinguishing characteristic of this age is the fulfillment of the contemplative

256. *Purg.*, II, 46.
257. *Ibid.*, XXVII, 142.
258. *De monarchia*, III, 13, 268.

life and the founding of the Church, whose apotheosis is presented in the pageant of the Earthly Paradise.

The Third Age: Ultimate earthly perfection. Reign of peace and Love. Goal of the universe in harmonious union of action and contemplation, Church and State, Eagle and Ladder. The Light of the Son had already shown the way. All that is needed is the Will to bring it about; and Will, or Fruition, as Aquinas said, corresponds to Love, as comprehension to Hope, and vision to Faith.[259] Dante likewise believes that Love is the motivating force of human activity,[260] just as it is Love that moves Beatrice to instigate the salvation of Dante.[261] This is the "activity of charity" and, informed with this Love, Dominic

> con dottrina e con volere insieme
> con l' officio apostolico si mosse
> quasi torrente ch' alta vena preme;
> e ne li sterpi eretici percosse
> l' impeto suo, più vivamente quivi
> dove le resistenze eran più grosse.[262]

> Joining . . . will with doctrine to sustain
> The office apostolic, he went forth,
> As pours a torrent from a lofty vein
> And ever on the stocks of heresy
> His onset most inexorably fell
> Where most stiff-necked was the contumacy.

The culminating "life" of combined action and contemplation had already been defined in the Prelative Life of the Middle Ages, which is *active* in teaching *contemplation* — so Beatrice. Its type is Christ. This is the teaching of *Piers Plowman*.[263] It is summarized as follows:

259. *Summa Theologica*, I, qu. 12, art. 7; cp. Bonaventura, *Sentences*, I, dist. II, pars. 2, art. 1, qu. 1. This progression also corresponds in function to the degrees of good and evil; in heart, word, deed; or to the 3 steps to virtue: contrition, confession, satisfaction.

260. *Purg.*, XVII.

261. *Inf.*, II, 72.

262. *Par.*, XII, 97-102.

263. See above, p. 189.

Do-wel my friend is,
To doon as lawe techeth;
To love thi frend and thi foo,
Leve me, that is Do-bet;
To gyven and to yemen
Bothe yonge and olde,
To helen and to helpen,
Is Do-best of alle.
    And Do-wel is to drede God,
And Do-bet is to suffre,
And so cometh Do-best of bothe.[264]

This is a succinct version of Dante's 3 ages: the first of fear and law under the Father; the second defined by the humility of Christ; the third distinguished by charity, virtue of the Holy Spirit, and the crown of the preceding two.

As has already been indicated, love, or 3, is the uniting force which harmonizes the members of the unstable duad:

con l' atto sol del suo etterno amore.[265]

By the sole act of His eternal love.

So, throughout the *Comedy*, Dante's many duads become unified at last. Dante's course through Hell is to the left; through Purgatory, to the right. In Paradise he turns no more, but rises upward, without motion of his own, as he is wheeled with the heavens. In the Golden Age, left and right, tree and cross are united, so that there is no longer any turning. As Augustine had said, both right and left are necessary for completeness.[266]

Dante himself had two precursors, Aeneas and Paul, who represent State and Church. Dante, the third, sings of both. Dante is also the third of the poets in Purgatory. Of this

264. Lines 5580-90 (Wright ed.). These lives were understood to be defined in Luke 17: 24-26. Cf. the commentaries on Luke of Bonaventura and Albertus Magnus.

265. *Par.*, VII, 33. The uniting force of the Holy Ghost is implied also in Skelton's *Prayer* to the Members of the Trinity.

266. *A Treatise on Grace and Freewill*; Letter II, 6-7; *Anti-Pelagian Writings*, III, 10-11; "Turn not to the right hand nor to the left" (Prov. 4: 27; *Civ. Dei*, II, 57).

triad, Virgil is the poet of Empire, which flourished under the rule of the Father.[267] The epitome of this age is seen in the Noble Castle, where the cardinal virtues may be said to rule, even as they enlighten the face of Cato. There also are the singers of the Eagle, who accept Dante as sixth of their brotherhood, completing the number of earthly perfection.

Statius, the second poet, does not appear until Purgatory and is there used as an example of the soul rising to the Spiritual Life. This is the domain of Wisdom, Lucia, and Christ, wherefore Statius is revealed

> che Cristo apparve a' due ch' erano in via.[268]

> as Christ
> Showed Himself unto two upon their way.

To reach Purgatory one must ascend the 3 steps which complete the first cycle.[269] Purgation of sin is the Hope advanced by Christ, and there Lucia, the Light, advances Dante on his way. The glory of the summit of Purgatory is the pageant of the Church. There Dante sees the second blossoming of the tree at the coming of Christ. The entire canticle bears witness to the dispensation of the Son. The Noble Castle of the *Inferno* was "without Christ." Contrariwise, perfect Church, or the guide to the true Contemplative Life, could exist only with the advent of the Son.

Dante alone, on the other hand, is the poet of Paradise. There he sees the eternal blossoming in the Celestial Rose. But even this final symbol of the eternal Spiritual Life is tinged with earthly memories in the first-seen throne of the Imperial Henry. Nor is it strange, in view of the polysemous nature of the *Comedy*, that the ultimate perfection of Heaven should hold intimations of the anticipated perfection of earth. In the Heavenly Rose is prefigured, perhaps, the third

267. Scartazzini believes, rightly I think, that Virgil is the symbol of Roman Universal Monarchy; *A Companion to Dante*, p. 444.

268. *Purg.*, XXI, 8.

269. See above, p. 182.

flowering of the tree of Adam. In it are united Old and New Testaments, action and contemplation in the harmony already seen in the Eagle. Similarly, in contrast to Hell and Purgatory, the dominating spirit of Love infuses this third realm, as it infused the emblem of the Eagle. Not, therefore, in a precisely symbolical sense, but as a result of the uniformity of the Great Design, the ultimate goal of Dante's spiritual journey may be said to mirror the goal of Dante's temporal aims: the harmonic union of Father and Son, action and contemplation, State and Church, bound together by the breath of the Holy Spirit.

We have already noted the correlation of Beatrice with Love and the Holy Spirit. It is significant, therefore, that in the *Earthly* Paradise it is Beatrice, earthly representative of the Third Person, who assumes the supervision of the Church *after* Christ has performed His function of renewing the tree of Adam. It is Beatrice who guides Dante to Paradise, Beatrice who commissions him to repeat to the world that he has seen

> la pianta
> ch' e or due volte dirubata quivi.[270]

> the tree
> Which now twice over hath been plundered here.

He is also to repeat her prophecy of the forthcoming salvation [271] and (presumably) the third restoration of the tree.

The image of the circle, which appears in the circling of the 3 apostles, as in the ultimate vision of Trinity, is repeated a third time in an enigmatic form in the Heaven of the Sun. Here again are 2 circles joined later by a third. The first two, in order of their appearance are identifiable as:[272]

1. Dominican, Active, State, Cherubic, Wisdom.
2. Franciscan, Contemplative, Church, Seraphic, Love.

270. *Purg.*, XXXIII, 56-57.
271. *Ibid.*, XXXIII, 43-45, 52.
272. See above, pp. 178-79.

Most puzzling, then, is the appearance of a third circle, as the light of John (Love) appeared to Peter (Faith) and James (Hope). This circle is greeted by Dante's exclamation:

> Oh vero sfavillar del Santo Spiro.[273]
>
> O sparkling truly of the Holy Spirit!

The lights which inform the figure of the Eagle are also to be described as

> lo sfavillar de l' amor.[274]
>
> the sparkling of love.

In contrast to the other circles, the lights which compose the third are unnamed, as if to imply that the individuals who should fill the places either could not yet be known, or had not yet come to their Heavenly abodes. The very mystery which attends it links it to Dante's other veiled prophetic utterances concerning the yet-unrealized third perfection of Earth. It follows that this third circle seems to imply the principle of the ultimate perfection of Love or the Holy Spirit, circumscribing the kings and the prophets, the doctors and the mystics, and binding them together in its Unity or, rather, Trinity.

The explicit relationship of the two named circles to the highest of the angelic orders serves to support this conception. If taken in order of appearance, Cherubim and then Seraphim, there is no higher circle possible. The alternative solution is to consider the third circle as representing the third order of the first hierarchy, the Thrones. In the *Convivio*, Dante had delegated to this order the contemplation of the Holy Spirit.[275] It is certain that Beatrice's description of the first 3 orders is very similar to the appearance of the 3 circles:

273. *Par.*, XIV, 76.
274. *Ibid.*, XVIII, 71.
275. *Convivio*, II, 6, 85-89. He changes the order in the *Comedy*, but the function remains the same.

I cerchi primi
t' hanno mostrati Serafi e Cherubi.
Così veloci sequono i suoi vimi,
per somigliarsi al punto quanto ponno;
e posson quanto a veder son sublimi.
Quelli altri amor che dintorno li vonno,
si chiaman Troni del divino aspetto,
per che 'l primo ternaro terminno.[276]

The first two circles here
Have shown thee Seraphim and Cherubim.
So swiftly follow they their bound to be
As like the Point as most they may, and most
May they which are exalted most to see.
Those other loves which round about them fleet,
Thrones of the Providence divine are named,
Because the primal triad they complete.

Notice that the Cherubim and Seraphim are coupled, and that
the Thrones complete the triad, including the other two in
their circling, which is precisely the figure in the Sun. Strictly speaking, the Seraphim should have been seen first and
should have been the inner circle, but at this point Dante is
stressing not angelic functions, but angelic representations
of action and contemplation, in which scheme action must
always come first, to be followed by contemplation, to be
completed, encircled, by their harmonious union.

Dominic and Francis, types of the first 2 circles, were ordained as guides to the 2 felicities:

due principi ordino in suo favore,
que quinci e quindi le fosser per guida.
L' un fu tutto serafico in ardore;
l' altro per sapienza in terra fue
di cherubica luce uno splendore.[277]

ordained in her behalf two Princes
To be, on either side, as guides to her.
One was, in ardor, of the Seraphim;

---

276. *Par.*, XXVIII, 98-105.
277. *Ibid.*, XI, 35-39.

The other by his wisdom upon earth
A splendor of the light of Cherubim.

The principle on which human felicity rests has been in them
set forth. All that is needed is the will to make this principle effective, to bring to full fruition the discrete functions
of action and contemplation, as actualized in State and
Church. For this reason, there is need for a third circle, a
circle of Love which corresponds to Will,[278] a circle of
Thrones who contemplate the Holy Spirit, whose procession
is by way of Will,[279] and in whose charge is the *execution* of
the Divine Will.[280] It is here implied that this third circle
will be the spring to the earthly action which is to come, and
that it is composed of places for figures who are yet on earth.
If so, Dante, whose *Comedy* is in part an exhortation to this
action, is the spokesman of this circle.

In respect to this series of images, the 3 dreams of Dante
in Purgatory take on an added and interrelated significance.
In one sense, the cycle of Dante's own salvation may be
figured. In the first dream he is snatched on high, as originally his spirit (literally, "sighs") had been uplifted by the
vision of Beatrice in the *Vita nuova*.[281] The second dream con-
jures up the picture of the siren who draws men from the
True Path,[282] even as "Philosophy" had misled Dante. Here
the true nature of the Siren is revealed to him, presumably by
the Light of Lucia. In the third dream, the vision of Leah
and Rachel presents Dante's ultimate realization that "human
nature, as it here exists, hath not only one blessedness but two,
to wit that of the civil life and that of the contemplative
life."

It is interesting, also, to observe that the first dream comes

278. See above, p. 191.

279. Cf. Aquinas, *Summa Theologica*, II-II, qu. 17, art. 7-8.

280. *Ibid.*, I, qu. 108, art. 6; "Throni dicuntur secundam Gregorium, per quos
Deus sua judicia exercet."

281. *Vita nuova*, XL, 21 *et seq.*

282. *Purg.*, XIX, 22-23.

to the poet as he sleeps, one of 5 (number of figures forming the eyelid of the Eagle), in the valley of the Kings. In this dream, the Eagle, symbol of Rome and Empire, seizes upon him as it had once seized Ganymede, son of Tros, an ancestor of Aeneas; as Lucia, Enlightenment, Hope, is later to guide him to the 3 steps of the first cycle. Under the tutelage of Wisdom, he learns of the defection of the second cycle, which pursued, in the Siren, false visions of good. It would fit the scheme perfectly if we might see in the stuttering old woman an intimation of the harlot of the defective Church. For the third dream takes place under Cytherea,

che di foco d' amor par sempre ardente.[283]

Who in the fire of love seems ever burning.

This planet Dante had once thought to represent the Love of the Holy Ghost,[284] as he had once believed its guidance to be delegated to the Thrones. Under the planet of love, he envisions the ultimate principle of duality. At the conclusion of the dream, Dante is himself crowned and mitred as, in figure, he reaches the perfection of the Third Age and Earthly Paradise.

Throughout this complex web of symbolism there is woven the intrinsic spiritual or moral motive of Dante, "to remove those living in this life from the state of misery and lead them to the state of felicity." The state of felicity is most uniquely emblemized by the number 8. We have seen it in the eighth step of Purgatory and in the 8 topmost figures of the Rose. The number, unlike 1 or 3, signalizes not a beginning, but a return to original unity, as the eighth beatitude repeats the first and as the eighth day is the first day of the second week.[285] It is this ultimate octave which binds together the multifarious events and images of the *Comedy*. Furthermore, in the carefully articulated time schedule of

283. *Ibid.*, XXVII, 96.
284. *Convivio*, II, 6, 109-26.
285. See above, p. 85.

the poet's journey may be envisioned, whether spiritually or temporally, the preordained course of man.

The 6 days consumed in traversing Hell and Purgatory suggests strongly the journey of humanity through the 6 earthly ages. The seventh is the Final Sabbath of the world, the age of the Final Resurrection, and accordingly the seventh day finds Dante in the Earthly Paradise.[286] At noon of this day he rises to the Eternal Paradise, having ascended from the temporal to the spiritual world.[287] In this same seventh day, he moves upward through all the heavens. No further mention of time is given until he reaches the starry heaven of the Redeemed.

The eighth age is the age of Final Redemption, eternal and timeless. Dante, by his rolling with the heavens, has been unconscious of time, but here he is told to observe the extent of the celestial movement. He discovers that he has moved

per tutto l' arco
che fa dal mezzo al fine il primo clima [288]

From middle unto end of the first Clime

since he formerly looked down. His previous view occurred in the eighth heaven, when he was over Jerusalem, the middle (from East to West) of the first climate.[289] Since he ascended to Paradise over Mount Purgatory, at noon of the seventh day, and no earlier mention of time is given, the meaning of the first downward vision, if it means anything at all in point of time, is that at least 12 hours have elapsed since his ascension (Purgatory to Jerusalem = 180° or 12 hours, if Dante moved with the sun. Actually, the sun is some 40° ahead of him at this point,[290] making the time 12 hours +). Exactly when the transition from the seventh to

286. *Purg.*, XXVII, 94-95.
287. *Par.*, I, 43-45.
288. *Ibid.*, XXVII, 80-81.
289. *Ibid.*, XXII, 151-53; XXVII, 81. See note and *argument* in Grandgent ed.; also Torraca ed. XXVII, 79-87 notes; also Moore, *Studies*, III, 62-71.
290. *Par.*, XXII, 152.

the eighth day occurred is difficult to say, but it is clear that, in his two visions in the eighth heaven of the Redeemed, Dante has reached the eighth or Final Age of Redemption.

In this same twenty-seventh canto which introduces the eighth day is the final expression of the cyclical theory. In the presence of Dante, the "light" of Adam is joined to the 3 "torches" of the theological virtues, as the cross was formerly joined to the tree.[291] Dante has seen the perfection of the first age in the Noble Castle of Limbus, in the person of Cato, and in Eden. He has witnessed the perfection of the second age at the advent of Christ in the flowering tree of the Earthly Paradise, restored after its long barrenness to its pristine splendour.

The third perfection has been predicted by Beatrice, who is now in charge of the chariot, and is imaged in Paradise in the circles, the Eagle, the 3 apostles, and the Rose. Here, however, he sees the actual event symbolically represented. Peter recounts, as Beatrice had formerly done, the history of the second era, with its 300 years of obedience and its succeeding adultery, which Dante is bidden to disclose.[292] It is at this point that Dante is told to look downward, to observe that he has moved "to the end." [293] As he looks backward to "the mad road Ulysses took," [294] Ulysses, who sailed ever to the left,[295] he has indeed come to the end in every sense — the end which is also the beginning, the Primum Mobile.

The cycle is completed, as Primal Love, which created Adam, is returned to its source by the agency of the theological virtues. Similarly, in the Rose Beatrice is returned to the

291. *Ibid.*, XXVII, 10-12.
292. *Ibid.*, XXVII, 43-46, 64-66.
293. *Ibid.*, XXVII, 81.
294. *Ibid.*, XXVII, 82-83.
295. *Inf.*, XXVI, 126. Ulysses, representing the search for wisdom before the Light had come, was never able to reverse his course as Dante had done, countering left with right until the balance was reached and he might go straight ahead. Ulysses whirled about 3 times and sank. Dante met 3 beasts, but was saved by Beatrice.

side of the originating power of Mary. Enlinked with the discourse on the nature of time, Beatrice tells Dante that the white skin of the "daughter" of the sun is blackened.[296] By Peter's previous remarks in the canto, the defective Church seems to be indicated, or possibly Rome, which flourished under the suns of both Church and State. Dante is assured, however, that time will inevitably bring about a restoration when

> verro frutta verrà dopo 'l fiore.[297]

> the true fruit shall follow on the flower.

The "flower" can hardly apply to Dante's own blackened age. Rather, it recalls the flowering tree of the time of Christ, and again proclaims a third generation after the second barrenness. Thus will be completed the perfection of the 3, which is both 1 and all, as in Heaven, so on earth.

296. *Par.*, XXVII, 136.
297. *Ibid.*, XXVII, 148.

NUMBER SYMBOLS OF NORTHERN PAGANISM

LIMITATIONS of time, as well as knowledge, have forced me to ignore certain scattered number symbols which are not clearly connected with the Babylonian-Pythagorean-Christian tradition. These appear to be Teutonic or Celtic in origin, since they are most prominent in the surviving fragments of northern pagan literatures. I am here setting down such random observations as I have made of these pagan number symbols, bequeathing further investigation (if it seem desirable) to those more fully acquainted with the field.

It is not surprising anywhere to find the triad an important number symbol, generally statistical and often connected with religion. The Scandinavian races, among innumerable trios, elevated the 3 norns, 3 colors of the rainbow, 3 roots of Igdrasil,[1] and 3 gods, Odin, Thor, and Frey.[2] Much of Teutonic mythology follows this triadic pattern. The Celtic races also worshiped 3-headed deities.[3] The ancient Goidals reckoned by a tripartite day.[4] The ancient Irish held 3 annual festivals.[5] Among the Welsh, triads were extraordinarily popular, both narrator and audience apparently delighting in the "3 costly pillages," "the 3 ill resolutions," "the 3 frivolous bards," "the 3 inventors," and so on.[6] Even the letters of the Welsh alphabet were composed of 3 elements.[7]

1. Thorpe, *Northern Mythology*, I, 11-12.
2. Olrik, *Viking Civilization*, pp. 44-45; MacCulloch, *Mythology of All Races*, III, 68.
3. MacCulloch, *The Religion of the Ancient Celts*, p. 34.
4. Rhys, *Lectures on the Origin and Growth of Religion*, p. 354.
5. Joyce, *A Social History of Ancient Ireland*, II, 388.
6. Chambers, *Arthur of Britain*, p. 78-80.
7. Rhys, *Lectures*, p. 268.

Similarly, the zodiacal 12 seems to have been firmly established among most of the northern peoples. Eddic mythology
exhibits considerable astrological knowledge. There are the
4 regions and the 4 streams of milk, which flowed from the
sacred cow, the same creation myth speaking of 12 rivers.[8]
Twelve gods and Odin inhabited Gladsheim, and Odin was
known by 12 names.[9] One account numbers the Valkyrie as
12, of which 6 ride northward and 6 to the south,[10] implying
the habitual division of the houses of the zodiac.[11] Thorpe
states that the earliest mention of regular computation by the
solar year of 364 days, or 12 months, is from 950 to 970
A.D.,[12] but the prominence of the number 12 over and above
any comparable usage in Christian narratives strongly indicates something more than a late borrowing. This does not
hold true in Celtic mythology, where the dozen holds no such
striking eminence and may easily have been appropriated
from southern civilization.

Similarly suspect is the number 7 which, though often
used, holds neither the connotations nor the emphasis given
the sacred integer through so many centuries in the Levant.
Comparable veneration is paid, instead, to the numbers 8 and
9, which appear to be used in the same sense of a "fated"
period or grouping as distinguishes the number 7 in southern
tradition.

One explanation of this substitution is found in the sugges-
tion, offered by Rhys,[13] of an ancient 8-day Aryan week.
Nine becomes easily connected with this week through the
northern idiosyncracy of computing time by beginning with
night instead of day, winter instead of summer, and ending
with those same unfavorable periods which northern climates

8. Thorpe, *op. cit.*, I, 3-5.
9. *Ibid.*, p. 15.
10. *Ibid.*, p. 12.
11. See above, p. 22.
12. Thorpe, *op. cit.*, I, 129.
13. *Lectures*, 360-64.

made so conspicuous. This kind of measurement is observable in the Irish word for *fortnight, coicthiges,* which literally means 15 nights.[14] Similarly, the Welsh *wythnos* denotes a 7-day week, though its literal translation is *8 nights.*[15] This would account for the use of 8 and 9 together to connote an 8-day week, as it seems to in the legend that 8 rings dropped from Odin's ring on every ninth night.[16] Perhaps this same week is referred to in the tradition that Odin rode an 8-footed steed.[17]

In the Scandinavian countries, the numbers 8 and 9 held a further significance, unknown in more southerly climates, because of the prolonged winter of 8 or 9 months. Gering and Golther explain that for 9 months the sea in the extreme north is sealed by ice and winter storms.[18] The conflict of heat and cold plays a dominant part in Eddic mythology, and, as in all primitive traditions, the fertility cycle is the basis for many of the most prominent legends. The *Lokasenna* narrates how Loki remained 8 winters under the earth, milking cows in woman's form and even giving birth to children.[19] Gering interprets Loki as the subterranean fire, regarded as female and producing vegetation through warmth. The 8 winters are the 8 winter months, during which frost reigns and the warmth retreats within the earth. The cows, then, are warm springs.[20] This interpretation is substantiated in the

14. Joyce, *op. cit.,* II, 391.

15. MacBain, *Celtic Mythology and Religion,* p. 64. There is evidence of the same sort of reckoning by half years, beginning and ending with winter. The term of 3 half years is used as a period in the Irish life of Saint Molaisus (O'Grady, *Silva Gadelica,* II, 34). In the *Guthrunarkvitha* II, 7 half years denotes a period (st. 14). The implication in both instances is that of a time unit of 3 half-years, which offers itself as a possible explanation of the 540 doors and rooms of Valhalla (*Grimnismol,* st. 23-24) which, granting further a simple 360-day year, would be the exact total of days of one cycle of winter-summer-winter.

16. *Skirnismol,* st. 21.

17. Olrik, *op. cit.,* p. 31.

18. MacCulloch, *Eddic Mythology,* pp. 105-6, n. 20.

19. Stanza 23.

20. MacCulloch, *Mythology of All Races,* II, 145-46.

Thrymskvitha, where Thrym, the frost giant, hides Thor's hammer 8 miles down in the earth. As Gering says, thunderstorms do not occur in the winter. Furthermore, the hammer is not to be returned unless Freya, goddess of Spring, is won for his wife.[21]

A variation of this northern Proserpine legend tells of the dissension in the marriage of Niörd, patron of the sea, and Skaldi, goddess of the snow-skates. Skaldi wanted to live in the mountains, in her father's abode, Thrymheim. Niörd preferred the sea. It was finally agreed that they should stay alternately 9 days in Thrymheim and 3 in Noatun. When Niörd came from the mountains to Noatun, he sang,

> I love not the mountains, I dwelt not long in them,
> Nine nights only;
> Sweeter to me is the song of the swan than the
> wild wolf's howl.[22]

To this Skaldi replied,

> My sleep was troubled on the shore of the sea
> By the screaming of sea-birds
> Every morning the sea-mew awakes me
> Returning from the deep.

The goddess of the snow-skates was as much out of her element during the 3 summer months as the patron of the sea was during the winter.

Nine came to be preferred to 8 as a symbol for the winter period, possibly because the sea remained locked for 9 months, but more probably because of the coincidence of this approximation of winter with the observed period of human gestation.[23] By this reckoning, both human and vegetable life remain hidden in the womb for the same period of time. Such a partition of the year is also preferable by virtue of its use of the important base 3. That this consideration might

21. Stanza 7; MacCulloch, *ibid.*, pp. 88-89.
22. *Ibid.*, p. 104.
23. *Rigsthula*, st. 20, 33.

have been of importance is borne out by the number of the Valkyries, which is sometimes given as 3, sometimes as 9, and sometimes as thrice 9.[24]

Even Odin must suffer the torture of these 9 months, as he confesses in the famous lines of the Havamal:

> I know that I hung
> On the wind-stirred tree
> Nine nights long,
> Wounded by spear,
> Consecrated to Odin,
> Myself to myself;
> On the mighty tree
> Of which no man knows
> Out of what root it springs.

At the roots of the world-tree are the 9 worlds of Niflhel — "dark hell" — "where the dead men dwell."[25] Adam of Bremen speaks of a 9-year festival at Upsala, thought to have been a fertility feast.[26] Olrik opines that it occurred every ninth year, about the time of the equinox, and lasted 9 days.[27] In the *Skirnismol* another fertility legend tells how Frey, brother of Freya and possessing similar attributes, was forced to wait 9 nights before his marriage with Gerda.[28] Heimdall, foe of Loki, watchman of the Norse gods, was born of 9 giantesses at the edge of the world where sea and land meet.[29] Presumably the same cycle is invoked in the 9 paces which Thor makes as he marches against the serpent sea, only to be defeated ("slain") at the approach of winter again.[30]

The number 9 thus became the northern counterpart of the southern magic 7, being particularly connected with fertility, religion, and magic. The Celtic need-fire was

24. MacCulloch, *Mythology of All Races*, II, 249.
25. *Voluspa*, st. 2; *Vafthrunthnismol*, st. 43.
26. MacCulloch, *Mythology of All Races*, II, 115.
27. *Viking Civilization*, pp. 44-45.
28. Stanza 40.
29. MacCulloch, *Mythology of All Races*, II, 153-54.
30. *Voluspa*, st. 55-56.

kindled by 81 men, 9 at a time being employed.[31] The number was also connected with the Beltane rites.[32] The Fortunate Isles were ruled over by 9 sisters, the first of whom was Morgen.[33] Nine witches of Gloucester are mentioned in *Peredur*,[34] 9 dragons in the *Vita Merlini*.[35] Nine *nicors* were slain by Beowulf.[36] Merlin had 9 bards.[37] One of the best known of the stone circles was the 9 maidens,[38] perhaps related to the wonderful Cauldron of the Head of Hades, kept boiling by the breath of 9 maidens.[39]

The use of 9 and thrice 9 is common in the *Mabinogion* as apparently little more than round numbers. In the Cuchullin Saga, the number is also prominent, with a hint of the fertility motif. Conchobar sent out 9 men to seek a wife for Cuchullin,[40] and his house had 9 compartments (like the 9 rooms of the world tree), each partition of which measured 30 feet.[41] Conchobar's connection with the calendar is substantiated by the account that it was he who divided the day into 3 parts.[42] The Irish are known to have used the word *nomaid*, or *nomad*, to denote a length of time, meaning 9 intervals of some kind, from *noi, nine*.[43] Tylor[44] knows no system of counting by 9's, and Webster[45] states that evidence for the existence of weeks of 9 days is very obscure. It is hard to avoid the inference that this is the same 9-month, 9-night period, common to the Scandinavians.

31. MacBain, *Celtic Mythology*, p. 159.
32. *Ibid.*, p. 165.
33. *Vita Merlini*, ll. 916-26.
34. MacCulloch, *Mythology of All Races*, III, 191.
35. Lines 629-30.
36. Line 575.
37. MacCulloch, *Mythology of All Races*, III, 201.
38. Lockyer, *Stonehenge*, p. 293.
39. Rhys, *Lectures*, p. 256.
40. Hull, *The Cuchullin Saga*, p. 60.
41. This is, incidentally, the only hint of a 30-day month to substantiate my hypothesis of a 360-day year of the northern peoples (see above, n. 15).
42. Rhys, *Lectures*, p. 141.
43. Joyce, *Social History of Ancient Ireland*, pp. 391-92.
44. *Primitive Culture.*
45. *Rest Days*, pp. 192-93.

The Arthurian chronicles of Layamon and Geoffrey of Monmouth all but ignore the number; but in the Welsh redactions it is very much in evidence. In the *Book of Taliessin*, Uther Pendragon claims "a ninth part in the prowess of Arthur." [46] Both 3 and 9 are common in the *Preiddeu Annwfn* and the *Black Book of Carmarthen*. In *Kulhwch and Olwen*, we are told that Kei could exist 9 nights and 9 days without sleep, and that Bedwyr had a spear which made 9 wounds when it was withdrawn. [47] Chambers connects both of these with the 9-night week of the Celts. It was possibly the same 9 which established the tradition of the 9 worthies and the phrase, "a nine-days' wonder."

The obscurity which envelops the origin and meaning of the pagan 9 is as broad daylight when compared to the mystery of the Irish predilection for the number 50. For in Irish folklore, along with 7's, dozens, and other conventional round numbers, appears the common usage of 50 or "thrice 50" as indicating not only a large group but apparently a fixed upper limit with decidedly traditional connotations. Cuchullin was loved by thrice 50 queens, [48] and in the *Voyage of Bran* was met by thrice 50 women. [49] Fifty maidens presided over his birth, [50] and on his head were 50 yellow tresses. [51] Caen, the bird maiden, wore a golden necklace from which hung thrice 50 chains. [52] Thrice 50 women welcome Loeg in Mag Mell. [53] Naisi and 2 brothers went to Scotland, with thrice 50 warriors, [54] and so on.

With the presence of other round numbers common to the decimal tradition, the emphasis on 50 is a little strange, espe-

46. Chambers, *Arthur of Britain*, p. 61.
47. *Ibid.*, pp. 61-62, 64, 73-74.
48. MacCulloch, *Mythology of All Races*, III, 209.
49. *Ibid.*, p. 143.
50. Rhys, *Lectures*, pp. 433-34.
51. Hull, *The Cuchullin Saga*, p. 154.
52. MacCulloch, *Mythology of All Races*, III, 79.
53. *Ibid.*, p. 87.
54. *Ibid.*, p. 24.

cially when used so obviously as a limit. Fifty fills of corn, milk, butter, and flour were exacted of the Nemedians by the Fomorians.[55] When a greater tribute is demanded, it reaches a limit not of 100 or 1,000, as might be expected, but thrice 50 hundred cows, thrice 50 hundred wethers, thrice 50 hundred swine.[56]

Fifty is a number which does not even approximately equate any known time period or natural phenomenon. As part of the decimal system, it is a useful round number, but by no means popular among the Christian romancers. In the Church it is the number of Pentecost, but no such implications are discernible in Irish usage. There is, in fact, but one body of tradition which exalts the number 50. The Babylonian Sun-god, Marduk, was known by 50 names:[57] "The gods name the fifty names of Nanib [= Marduk], and the name of 50 becomes sacred to him, so that even in the time of Gudea a temple was actually dedicated to the number 50."[58] The tradition of the solar hero in Celtic mythology has been widely recognized. If Nutt can find his prototype in Achilles,[59] and Rhys in Heracles,[60] it might not be entirely impossible to see an even earlier ancestor in Marduk, who also performed his cycle of "labours." For beside the tradition of Cuchullin, with his 50 tresses, we can place the fragment of a Chaldean tablet, which reads, "The sun with 50 faces, the raised weapons of divinity."[61]

But whatever the original significance of the number 50

55. *Ibid.*, p. 27.

56. O'Grady, "The Boromean Tribute," *Silva Gadelica*, II, 403.

57. The Babylonian gods were ranked according to a composite decimal and sexagesimal system. Anu, greatest of the gods, was honored by the base number 60. (Jastrow, *The Religion of Babylonia*, p. 465; Farbridge, *Studies*, p. 142). Marduk, who became second in importance, is designated by 50 names at the close of the *Epic of Creation* (VI, 98-100; VII, 124-25).

58. Farbridge, *Studies*, p. 177.

59. Nutt. *Cuchulainn, the Irish Achilles.*

60. Rhys, *Studies in the Arthurian Legend.*

61. Lenormant, *Chaldean Magic*, p. 162.

may have been, it carries nothing more than the faint impress of the traditional fiat when it occurs in Celtic narratives. Once, in the favorite form of thrice 50, it is connected with the 150 psalms which had been similarly divided. In the *Boromean Tribute*, Adamnan sends a cleric to summon Finnachta, who refuses to move until he has finished a game of chess in which he was engaged. The ecclesiastic returns to Adamnan with the answer. The saint responds, "Go and tell him that in the interval I will chant him 50 psalms, in which 50 is a single psalm that will deprive his children and grandchildren and even any namesake of his of the kingdom." Finnachta has started another game by the time the answer is returned. Adamnan chants another 50 psalms, one of which will confer shortness of life. Similarly, a third 50 are repeated, one of which will prevent Finnachta from attaining the Lord's Peace.[62]

The number eventually became associated with the knights of the Round Table. The *Roman de Merlin* gives 50 knights, the Huth *Merlin* 150, the *Roman de Brut*, 250.[63] Malory finally specifies the number of 150,[64] possibly influenced in his decision by the 150 psalms, and employs the number as a symbol in the parable of the 150 bulls which appear in Gawaine's dream.[65]

62. O'Grady, *Silva Gadelica*, II, 422.
63. Lewis F. Mott, "The Round Table," PMLA XX, 231-64.
64. *Morte d'Arthur*, VII, 1.
65. *Ibid.*, XVI, 1; interpretation, section 3.

BIBLIOGRAPHY

Abraham, the Apocalypse of, ed. by G. H. Box. London, 1918.

Absalon, Abbas Sprinckirsbacensis. Sermones. Migne, P. L., tom. 211.

Adam, James. The Nuptial Number of Plato; Its Meaning and Significance. London, 1891. (Emended in his ed. of the Republic of Plato, II, 264-312. Cambridge, 1902.)

Adamus, Abbas Perseniae. Adami abbatis Perseniae epistolae. Migne, P. L., tom. 211.

Agrippa von Nettesheim, Henricus Cornelius. Three Books of Occult Philosophy, trans. by "J. F." London, 1651.

———— Three Books of Occult philosophy, ed. by Willis F. Whitehead. (Revised version of the English trans. by "J. F.") New York, 1897.

See also Morley, Henry.

Alanus de Insulis, Bishop of Auxerre. Opera omnia. Migne, P. L., tom. 210.

Albertus Magnus, Bishop of Ratisbon. Opera omnia. ed. by Augustus Borgnet. 38 vols., Paris, 1890-99.

Alcuin. Opera omnia. Migne, P. L., tom. 100-1.

Aldhelm, Saint, Bishop of Sherborne. Opera omnia. Migne, P. L., tom. 89.

Ambrose, Saint, Bishop of Milan. Opera. Migne, P. L., tom. 14-17.

Ante-Nicene Christian Library. Translations of the writings of the fathers down to 325 A.D., ed. by Alexander Roberts and James Donaldson. 23 vols., Edinburgh, 1867-72.

Apocrypha and Pseudepigrapha, the, of the Old Testament, ed. by R. H. Charles. 2 vols., Oxford, 1913.

Apocryphal Gospels, Acts and Revelations, trans. by Alexander Walker. Edinburgh, 1873. (AN Vol. XVI.)

Apocryphal New Testament, the, trans. by Montague Rhodes James. Oxford, 1925.

Archelaus. The Acts of the Disputation of Archelaus with the Heresiarch Manes, trans. by S. D. F. Salmond. Edinburgh, 1871. (AN Vol. XX.)

Ariosto, Lodovico. Orlando furioso, ed. by Adriano Salani. 2 vols., Firenze, 1928.

———— Trans. by William Stewart Rose. 2 vols., London, 1895.

Aristotle. De caelo, trans. by J. L. Stocks. Oxford, 1922. (In his works, ed. by W. D. Ross. Vol. II.)

———— Metaphysics, trans. by W. D. Ross. Oxford, 1908. (In his Works, ed. by W. D. Ross, Vol. VIII.)

———— Physics, trans. by R. P. Hardie and R. K. Stocks. Oxford, 1922. (In his works, ed. by W. D. Ross, Vol. II.)

Arthurian Chronicles represented by Wace and Layamon. London, and New York, 1912. ("Everyman.").

Audsley, William James and George Ashdown Audsley. Handbook of Christian Symbolism. London, [1865].

Augustine, Saint, Bishop of Hippo. The Works of Aurelius Augustine, trans. by Marcus Dods. 15 vols., Edinburgh, 1871-76.

Austin, H. D. "Number and Geometrical Design in the Divine Comedy." *The Personalist*, XVI (1925), 310-30.

[Bacon, Roger.] The Opus Majus of Roger Bacon, trans. by Robert Belle Burke. 2 vols., Philadelphia, 1928.

Baruch, the Apocalypse of, ed. by R. H. Charles. London, 1896.

Basil, Saint, Archbishop of Caesarea in Cappodocia, Called the Great. The Treatise De spiritu sancto, the Nine Homilies of the Hexameron and the Letters of Saint Basil, trans. by Blomfield Jackson. Oxford and New York, 1895. (NPN, ser. 2, Vol. VIII.).

Bayley, Harold. The Lost Language of Symbolism; An Inquiry into the Origin of Certain Letters, Words, Names, Fairy-Tales, Folk-Lore and Mythologies. 2 vols., London, 1912.

Bede, the Venerable, Saint. Venerabilis Bedae opera omnia. Migne, P. L., tom. 90-95.

Bell, Eric Temple. Numerology. Baltimore, 1933.

Bension, Ariel. The Zohar. London, 1932.

Beowulf and the Fight at Finnsburg, ed. by Franz Klaeber. New York, 1922.

Bernard, Saint, Abbot of Clairvaux. Life and Works, ed. by John Mabillon; trans. and ed. by Samuel J. Eales. 4 vols., London, 1889.

Bible. The Holy, King James' version.

Blake, John Frederick. Astronomical Myths, Based on Flammarion's History of the Heavens. [London], 1877.

Boethius, Amicius Maulius Torquatus Severinus. Opera omnia. Migne, P. L., tom. 63-64.

Böklen, Ernst. Die unglückszahl Dreizehn und ihre mythische Bedeutung. Leipzig, 1913.

Bolton, Henry Carrington. The Literature of Alchemy. Reprinted from *The Pharmaceutical Review*, Vol. XIX, nos. 4, 5.

Bonaventura, Saint, Cardinal, Bishop of Albano, (Giovanni Fidenza). Opera omnia, edidit studio et cura P. P. collegii a S. Bonaventura. 10 vols., 1882-1902.

Bongus, Petrus. Mysticae numerorum significationis liber. 2 vols. in 1, Bergomi, 1585.

Book of the Dead, The, ed. and trans. by E. A. Wallis Budge. 3 vols., London, 1898.

Brèhaut, Ernest. An Encyclopaedist of the Dark Ages: Isidore of Seville. New York, 1912. ("Studies in History, Economics and Public Law," ed. by the Faculty of Political Science of Columbia University. Vol. XLVIII, no. 1, whole no. 120.)

Brown, C. A. "The Poem of the Philosopher Theophrastus upon the Sacred Art: A Metrical Translation with Comments upon the History of Alchemy." *Scientific Monthly*, XI (1920), 193-214.

Brown, J. Wood. The Life and Legend of Michael Scot. Edinburgh, 1897.

Browne, Sir Thomas. The Works of Sir Thomas Browne, ed. by Geoffrey Keynes. 6 vols., London, 1928.

Buckland, A. W. "Four as a Sacred Number." *Journal of the Anthropological Institute of Great Britain and Ireland*, XXV (1896), 96-102.

Budge, E. A. Wallis. Egyptian Magic. London, 1899.

———— The Babylonian Story of the Deluge and the Epic of Gilgamish. [London], 1920. (British Museum, Department of Egyptian and Assyrian Antiquities.)

———— The Literature of the Ancient Egyptians. London, 1914.

———— Osiris and the Egyptian Resurrection. 2 vols., New York, 1911.

Bungus, *see* Bongus.

Burkitt, F. C. Church and Gnosis. Cambridge, 1932. (Morse Lectures for 1931.)

———— The Religion of the Manichees. Cambridge, 1925.

Busnelli, Giovanni. Il concetto e l'ordine del "Paradiso" dantesco; indagini e studii preceduti da una lettera di Francesco Flamini. 2 vols., Citta de Castello, S. Lapi, 1911-12.

Cabala, *see* Bension, Ariel; Franck, Adolf; Ginsburg, Christine D; Mathers, S. L. Macgregor.

Cajori, Florian. History of Mathematics. 2d ed., New York, 1924.

Candler, Howard. On the Symbolic Use of Number in the Divine Comedy and Elsewhere. Royal Society of Literature, ser. 2, XXX (1910), 1-29.

Capella, Martianus Mineus Felix. De nuptiis philologiae et mercurii, ed. by Adolfus Dick. Leipzig, 1925.

Carnoy, Albert J. Iranian [Mythology]. Boston, 1917. (Mythology of All Races, Vol. VI.)

Carroll, Lewis "The Hunting of the Snark," pp. 391-426 in *The Lewis Carroll Book*, ed. by Richard Herrick. New York, 1931.

Cary, M. and E. H. Warmington. The Ancient Explorers. New York, 1929.

Cassiodorus, Magnus Aurelius. Opera omnia, Migne, P. L., tom. 69-70.

Celsus, Aulus Cornelius. Of Medicine, in Eight Books, trans. by James Greive. Edinburgh, 1814.

Chambers, Edmund Kerchever. Arthur of Britain. London, 1927.

Charlemagne, an Anglo-Norman Poem of the 12th Century, Containing Perlerinage de Charlemagne à Constantinople, ed. Francisque Michel. London, 1836.

Chaucer, Geoffrey. Complete works, ed. Walter W. Skeat. Oxford, 1894.

Chronicle of the Cid, trans. by Robert Southey, with an Introduction by Henry Morley. 3d. ed., London, 1885. ("Morley's Universal Classics.")

Cicero, Marcus Tullius. De divinatione, ed. by Arthur Stanley Pease. 2 vols. University of Illinois, 1920-23.

———— De natura deorum, trans. by H. Rackham. London and New York, 1933. ("Loeb Classical Library.")

———— De officiis, trans. by Walter Miller. London and New York, 1913. ("Loeb Classical Library.")

———— Republic, trans. by G. G. Hardingham. London, 1884.

Clay, Albert T. A Hebrew Deluge Story in Cuneiform and Other Epic Fragments in the Pierpont Morgan Library. New Haven, 1922. ("Yale Oriental Series." Researches, Vol. V, Part 3.)

———— The Origin of Biblical Traditions. New Haven, 1923. ("Yale Oriental Series," Vol. XII.)

Clement, Titus Flavius, Alexandrinus. The Writings of Clement of Alexandria, trans. by William Wilson. 2 vols., Edinburgh, 1867-69. (AN Vols. IV, XII.)

Clement, Pseudo-. Recognitions, trans. by B. P. Pratten, Marcus Dods, and Thomas Smith. Edinburgh, 1867. (AN Vol. III.)

Conant, Levi Leonard. The Number Concept; Its Origin and Development. New York and London, 1896.

Conway, Moncure Daniel. Demonology and Devil-Lore. New York, 1887.

Conybeare, Frederick Cornwallis. Myth, Magic and Morals. Boston, 1909.

Cumont, Franz. Astrology and Religion among the Greeks and Romans. New York, 1912. ("American Lectures on the History of Religions," ser. 1911-12.)

———— The Mysteries of Mithra, trans. by T. J. McCormack. Chicago, 1903.

———— The Oriental Religions in Roman Paganism. Chicago, 1911.

Cyprian, Saint, Bishop of Carthage, The Writings of Cyprian, trans. by Robert Ernest Wallis. 2 vols. Edinburgh, 1868-69. (AN Vols. VIII, XIII.)

Dante Alighieri. Tutte le opere, ed. by Edward Moore. 4th ed., Oxford, 1924.

———— Le opere di Dante. Testo critico della Societa Dantesca Italiana. Firenze, 1921.

———— The Convivio, trans. by P. H. Wicksteed. London, 1924. ("Temple Classics.")

———— La Divina Commedia, ed. and annotated by C. H. Grandgent. New York [1913].

———— The Divine Comedy of Dante Alighieri, trans. by Jefferson Butler Fletcher. New York, 1931.

———— The Early Lives of Dante, trans. by Philip Henry Wicksteed. London and Boston, 1907.

———— The Inferno, Purgatorio and Paradiso, text with trans. by Carlyle, Okey, and Wicksteed. 3 vols., London, 1900. ("Temple Classics.")

———— De Monarchia. London, 1924. (The Latin Works of Dante, "Temple Classics.")

———— The Vita Nuova and Canzoniere, trans. by Thomas Okey and P. H. Wicksteed. London, 1924. ("Temple Classics.")

Dantzig, Tobias. Number, the Language of Science. New York, 1930.

Definitions of Asclepius, the, trans. by G. R. S. Mead, in Thrice Greatest Hermes. London, 1906.

Dickson, Leonard Eugene. History of the Theory of Numbers. 2 vols., Washington, 1919-20.

Dill, Samuel. Roman Society in the Last Century of the Western Empire. 3d. ed., London, 1925.

Dinsmore, Charles Allen. Life of Dante Alighieri. Boston and New York, 1919.

Diogenes Laertius. Lives of Eminent Philosophers, trans. by R. D. Hicks. 3 vols., London and New York, 1925. ("Loeb Classical Library.")

Dionysius, Saint, called the Areopagite. Opera omnia. Migne, P. G., tom. 3-4.

———— Joannis Scoti versii operum S. Dionysii Areopagitae. Migne, P. L., tom. 122.

———— Oeuvres de St. Denys l'Areopagite, trans. by J. Dulac. Paris, 1865.

———— The Works of Dionysius the Areopagite, trans. by John Parker. 2 vols., London, 1897.

Dryer, J. L. E. History of the Planetary Systems from Thales to Kepler. Cambridge, 1906.

Duhem, Pierre. Le Système du monde, Histoire des doctrines cosmologiques de Platon à Copernic. 4 vols., Paris, 1913-17.

Dunbar, H. Flanders. Symbolism in Medieval Thought and Its Consummation in the Divine Comedy. New Haven, 1929.

Dunbar, William. Poems, ed. by J. Small. 3 vols., Edinburgh, 1893. ("Scottish Texts Society," Vol. X.)

Durandus, Gulielmus, Bishop of Mende. Durandus on the Sacred Vestments; an English Rendering of the Third Book of the Rationale divinorum officiorum of Durandus, Bishop of Mende, trans. by T. H. Passmore. London, 1899.

———— The Symbolism of Churches and Church Ornaments: A Translation of the First Book of the Rationale divinorum officiorum, trans. by John M. Neale and Benjamin Webb. Leeds, 1843.

Edda, the Poetic, trans. by Henry Adams Bellows. New York, 1923.

Ellworthy, Frederick Thomas. Horns of Honor and Other Studies in the By-Ways of Archeology. London, 1900.

Enoch, the Book of, ed. by R. H. Charles. Oxford, 1893.

Epic of Creation, the Babylonian, ed. by Stephen Herbert Langdon. Oxford, 1923.

Epic of Gilgamesh, see Budge, E. A. Wallis; Clay, Albert T.; Leonard, William Ellery.

Erigena, see Joannes Scotus, Erigena.

Erman, Adolf. The Literature of the Ancient Egyptians, trans. by A. M. Blackman. New York (1927).

Evans, Joan. Magical Jewels of the Middle Ages and the Renaissance Particularly in England. Oxford, 1922.

Evelyn, John. Diary, ed. by Austin Dobson. 3 vols., London, 1906.

Farbridge, Maurice H. Studies in Biblical and Semitic Symbolism. New York, 1923. ("Trubner's Oriental Series.")

Firmicus Maternus, Julius. Julii Firmici Materni matheseos, libri viii, ed. by W. Kroll and F. Skutsch. Leipzig, 1897.

Flamini, Francesco. Introduction to the Study of the Divine Comedy, trans. by Freeman M. Josselyn. Boston, 1910.

Fletcher, Banister. A History of Architecture. 9th ed., New York, 1931.

Fletcher, Jefferson Butler "Allegory of the Vita Nuova." MP XI (July, 1913), 19-37.

———— "The Crux of Dante's Comedy." *Romanic Review*, XVI (Jan.-Mar., 1925), 310-30.

———— "Dante's School of the Eagle." *Romanic Review*, XXII (July-Sept., 1931), 191-209.

———— "Left and Right Turns in the Divine Comedy." *Romanic Review*, XXIII (July-Sept., 1932), 236-37.

———— Literature of the Italian Renaissance. New York, 1934.

———— The Religion of Beauty in Women, and Other Essays on Platonic Love in Poetry and Society. New York, 1911.

———— Symbolism of the Divine Comedy. New York, 1921.

Forbes, George. History of Astronomy. New York and London, 1909.

Fournier, P. Études sur Joachim de Flore et ses doctrines. Paris, 1909.

Franck, Adolf. The Kabbalah, trans. by I. Sossnitz. New York, 1926.

Frazer, James. Folk-Lore in the Old Testament. Abridged ed., New York, 1923.

———— The Golden Bough. Abridged ed., New York, 1926.

———— The Worship of Nature. 2 vols., New York, 1926.

Fulbert, Saint, Bishop of Chartres. Opera quae reperiri potuerunt omnia. Migne, P. L., tom. 141.

Gardner, Edmund G. Dante. New York, 1923.

———— Dante and The Mystics; a Study of the Mystical Aspect of the Divina Commedia and Its Relations with Some of Its Mediaeval Sources. London and New York, 1913.

———— Dante's Ten Heavens, a Study of the Paradiso. Westminster, 1900.

Gaster, Moses. Studies and Texts in Folk-Lore, Magic, Medieval Romance, Hebrew Apocrypha and Samaritan Archaeology. 3 vols., London, 1925-28.

Gebhardt, Émile. Mystics and Heretics in Italy, trans. by Edward M. Hulme. New York, 1923.

Geoffrey of Monmouth. Historie of the Kings of Britain, trans. by Sebastian Evans. London, 1904. ("Temple Classics.")

Gerbert of Aurillac, see Sylvester II, Pope.

Ginsburg, Christine D. The Kabbalah. London, 1925.

Ginzberg, Louis. The Legends of the Jews. Philadelphia, 1909.

Gollancz, Hermann. The Book of Protection. London, 1912.

Gould, Sabine Baring —. Curious Myths of the Middle Ages. 2d ed., London, 1868.

Grandgent, Charles H. The Ladies of Dante's Lyrics. Cambridge, Mass., 1917.

Gregory I, Saint, surnamed the Great, Pope. S. Gregorii Papae i opera omnia. Migne, P. L., tom. 75-79.

———— Morals on the Book of Job, trans. by John Henry Parker. London, 1844. ("A Library of the Fathers of the Holy Catholic Church.")

Grillot de Givry, Émile Angelo. Witchcraft, Magic and Alchemy, trans. by J. Courtenay Locke. London, 1931.

Guazzo, Francesco Maria. Compendium malificarum, trans. by E. A. Ashwin, ed. by Montague Summers. London, 1929.

Guido Aretinus. Opuscula de musica. Migne, P. L., tom. 141.

Guntherus Cisterciensis. Opera omnia. Migne, P. L., tom. 212.

Gurteen, Stephen Humphrey Villiers. The Arthurian Epic, A Comparative Study of the Cambrian, Breton and Anglo-Norman Versions of the Story and Tennyson's Idylls of the King. New York and London, 1895.

Guthlac, Saint. The Anglo-Saxon Version of the Life of the Saint Guthlac, ed. by Charles Wycliffe Goodwin. London, 1848.

Guthrie, Kenneth Sylvan. Pythagorean Source Book and Library. Platonist Press, Alpine, New York, 1919.

Handcock, Percy. Babylonian Flood Stories. London and New York, 1921.

Hargrave, Catherine Perry. A History of Playing Cards. Boston and New York, 1930.

Harnack, Adolph. History of Dogma, trans. by Neil Buchanan. 7 vols., Boston, 1907.

Hastings, James, and John A. Selbie. Dictionary of the Bible. New York, 1900.

Heath, Sidney H. The Romance of Symbolism and Its Relation to Church Ornaments and Architecture. London, 1909.

Heath, Thomas L. Aristarchus of Samos, the Ancient Copernicus; a History of Greek Astronomy to Aristotle. Oxford, 1913.

———— Greek Astronomy. London, 1932.

———— A Manual of Greek Mathematics. Oxford, 1931.

Helinand. Opera omnia. Migne, P. L., tom. 212.

Herodotus. The Persian Wars, trans. by George Rawlinson. 2 vols. ("Everyman.")

Hesiod. Poems and Fragments, trans. by A. W. Mair. Oxford, 1908.

Hildegarde, Saint. S. Hildegarde abbatissae opera omnia. Migne, P. L., tom. 197.

Hippolytus, Saint, Bishop of the Port of Rome. The Writings of Hippolytus, trans. by J. H. Macmahon and S. D. F. Salmond. Edinburgh, 1868-69. (AN Vol. VI.)

Hoccleve, Thomas. The Regement of Princes, ed. by Frederick J. Furnivall. London, 1897. ("Early English Texts Society," Vol. LXXII.)

Holinshed, Raphaell. Chronicles of England, Scotland and Ireland. 6 vols., London, 1807.

Homer. Iliad, ed. by Walter Leaf. London, 1886.

———— Iliad, trans. by Lang, Leaf, and Myers. London, 1922.

———— Odyssey, ed. by Victor Berard. Paris, 1924.

———— Odyssey, trans. by Butcher and Lang. New York, 1921.

Honorius, Augustodunensis, called Solarius, of Autun. Opera omnia. Migne, P. L., tom. 172.

Hopkins, Edward Washburn. The Holy Numbers of the Rig-Veda. "Oriental Studies." Oriental Club of Philadelphia, 1888-94, pp. 141-59. Boston, 1894.

Hopper, Grace Murray. "The Ungenerated Seven as an Index to Pythagorean Number Theory." American Mathematical Monthly, XLIII (Aug.-Sept., 1936), 409-13.

Hopper, Vincent Foster. "Geryon and the Knotted Cord." MLN LI (Nov., 1936), 445-49.

Hrabanus, Magnentius, surnamed Maurus, Archbishop of Mentz. Opera omnia. Migne, P. L., tom. 107-12.

Hugo de Sancto Victore. Hugonis de S. Victore opera omnia. Migne, P. L., tom. 175-77.

Hull, Eleanor. The Cuchullin Saga in Irish Literature. London, 1898.

Hulme, F. Edward. The History, Principles and Practice of Heraldry. London, 1892.

———— The History, Principles, and Practice of Symbolism in Christian Art. London, 1899.

Iamblichus of Chalchis. Biography of Pythagoras, see Guthrie, K.S.

———— Iamblichus on the Mysteries of the Egyptians, Chaldeans and Assyrians, trans. by Thomas Taylor. Chicago, 1821.

———— Theologoumena Arithmeticae, ed. by Victorinus de Falco. Leipzig, 1922.

Innocent III, Pope (Gregorio Papi). Opera omnia. Migne, P. L., tom. 214-17.

Irenaeus, Saint, Bishop of Lyons. Against Heresies, trans. by Alexander Roberts and W. H. Rambaut. 2 vols., Edinburgh, 1868-69. (AN Vols. V, IX.)

Ascension of Isaiah, the, ed. by R. H. Charles. (London), 1917.

Isidore, Saint, Bishop of Seville. Opera omnia. Migne, P. L., tom. 81-84.

———— See also Brèhaut, Ernest.

Jackson, A. V. Williams. Researches in Manichaeism. New York, 1932.

———— Zoroaster: the Prophet of Ancient Iran. New York, 1899.

Jacobus de Voragine. The Golden Legend or Lives of the Saints, as Englished by William Caxton. 7 vols., London, 1900. ("Temple Classics.")

Jastrow, Morris. The Religion of Babylonia and Assyria. Boston, 1898. ("Handbooks on the History of Religion.")

Joachim of Flora, Abbot of Fiore. Gioachino da Fiore tractatus super quatuor Evangelia, ed. by Ernesto B. Buonaiti in Fonti per la storia d'Italia, Vol. LXVII. Rome, 1930.

———— See also Fournier, P; Rousselot, X.

Joannes Scotus, Erigena. Joannis Scoti opera. Migne, P. L., tom. 122.

John, Ivor B. The Mabinogion. London, 1901. ("Popular Studies in Mythology, Romance and Folk-Lore," No. 11.)

Josephus, Flavius. The Works of Flavius Josephus, trans. by William Whisten, revised by A. R. Shilleto. London, 1889-90.

Jourdain, Eleanor Frances. Le Symbolisme dans la divine comedie de Dante. Oxford and Paris, 1904.

Joyce, P. W., and Patrick Weston. A Social History of Ancient Ireland. 2d ed., 2 vols., London and Dublin, 1913.

Jubilees, the Book of, or the Little Genesis, ed. by R. H. Charles. London, 1902.

Justin Martyr, Saint. Hortatory Address to the Greeks, trans. by Marcus Dods, George Reith, and B. P. Patten. Edinburgh, 1867. (AN Vol. II.)

Kalendar and Compost of Shepherds, the, ed. by G. C. Heseltine. London, 1931.

Karpinski, Louis C. "Number." *American Mathematical Monthly*, XVIII (1911), 97-102.

Keith, A. Berriedale. Indian [Mythology]. Boston, 1917. (Mythology of All Races, Vol. VI.)

King, Charles William. Antique Gems; Their Origin, Uses and Value as Interpreters of Ancient History and as Illustrative of Ancient Art. London, 1860.

———— The Gnostics and Their Remains, Ancient and Medieval. 2d ed., New York, 1887.

Knight, Richard Payne. The Symbolical Language of Ancient Art and Mythology, ed. by Alexander Wilder. New York, 1876.

Kraeling, Carl H. Anthropos and Son of Man: a Study in the Religious Syncretism of the Hellenistic Orient. New York, 1927. ("Columbia University Oriental Studies," Vol. XXV.)

Kramer, Henry, and James Sprenger. Malleus maleficarum, ed. by Montague Summers. London, 1928.

Kunz, George Frederick. The Curious Lore of Precious Stones. Philadelphia and London, 1913.

Lactantius, Lucius Coelius Firmianus. The Works of Lactantius, trans. by William Fletcher. 2 vols., Edinburgh, 1871. (AN Vols. XXI, XXII.)

Lang, Andrew. Myth, Ritual and Religion. 2 vols., New York, 1901.

Langdon, Stephen Herbert, Semitic [Mythology]. Boston, 1918. (Mythology of All Races, Vol. V.)

Langland, William. Piers the Ploughman, ed. by W. A. Neilson. Cambridge, Mass., 1917.

———— Ed. by W. W. Skeat. 10th ed., rev., Oxford, 1924.

———— Ed. by Thomas Wright. London, 1856.

Launcelot del lac, le Livre de, a French Prose Romance of the 13th Century, trans. by Lucy Allen Paton. New York, 1929.

Lea, Henry Charles. A History of the Inquisition of the Middle Ages. 3 vols., New York, 1887.

Lease, Emory B. "The Number Three: Mysterious, Mystic, Magic." *Classical Philology*, XIV (1919), 56-73.

Legenda aurea, *see* Jacobus de Voragine.

Lenormant, François. Chaldean Magic, Its Origin and Development, trans. by W. R. Cooper. London [1878].

Leonard, William Ellery. Gilgamesh, Epic of Old Babylonia, A Rendering in Free Verse. New York, 1934.

Lewis, George Cornewall. A Historical Survey of the Astronomy of the Ancients. London, 1862.

Levy-Bruhl, L. Les Fonctions mentales dans les sociétés infèrieures. Paris, 1910.

Lilly, William. An Introduction to Astrology, Rewritten by Zadkiel. London, 1913.

Lockyer, Norman. Stonehenge and Other British Stone Monuments Astronomically Considered. London, 1906.

Loomis, Roger S. Celtic Myth and Arthurian Romance. New York, 1927.

Loria, Gino. Histoire des sciences mathématiques dans l'antiquité héllenique. Paris, 1929.

Lorris, W., and J. Clopinel, Roman de la rose, trans. by F. S. Ellis. London, 1900. ("Temple classics.")

Lucian. Philosophies for Sale. In his Works ed. by Capps, Page, and Rowse. New York, 1919. ("Loeb Classical Library.")

Lull, Raymón. The Book of the Lover and the Beloved, trans. by E. Allison Peers. London, 1923.

Mabinogion, the, trans. by Charlotte Guest. London, 1877.

———— Another ed. 1927.

———— Another ed. New York, 1919. ("Everyman.")

———— Trans. by T. P. Ellis and John Lloyd. 2 vols., Oxford, 1929.

Macalister, Robert A. S. Ireland in Pre-Celtic Times. London, 1921.

MacBain, Alexander. Celtic Mythology and Religion, with a Chapter on the Druid Circles. New York, 1917.

MacCulloch, John Arnorth. Celtic [Mythology]. Boston, 1918. (Mythology of All Races, Vol. III.)

———— Eddic [Mythology]. Boston, 1930. (Mythology of All Races, Vol. II.)

McGee, W. J. "Primitive Numbers." United States Bureau of Ethnology, *Nineteenth Annual Report*, Part 2, pp. 821-53. Smithsonian Institution, 1897-1898. Washington, 1900.

Mackenzie, Donald A. The Migration of Symbols and Their Relations to Beliefs and Customs. New York, 1926.

Mackintosh, Hugh Ross. The Doctrine of the Person of Jesus Christ. ("International Theological Library.") New York, 1912.

McLean, Charles Victor. Babylonian Astrology and Its Relation to the Old Testament. Toronto, 1929.

Macrobius. In somnium Scipionis, in Macrobe. Oeuvres complètes, trans. by A. J. Mahul. Paris, 1863. ("Collection des auteurs latins," ed. Nisard.)

Maeterlinck, Maurice. Le Grand Sécret. Paris, 1921.

Malory, Thomas. The Arthurian Tales, the Greatest Romances Which Recount the Noble and Valorous Deeds of King Arthur and the Knights of the Round Table. Comp. by Sir Thomas Malory, knt., and ed. from the Text of 1634 with an Introduction by Ernest Rhys. London, 1906. (Norroena Society.)

Mankind, An Interlude, ed. by John S. Farmer, *in* Lost Tudor Plays with Some Others. London, 1907. (Early English Drama Society.)

Mansel, Henry Longueville. The Gnostic Heresies of the First and Second Centuries, ed. by J. B. Lightfoot. London, 1875.

Marot, Clement. Oeuvres complètes, ed. by Abel Grenier. 2 vols., Paris, [no date].

Martinus, Saint, of Leon. Opera, Migne, P. L., tom. 208-9.

Mason, Eugene, translator. French Medieval Romances from the Lais of Marie de France. London and New York, 1911. ("Everyman.")

Mathers, S. L. MacGregor. The Kabbalah Unveiled; translated from the Latin Version of Knorr von Rosenroth (Kabbalah Denudata) and Collated with the Original Chaldee and Hebrew. London, 1926.

Maynadier, Howard. The Arthur of the English Poets. Boston, 1907.

Mead, G. R. S., Thrice Greatest Hermes. 3 vols., London, 1906.

———— Orpheus, the Theosophy of the Greeks, London, 1896.

Methodius, Saint, Successively Bishop of Olympus and Patam, and of Tyre. Banquet of the Ten Virgins or Concerning Chastity, trans. by W. R. Clark. Edinburgh, 1869. (AN Vol. XIV.)

Migne, Jacques Paul, editor. Patrologiae cursus completus, sive bibliotheca universalis, integra, uniformis, commoda, oeconomica, omnium S. S. Patrum, doctorum, scriptorumque ecclesiasticorum, qui ab aevo apostolico ad usque Innocentii III tempora floruerunt. Series latina prima. 221 tom., Paris, 1844-64.

———— Patrologiae cursus completus. . . . Series graeca. 162 tom., Paris, 1857-66.

Montaigne, Michael Eyquem de. Essays, trans. by John Florio. 3 vols., Oxford, 1906-24. ("Worlds Classics.")

Moore, Edward. Studies in Dante. First Series, Scripture and Classical Authors in Dante. Oxford, 1896.

———— Studies in Dante. Second Series, Miscellaneous Essays. Oxford, 1903.

———— Studies in Dante. Third Series, Miscellaneous Essays. Oxford, 1903.

Moret, Alexandre. The Nile and Egyptian Civilization, trans. by M. R. Dobie. New York, 1927.

Morley, Henry. Cornelius Agrippa: the Life of Henry Cornelius Agrippa von Nettesheim. 2 vols., London, 1856.

———— Medieval Tales. London, 1884.

Moses, the Assumption of, ed. by R. H. Charles. London, 1897.

Mott, Lewis F. "The Round Table." PMLA XX (1905), 231-64.

Müller, W. Max. Egyptian [Mythology]. Boston, 1918. (Mythology of All Races. Vol. XII.)

Murray, Margaret Alice. The Witch-Cult in Western Europe; A Study in Anthropology. Oxford, 1921.

Mythology of All Races, the, ed. by L. H. Gray and G. F. Moore. 13 vols., Boston, 1916-32.

Narrien, John. An Historical Account of the Origin and Progress of Astronomy. London, 1833.

Newman, Albert. Introductory Essay on the Manichean Heresy. [No place or date.]

Nibelungenlied, the, trans. by George Henry Needler. New York, 1904.

Nicene and Post-Nicene Fathers of the Christian Church, a Select Library of the, ed. by Philip Schaff and Henry Wace. 2d series, 14 vols., New York, 1890-1900.

Nicomachus of Gerasa. Introduction to Arithmetic, trans. by Martin

Luther D'Ooge. New York, 1926. ("University of Michigan Studies, Humanistic Series," Vol. XVI.)

Nutt, Alfred. Celtic and Mediaeval Romance. 2d ed., London, 1904. ("Popular Studies in Mythology, Romance and Folk-Lore," No. 1.)

O'Grady, Standish H., editor and translator. Silva Gadelica, A Collection of Tales in Irish with Extracts Illustrating Persons and Places, Vol. II, Translation and Notes. London and Edinburgh, 1892.

Olrik, Axel. Viking Civilization, trans. by Jacob Wittmer Hartmann and Hanna Astrup Larsen. New York, 1930.

[Origen.] The Writings of Origen, trans. by Frederick Crombie. 2 vols., Edinburgh, 1869-72. (AN Vols. X, XXIII.)

Orr, Mary Acworthy. Dante and the Early Astronomers. London, [1914].

Papini, Giovanni. Dante vivo, trans. by Eleanor Hammond Broadus and Anna Benedetti. New York, 1935.

Pastor of Hermas, the. In Writings of the Apostolic Fathers, trans. by Roberts, Donaldson and Crombie. Edinburgh, 1867. (AN Vol. I.)

[Pepys, Samuel]. Everybody's Pepys, ed. by O. F. Morshead. New York, 1936.

Perfect Sermon, the, or the Asclepius, trans. by G. R. S. Mead. In Thrice Greatest Hermes. London, 1906.

Peter Pictaviensis. Sententiarum libri V. Migne, P. L., tom. 212.

[Philo Judaeus]. The Works of Philo Judaeus, the Contemporary of Josephus, trans. by C. D. Yonge. 4 vols., London, 1855. ("Bohn's Ecclesiastical Library.")

Philolaus. Fragments, see Guthrie, K. S.

Philostratus, Flavius. In Honor of Apollonius of Tyana, trans. by J. S. Phillmore. 2 vols., Oxford, 1912.

Phoenix, ed. by Albert Stanburrough Cook in The Old English Elene, Phoenix and Physiologus. New Haven, 1919.

Photius. Anonymous Biography of Pythagoras, preserved by Photius, see Guthrie, K. S.

Pistis Sophia, the, trans. by G. R. S. Mead. London, 1896.

Plato. Dialogues, trans. by Benjamin Jowett. 3d ed. 5 vols., New York, 1892.

———— The Republic of Plato, trans. by Benjamin Jowett. 3d ed. Oxford, 1921. ("Oxford Translation Series.")

———— Timaeus, trans. by A. E. Taylor. London, 1929.

Plinius, Caecilius Secundus. The Natural History of Pliny, trans. by J. Bostock and H. T. Riley. 6 vols., London, 1855-57. ("Bohn's Classical Library.")

[Plotinus.] Plotinos; Complete Works, ed. and trans. by Kenneth Sylvan Guthrie. London, 1918.

Plutarch. Miscellanies and Essays, Comprising All His Works Collected under the Title of "Morals," ed. by William W. Godwin. 6th ed. 5 vols., Boston, 1898.

———— Plutarch's Lives, trans. by Bernadotte Perrin. 11 vols., London, [1914-26]. ("Loeb Classical Library.")

Poimandres, the, trans. by G. R. S. Mead. *In* Thrice Greatest Hermes. London, 1906.

———— Trans. by W. Scott. *In* Hermetica. Oxford, 1924.

Porena, Manfredi. Commento grafico alla Divina Commedia. Milan, 1902.

Porphyry. Biography of Plotinus. *In* Plotinus, Works, ed. by K. S. Guthrie. London, 1918.

———— Biography of Pythagoras, *see* Guthrie, K. S.

———— Select Works of Porphyry, trans. by Thomas Taylor. London, 1823.

Proclus Diadochus. Elements of Theology, trans. by E. R. Dods. Oxford, 1933.

Rabanus, *see* Hrabanus.

Rand, Edward Kennard. Founders of the Middle Ages, Cambridge, Mass., 1928.

Reade, W. H. V. The Moral System of Dante's Inferno. Oxford, 1909.

Reinach, Salomon. Orpheus: A General History of Religions, trans. by Florence Simmonds. London, 1909.

Rhys, John. Lectures on the Origin and Growth of Religion as Illustrated by the Celtic Heathendom. 2d ed., Edinburgh, 1892.

———— Studies in the Arthurian Legend. Oxford, 1891.

Ritter, Heinrich. Geschichte der Pythagorischen Philosophie. Hamburg, 1826.

Rivers, W. H. R. Medicine, Magic and Religion. New York, 1924. (Fitzpatrick Lectures, 1915-16).

Robbins, F. E., and L. C. Karpinski. Studies in Greek Arithmetic, *in* Nicomachus of Gerasa. New York, 1926.

Robin, Léon. Greek Thought and the Origins of the Scientific Spirit. New York, 1928.

Rodkinson, Michael L. The History of the Talmud. In his edition of the Babylonian Talmud. Vols. XIX-XX. Boston, 1918.

Rogers, Robert William. Cuneiform Parallels to the Old Testament. New York and Cincinnati, 1912.

Roland, le Chanson de, ed. by L. Petit de Julleville. Paris, 1878.

———— Trans. by Isabel Butler. Cambridge, 1904.

Roman de la rose, by W. Lorris and J. Clopinel, trans. by F. S. Ellis. 3 vols., London, 1900. ("Temple Classics.")

Rousselot, Xavier. Joachim de Flore, Jean de Parme et la doctrine de l'évangile éternal. In Étude d'histoire religieuse aux XIIe et XIIIe siècles. 2d ed., Paris, 1867.

Saga of the Volsungs, the. The Saga of Ragnar Ladbrok, Together with the Lay of Kraka, trans. by Margaret Schlauch. New York, 1930.

Salvio, Alfonso de. Dante and Heresy. Boston, 1936.

Sanders, Henry A. "The Number of the Beast in Revelations." Journal of Biblical Literature, XXXVI (1918), 95-99.

Scartazzini, Giovanni Andrea. A Companion to Dante, trans. by Arthur John Butler. London, 1893.

Scoon, Robert Maxwell. Greek Philosophy before Plato. Princeton, 1928.

Scot, Michael, see Brown, J. W.

Scott, Walter. Hermetica. Oxford, 1924.

Secrets of Enoch, the Book of the, ed. by R. H. Charles and W. R. Morfil. Oxford, 1896.

[Seneca, Lucius Annaeus.] The Works of Lucius Annaeus Seneca Both Morrall and Naturall, trans. by Thomas Lodge. Newly Enlarged and Corrected. London, 1620.

Sextus Empiricus. Outlines of Pyrrhonism, trans. by R. G. Bury. London and New York, 1933. ("Loeb Classical Library," Vol. I.)

———— Against the Physicists, trans. by R. G. Bury. London and Cambridge, Mass., 1936. ("Loeb Classical Library," Vol. III.)

Sibylline Oracles, trans. by R. H. Charles. In his Apocrypha and Pseudepigrapha of the Old Testament. Oxford, 1913.

Sicardus, Bishop of Cremona. Mitrale, sive summa de officiis ecclesiasticis chronicon. Migne, P. L., tom. 213.

[Skelton, John]. The Complete Poems of John Skelton, ed. by Philip Henderson. London, 1931.

Smith, David Eugene. History of Mathematics. 2 vols., New York, 1923.

———— Rara Mathematica. Boston, 1908.

Smith, Henry Preserved. Old Testament History. New York, 1903.

Spaeth, J. Duncan. Old English Poetry, Translations into Alliterative Verse. Princeton, 1922.

Spenser, Edmund. The Faerie Queene. *In his* Works, ed. by Edwin Greenlaw, Charles Grosvenor Osgood, Frederick Morgan Padelford. Vols. I-IV., Baltimore, 1932-35. (Variorum Edition.)

———— The Oxford Spenser, ed. by J. C. Smith and E. de Selincourt. Oxford, 1924.

Stobaeus, Joannes. Excerpts *in* G. R. S. Mead, Thrice Greatest Hermes; W. Scott, Hermetica; K. S. Guthrie, Pythagorean Source Book and Library.

Sylvester II, Pope, called Gerbert. Opera. Migne, P. L., tom. 139.

Talmud, the Babylonian, ed. by Michael L. Rodkinson. 20 vols., Boston, 1918.

Tannery, Paul. Recherches sur l'histoire de l'astronomie ancienne. Paris, 1893.

Taylor, Henry Osborne. The Classical Heritage of the Middle Ages. New York, 1901.

———— The Medieval Mind, A History of the Development of Thought and Emotion in the Middle Ages. 4th ed., 2 vols., London, 1927.

[Tertullianus, Quintus Septimus Florens.] The Writings of Tertullianus, trans. by S. Thewwall, P. Holmes, and others. Edinburgh, 1869-70. (AN Vols. XI, XV, XVIII.)

Testaments of the Twelve Patriarchs, the, ed. by R. H. Charles. London, 1908.

Theon of Smyrna. Espositio rerum mathematicarum ad legendum Platonem utilium, ed. by Eduardus Hiller. Leipzig, 1928.

Theophilus, Saint, Bishop of Antioch. The Three Books of Theophilus of Antioch to Autolycus, trans. by Marcus Dods. Edinburgh, 1867. (AN Vol. III.)

Thomas of Britain. The Romance of Tristram and Ysolt, trans. by Roger Sherman Loomis. Rev. ed., New York, 1931.

Thomas Aquinas, Saint. Opera omnia; sive antehac excusa, sive etiam anecdota; ex editionibus vetustis et decimi tertii saeculi codicibus religiose castigata . . . notis . . . ornata studio ac labore Stanislai Eduardi Fretté et Pauli Maré. 34 vols., Parisiis, 1871-80. (Vols. XI-XXXIV are edited by Fretté alone.)

———— Summa contra Gentiles, trans. by the English Dominican Fathers. London, 1924.

—— Summa Theologica, trans. by the English Dominican Fathers. 20 vols., London, 1911-25.

Thompson, D'Arcy W. "The Greek Winds." *Classical Review*, XXXII (1918), 49-56.

—— "Science and the Classics." *Proceedings of the Classical Association*, XXXVI (1929), 14-35.

Thompson, R. Campbell. Semitic Magic, Its Origin and Development. London, 1908.

Thoms, William John, editor. Early English Prose Romances. London, 1906. (Containing the Famous Historie of Fryer Bacon.)

Thorndike, Lynn. A History of Magic and Experimental Science. 4 vols., New York, 1923-34.

Thorpe, Benjamin. Northern Mythology. 3 vols., London, 1851.

Thoth, the Books of, trans. by G. R. S. Mead. *In* Thrice Greatest Hermes. London, 1906.

[Timaeus Locrus.] Timée de Locres, De l'ame du monde, trans. by M. l'abbe Batteux. Paris, 1768.

Tobit, the Book of, trans. by Moses Gaster. *In his* Studies and Texts. London, 1925-28.

Toynbee, Paget. Concise Dictionary of Proper Names and Notable Matters in the Works of Dante. Oxford, 1914.

—— Dante Alighieri, His Life and Works. 4th ed., New York, 1910.

—— Dante Studies and Researches. London, 1902.

Tozer, H. F. A History of Ancient Geography. Cambridge, 1897.

Turberville, A. S. Medieval Heresy and the Inquisition. London, 1920.

Tylor, Edward B. Primitive Culture. 7th ed., New York, 1924.

Vaughan, Magical Writings, ed. by Arthur Edward Waite. London, 1888.

Vergilius Maro, Publius. The Aeneid, ed. by J. W. Mackail. Oxford, 1930.

Victorinus, Caius Marius. A Fragment on the Creation of the World, trans. by Peter Holmes, Edinburgh, 1870. (AN Vol. XVIII.)

Vita Merlini, the, ed. by John Jay Penny. University of Illinois, 1925.

[Vitruvius Pollio, Marcus]. Vitruvius, the Ten Books on Architecture, trans. by Morris Hicky Morgan. Cambridge, Mass., 1914.

Vossler, Karl. Mediaeval Culture; An Introduction to Dante and

His Times, trans. by William Cranston Lawton. 2 vols., New York, (1929).

Waite, Arthur Edward. Lives of the Alchemystical Philosophers. London, 1888.

Webster, Hutton. Rest Days; A Study in Early Law and Morality. New York, 1916.

Wedel, Theodore Otto. Medieval Attitude toward Astrology. New Haven, 1920. ("Yale Studies in English, Vol. XX.)

Wells, Henry W. "The Construction of 'Piers Plowman'." PMLA XLIV (March, 1929), 123-40.

Westcott, William Wynn. Numbers: Their Occult Power and Mystic Virtues. London, 1890.

Weston, Jessie L. From Ritual to Romance. Cambridge, 1920.

—— King Arthur and His Knights. 2d ed., London, 1906. ("Popular Studies in Mythology, Romance and Folk-Lore," No. 4.)

—— The Legend of Sir Perceval. 2 vols., London, 1906-9.

—— The Romance Cycle of Charlemagne and His Peers. 2d ed. London, 1905. ("Popular Studies in Mythology, Romance and Folk-Lore," No. 10.)

Weston, Patrick, and P. W. Joyce. A Social History of Ancient Ireland. 2d ed., 2 vols., London and Dublin, 1913.

Wicksteed, Philip Henry. Dante and Aquinas. London and New York, 1913. (Jowett Lectures, 1911.)

Wiedemann, Alfred. Realms of the Egyptian Dead, trans. by J. Hutchison. London, 1901.

—— Religion of the Ancient Egyptians. New York and London, 1897.

Witte, Johann Heinrich Freidrich Karl. Essays on Dante, trans. by C. Mabel Lawrence and Philip H. Wicksteed. London, 1898.

Wulf, Maurice de. History of Medieval Philosophy, trans. by P. Coffey. London, 1909.

Young, Grace Chisholm, "On the Solution of a Pair of Simultaneous Diophantine Equations Connected with the Nuptial Number of Plato." Proceedings of the London Mathematical Society, Series 2, XXIII (1925), 27-44.

Zeller, Eduard, A History of Greek Philosophy. 2 vols., London, 1881.

Zend-Avesta, the. Part 1., the Vendidad, trans. by James Darmestater. Oxford, 1880. ("Sacred Books of the East," ed. by Max Müller, Vol. IV.)

INDEX

Abundant numbers, 37

Active and contemplative lives, 167 ff.

Aeons, of Valentinian Gnosticism, 57, 58

Ages, *see* Golden ages

Agrippa, Cornelius, *Second Book of Occult Philosophy*, 105

Albertus Magnus, 94, 157; quoted, 90, 112

Alchemy, symbol of chemical change, 117

Allegory, 136

Angelic host, theological position, 105; spiral movement, 109

Apocalypse of John, symbolic numbers, 109

Apostles, 151, 152, 195, 200

Aquinas, *see* Thomas Aquinas

Ariosto, *Orlando Furioso*, excerpt, 66

Arithmancy, 125

Arithmetic, as design for material creations, 97; method by which Divine Intellect becomes intelligible, 99

Arithmology, defined, 104

Astrological numbers, 12-32; stubborn vitality of, ix; reintroduced to West as Divine revelation, 50 f.; recognized by Pythagoreanism, 51; in Manicheanism, 59; combined with Pythagoreanism in attempt to define cosmic pattern, 89; all manifestation of number science traced to, 90; casting of horoscope, 118

3: Babylonian triads, 20; statistical, 26, 27; divine, 27

4: lunar phases, 13, 14; earth, cardinal points, 14, 22, 28, 31; 4-7 relationship, 14; in creation legend, 28; archetypal pattern for macrocosm, 31; popularity of, 127

5: zones of the earth, 22

6: ages of duration of world, 23

7: of Babylonian cosmogony and religion, 13-19; week, 13, 23; baleful aspect of seventh day, 13; Sabbath of eternal rest, 13, 23; stars, planets, 14, 16, 22; wisdom, godliness, gods, 15, 16; of evil and good, 16, 24; tree of life ancestor of 7-branched candlestick, 17; steps symbolize ascent to heaven; steps to perfection, 17, 18; descent of soul, 18; recognizable as round number, 19 f.; creative acts, 23; sin and expiation; servitude; sacrifice, 24; age of world, 31 f.; popularity of, 127

8: eighth heaven, eternal bliss, 18; eighth step of purgatory, 19; sanctity, 25; eighth sphere that of fixed stars, 56

9: 9-10 relationship, 25; ninth house, 139

10: month ruled over by decan stars, 20; decans become the horoscopi, 21; infinity, quantity, perfection, 29; in ceremonial, 30

12: complete cycle, 19; zodiac, 19, 31; double-hour division of day, 19, 20; in ancient civilizations, 21; in time and space divisions, 21, 28, 32; in legend of the tribes, 28, 29; popularity of, 127; a round number where calendar is important, 129

14: evil day, 13

19: evil day, 13

21: evil day, 13

24: hours of day and night, 20, 29; occasional appearance of, 128; a round number, 129

28: evil day, 13; moon, 22

30: in symbol for month and for moon god, 19

40: trial and privation, 15, 25; fated period, 15, 26

49: baleful aspect, 13

50: hallowed year, 25

70: important Hebrew number, 25

360: in calendar, 19, 21

Augustine gave final stamp of approval to number symbolism, 78; treatment of seventh day, 79; interpretation of flood legend, 80; interpretation of 153 fish, 82

Averroism, 89

Bacon, Roger, quoted, 106 f., 116, 117, 139

Beast in Revelations, number of the, 9, 64 ff.

Bible, New Testament references to a triad and to Trinity, 3; early explanations of numbers forced, 76; Old and New Testaments, 170, 173 ff., 180, 181; *see also* Christian writers, early

Black arts, 125

Bonaventura, 113; quoted, 185, 187

Books, Christian, formal arrangement pays tribute to science of number, 87

Budge, E. A. Wallis, quoted, 67

Bungus, Petrus, *Mysticae numerorum,* 105, 131

Cabala, 60; use of gematria, 62 ff.

Can Grande, 137, 181

Capella, Martianus, *Textbook of the Seven Arts*; *De nuptiis,* 98, 104

Cathedral architecture, number symbolism recognized in, 114

Celestial rose of the church triumphant, 174 ff., 186, 200

Celtic mythology, triadic pattern, 203

Chanson de Roland, 128

Cherubim, 152, 179, 195 ff.

Christianity, the dominating factor in medieval equation, 93

Christian writers, early, 69-88; number theory, influence of Gnostics and Neo-Pythagoreans, x; exaggerated number mysticism of early years, 50; church fathers zealous in combating heresies of Gnostic literature, 52; path of numerical theology not the road chosen by, 72; explanation of scriptural numbers, 75, 76; attitude toward number dominant through

Middle Ages, 76, 89; used numbers in a symbolic sense, 87

1: unity of Godhead provided by addition of Holy Ghost, 73; God One and alone, 74; no longer First Cause; specifically God, 82

2: duality of Godhead the doctrinal weakness of Christianity, 73; nature of Christian dualism, 83

3: Trinity, viii, 7; holiness, sanctity, viii, 70; Father, Son, and Holy Spirit — one by virtue of being three, 73; Gnostic triads a factor in creation of Trinity, 73; triplicity in spiritual world, 74; trinity; number of perfection, 83; *3* and *4,* identification of spiritual-temporal duality, 83

4: mundane sphere; man, 84

5: manifest in true faith, 74; symbol of the flesh, 86

6: earthly perfection, 86

7: of evil and repentance, 71; 7-fold nature of world; final glory, 77; symbol of all numbers, 79; universe, 84, 85; man; creature as opposed to Creator, 84; Sabbath and salvation; sin, 85

8: regeneration; final glory, 77; immortality; resurrection and circumcision, 85

10: totality, 69; unity, 85

11: sin, 87

12: in New Testament, 70; in Old Testament, 71, 74; universal symbol, 84; great astrological and scriptural number, 85; another form of seven, 86

40: days of trial, 71

70: juncture with 12 in Bible, 70, 71

100: expression of totality, 70

300: or T, symbol of the cross, 75, 76

318: interpretation of, 75, 76; becomes established tradition, 87

1,000 years the length of an age, 77

6,000 years the limit of the world, 77

Church, acceptance of number theory, 93, 105, 114, 115

Church and state, 167 ff., 179 ff.

Church militant, 168, 173, 178, 180, 181

Church triumphant, 168, 173, 174, 178, 181, 186

Cid, Chronicle of the, 128

Circle, perfect spirituality, 165, 173, 179, 200; image of the, 165, 168, 178, 194

Circles, of the moon, 149; about Dante and Beatrice, 150; of hell, 151; Dante's vision of, 159; circling dance of heavenly lights, 152, 160

Circular numbers, 102

Civil life, 167 ff.

Classification of numbers, 37

Clementine *Recognitions,* 72, 76

Colors partake nature of number, 143, 158, 160

Contemplative life, 167 ff.

Cosmic pattern, 89, 96

Cross, six orders of the, 115; magic of Christian cross, 121; use in magic, 124

Cubing, adds dimension of height, 102

Cyclical theory of Dante, 182 ff.

Dante, use of significant numbers; comprehension of universal harmony, 136-201; subtlety, 136, 137; love of allegory, 137; Pythagoreanism, 142; works: *Convivio,* 137, 140, 142, 149, 154, 160, 161, 163, 167, 168, 172, 180, 195; *De monarchia,* 137, 138, 145, 149, 168, 180; *Divine Comedy,* 105, 136, 145; numerical framework, 146 ff.; triads, 149 ff.; duads, 170 ff.; cyclical theory, 182 ff.; *Vita nuova,* 137, 138, 163, 176, 197

1: God, first cause, 138, 142, 144, 147; Godhead, 164; Father (power, creator), 144, 147, 154, 164, 186, 187, 188, 190; (faith), 159, 161; universal duality of God, 168; unity, essence, 138; unity the root of good, 143; unity of the Trinity, 144, 165; unity recovered from diversity by addition of 1 and 2, 147; unity figured by

circular revolution, 150; alpha and omega of all things, 146; hell, 149, 151 ff., 165; first day (age), before Christ, 156, 165, 188, 190, 192; pale, symbolic of impotence; Cassius, 158, 164; faith, 159 ff., 176, represented by Peter, 195; white, symbolic of faith, 160, 161, 176; Mary, Mother of Christ, 162, 165, 172, 174, 201; Lucifer, antitype of Godhead, 164; white, symbolic of innocence, 182; origin, perfect, 185 ff.

2: dualism of body and soul, 141; plurality the root of evil, 143; Jesus Christ, Son (wisdom, light), 144, 147, 154, 159, 161, 164, 186, 187, 188, 190, 193, 200; (hope), 159; unity recovered from diversity by addition 1 and 2, 147; second day (age), 156, 165, 188, 190, 192; black, symbolic of ignorance; Brutus, 158, 164; hope, 159 ff., 176; hope represented by James, 160, 195; green, symbolic of hope, 160, 161, 176; Lucia, light, intercessor, 162, 165, 197; inclusion of imperfect duad effects unity of Trinity, 165; Dante's representations of duality, 165 ff.; image (dual, imperfect), 165, 168, 178, 194; God-man, archetype of cosmic dualism, 166; antithetical duads, 166 ff.; archetypal duad imperfect in relation to Unity (or Trinity), 168; cardinal and speculative virtues, 168, 172, 173, 184; imperfect periods between golden ages, 182, 185 ff.

3: Beatrice (miracle), earthly symbol of ultimate perfection, 138, 149, 176, 200; as love, the way, 163, 165, 175, 194; as revelation, 171; function of, 175 ff. (*see also* 9: Beatrice); God, three dimensions of, 144; God (power), 154; (faith), 159; Holy Spirit (love), 144, 147, 154, 159, 164, 186, 187, 188, 191, 192; Trinity, beginning and end; Dante's vision, 146; manifest in triad of heaven, purgatory, and hell, 149; revolving images and emblems of Trinity, 150; representations in paradise, 151; *Divine Comedy*, 3 in 1 the external form of, 146, 147, 149; purgatory, 149, 153 ff., 165, 181, 193; 3 steps to, 182 ff.; Dante's 3 dreams in, 197; miracle, sanctity of, rooted in, 149; heaven, 149, 151 ff., 165, 173; infernal triads, 151; paradise, 151 ff., 181, 185, 198, 199, 200; third day (age), 156, 165, 188, 190, 192; anti-Trinity, impotence, ignorance, 158; Judas, 158, 164; red, symbolic of malice, 158, 164; symbolic of love, 160, 162, 176; red of redemption by passion of Christ, 182; theological virtues, 159, 173, 200; love, represented by John, 160, 195; circle (perfect spirituality), 165, 168, 178, 194; soul, 171; golden ages, 182 ff; perfect, both *one* and *all*, 201

4: of the body, 171

6: age of earthly perfection, 179

7: earth, spiritual life of microcosm, 154; image of man, 171; age of final resurrection, 199

8: baptism, regeneration, 154, 178; state of felicity, return to original unity, 198; age of final redemption, 199, 200

9: Beatrice, recurrence of 9 in Dante's relationship to, viii, 138, 139, 143; as ultimate effect of miracle of Beatrice, 9 becomes 10, 149 (*see also 3:* Beatrice); the angelic number, 138, 143, 144; earthly mirror of First Cause; astrological place, 139

10: tenth angelic order, Empyrean, 144; as end of all things, 146; ultimate effect of miracle of Beatrice; 9 moving spheres and the Empyrean, 149

11: sin, 152

35: apex of life, 180

100: as end of all things, 146

515: DVX interpretation of number of the beast, 65

1,000: as end of all things, 146; perfection, 180

Deficient numbers, 37

Dionysius the Areopagite, writings, 107

Divination, 125

Divine plan, *see* Universal order

Dominic, 194, 196

Eagle, symbol of Rome and Empire, 179 ff., 187, 193 ff. 198, 200

East, magic of the, 119

Eddic mythology, astrological knowledge exhibited in, 204; conflict of heat and cold, 205

Elementary number symbolism, 3-11; basic in all number symbolism, ix

1: alone, 3; positive degree, 4

2: duals of nature, 3 f.; dual and plural distinguished; comparative degree, 4; diversity; antithetical pairs, 4, 11

3: many, 4; all; superlative, 4, 5, 7, 11; cumulative or statistical, 5; holy, deities (triads of gods), 6, 7, 11; triad of family; divisions of physical world, 6; in sun worship; in human cycle, 7

4: earth; cardinal points, 8, 11; cult of; cruciform emblems, 8

5: hand, ix, 9

8: sanctity of, 9

9: triple triad of Heliopolis, 6; all-but-complete, all-but-perfect, 10, 11

10: two hands; adoption of decimal system, 9; finality, completeness, perfection, 10, 11

18: 3 in spirit and, mystically, in number, 6

20: man, ix, 9

27: 3 in spirit and, mystically in number, 6

100: basic 10 implied in, 9; finality, completeness, 10

300: extension of 3, 9

666: number of the beast in Revelations, 9

1,000: basic *10* implied in, 9; finality, completeness, 10

Emanations, doctrine of, 51, 52

Empyrean, 10th angelic order, 144

Erigena, 108

Even numbers (feminine) of ill omen, 39, 40; less godlike, perfect, and powerful than the odd, 101

Faust, *Miraculous Art*, 132

Fletcher, J. B., 139, 149, 185

Flood legend, importance, 80

Francis, 194, 196

Gardner, E. G., quoted, 157

Gawain and the Green Knight, use of pentacle, 124

Gematria, numerical system, 62 ff.

Gesta Romanorum, 133

Gnostics, 50-68; essential heresies, 56; influence in formation of Christian number theory, x; origin of Christian Gnosticism ascribed to Simon Magus, 56; Valentinian Gnosticism, 57; Manicheanism, 59, 68; scheme of world in all philosophies of, 62; suppressed by true church, 68; numerical scheme incorrect, 74

1: separation of the one from the many, 55; fire, the first cause, 56; first sephira, 60; unity, 61

2: creative pairs, 56; zoroastrian duality preserved in rulers of light and of darkness, 59; first sephira reflects itself to produce Jahveh, 60

3: triadic groups of Greek pantheon; of Egyptian and Babylonian gods, 52; a basic symbol in Gnostic theology, 52; divine triad, 56; a Trinity in doctrines of many sects, 57; in scheme of the pleroma, 58, 59; third sephira completes primal trinity, 60; mothers (elements, division of year, parts of body), 62 f.

4: a basic symbol in Gnostic theology, 52; Pythagorean tetrad, 57; in scheme of the pleroma, 58

5: in working of the zodiac, 54; in scheme of the pleroma; eastern holy number, 59

7: related to planets, established order of worlds and gods, 53; in working of the zodiac, 54; mystic hebdomad by which world is generated, 56; in scheme of the pleroma, 58, 59; Pythagorean, harmony, 61; doubles, 61, 62

8: in Hermetic theology, 54; method of generation of the ogdoad, 55; ogdoad duplicated in human body; symbol of blessedness, 56; first begotten ogdoad, 57; in scheme of the pleroma, 58

9: in scheme of the pleroma, 59; sephiroth composed of 3 trinities, 60

10: decans made spiritual rulers over 7 Fates, 55; decans the highest controllers of the heavens, 56; in scheme of the pleroma, 58; sephiroth, most abstract forms of Pythagorean decad, 60; in cabalistic theology, 61

12: zodiac, 53; signs of zodiac, forces of evil, 54; tormentors; superiority of decad to, 56; Logos and Zoe form perfect number by creation of 10 aeons, 57; in scheme of the pleroma, 58, 59

13: conformations of the holy beard, 61; love of unity, 64

24: in scheme of the pleroma, 59

30: triacontad of the pleroma; years of Christ's preparation for teaching, 58

32: paths of wisdom, 61

36: in working of the zodiac, 54; cosmos, 55

42: a traditional Egyptian number; Hermetic books, 53

49: sacred number of Orphism composed of 7 septenaries, 53

60: ripe age, 63

91: Amen, Jahveh Adonai, 64

100: Sarra, 63

318: Eliezer, 63

358: Shiloh shall come; Messiah, 64

365: zones of zodiac; numerical value of Abraxas, 54; in scheme of the pleroma, 58, 59

801: Christ, the dove, 63

888: Jesus, 63

God, use of number, 74, 78

Goidals, tripartite day, 203

Golden ages, 182 ff.

Heavenly rose, *see* Celestial rose

Hebrews, adherence to number symbolism, 23 ff.

Hermes Trismegistus, 53, 96; a master in regard to numbers, 79

Hermetic philosophy, Pythagorean aspect of, 56

Hildegard of Bingen, 107

Hippolytus, 57

Hoccleve, Thomas, 96

Hugo of St. Victor, 108, 109; quoted, 100, 102; attempt to organize principles of number science, 103

Identical number groups, relations between, 95

Image conforms to circle, 165, 168, 178, 194

Ineffable name, 67

Innocent III, 111, 113

Irenaeus, refutation of Gnostic numerical scheme, 74

Irish, ancient, use of triad, 203; use of, 9, 208; predilection for 50, 209

Isidore of Seville, *Liber numerorum,* 104; quoted, 113

Jesus, numerical secrets in life and preachings, at variance with spirit of Scriptures, 69

Joachim of Flora, 109, 187

Joannes Turpini historia de vita Caroli Magni et Rolandi, 134

John, Gospel of, approach to number symbolism, 71

Kalandar and Compost of Shepherds, The, 94; excerpt, 91

Langland, William, *Piers the Plowman,* 106; excerpt, 188, 191

Left hand in gematria, 63

Lewis, Caspar, 62

Lull, Raymon, *Book of the Lover and the Beloved,* excerpt, 100

Macrocosm and microcosm, relation of, 22, 92; archetypal pattern reproduced in, 94

Magic, eastern, 119; most potent numbers, 122

Malleus maleficarum, excerpt, 120

Man, influenced by celestial bodies, 90

Manicheanism, 59, 68

Marie de France, *Lay of the Ash Tree,* 134

Mathematical aspects of number of divine origin, 98

Matter and spirit, dualism of, 51

Medico concerned with numerical science, 118

Medieval number philosophy, 89-135

   1: and *3* relationship, 90; First Mover, First Cause, 96; unity, multiplicity proceeds, 96; regulates plurality; numbers become more imperfect as they recede from unity, 100; all things *One* with God, 99; point, 101; *10* is *1,* 102; superessential, 108; Dionysian distinction between unity and diversity, 109; form, 117

   2: corruptible and transitory, 101; love of God, 102; evil symbolized as diversity, or the duad, 108; matter, 117

   3: and *1* relationship, 90; trinity of natural phenomena, 94; first visible number, 99; Trinity, 100, 103, 107; indissoluble and incorruptible, 101; perfection, beginning, middle, end, 107; celestial and ecclesiastical hierarchies constructed on basis of Divine Triad, 109; ages, under Adam, in Christ, with Christ, 110; division of Commandments into tables of *3* and *7;* altar steps, 114; composition; unity of 3 and 7, 117; in magic, 122; modern use of, 127; favorite number of the Middle Ages, 128

4: times of year, 103; cardinal virtues, 113; in magic, 122; popularity of, 127

5: circular or spherical, 102; senses, 103, 126; in magic, 122 ff.; incorruptibility, 124; modern use of, 127

6: perfect, 98, 99, 102; circular or spherical, 102

7: and 8 relationship, 90; universality, 95, 102; sacred, 100; beyond 6, rest after work, 101; Hugo's *De quinque septenis*, 109; as an attribute of the pillars, 111; the cosmic period, 112; division of Commandments into tables of 3 and 7, 114; 7 and 3 revert to unity of decad, 117; in eastern magic, 119 ff.; ages, 126; modern use of; popularity, 127; wide significance of heptad, 129; of repentence; stages of contemplation, 134

8: and 7 relationship, 90; deficient number, occasioned second origin of human race, 98; beyond 7, eternity after mutability, 101; day of justice, 112; baptismal font octagonal, symbol of salvation, 114

9: before 10, defect among perfection, 101; a circular number, 102; orders of angels, 105; more expressive than Trinity, 106; in magic, 122; Arabic numerals add virtue of incorruptibility, 123

10: Pythagorean most perfect, 98; decad includes essential numbers of Divine plan, 99; rectitude in faith; linear, 101; perfect, 102, 117; circular, 102; order of fallen angels, 106; sum of 3 and 7 reverts to unity, 117; modern use of, 127

11: beyond 10, transgression outside of measure, 101; a number of transgression, 131

12: sacred, 101; universality, 102; 103; faith in Trinity; doctrine of 12 apostles or 12 tribes; abundant, 102; associated with Christ, 111; popularity of, 127; a round number where calendar is important, 129

13: sacred, or number of sin, 103; unlucky, 130 ff.; at table, 130, 132; associated with Epiphany; transgression, 131; associated with witchcraft, 132

15: popular through liturgical and scientific use, 127

24: occasional appearance of, 128; a round number, 129

30: of parable of the sower, 104

40: popular through liturgical and scientific use, 127

48: occasional appearance of, 128

50: unity, signifies 1 Jubilee, 101

60: of parable of the sower, 104; made familiar through use of the score, 128

100: a return to unity; amplitude of charity; two-dimensional, 101; of the parable of the sower, 104

120: popular through liturgical and scientific use, 127; made familiar through use of the score, 128

1,000: return to unity; height of hope; three-dimensional, or solid, 101; ultimate boundary of number; perfection, 102; perfect number of all virtues, 107

7,000: universal perfection, 102

144,000: of the Apocalypse, 102; final number of the elect, 103

Miracle, 138

Montaigne, Michel Eyquem, quoted, 131

Moore, Edward, 65

Mysticism, in early Christian Era; of the Orient, 50

Naaseni, 57

Name, ineffable, 67

Neo-Pythagorean number theory, Augustine a source of information concerning, 79

Nicomachus, *Introduction to Arithmetic*, 97, 98

Noble Castle of Limbus, 171, 190, 193, 200

Odd numbers (masculine), mastery, 39, 40; more godlike, perfect, and powerful than the even, 101

Olivi, Pierre, *Postil on the Apocalypse*, 179

One Cause and diversified effects, correlation between, 96

Order, beauty of, 136-201

Origen, theory of creation according to number, 74

Pagan number symbols, 203-11

  3: in pagan number symbolism, 203; use in partition of year, 206

  6: division of houses of zodiac, 204

  8: fated period, 204

  9: fated period, 204; symbol for winter, 206; fertility, religion, magic, 207

  12: zodiacal, established among northern pagans, 204

  50: in Irish folklore, 209; in Christian church and Chaldean magic, 210; associated with knights of the Round Table, 211

Pastor of Hermas, filled with numerical allegory, 72

Pauline epistles innocent of number theory, 69

Pelérinage de Charlemagne à Constantinople, excerpt, 130

Pentacle, magical significance, 124

Perfect numbers, 36, 37

Phoenix, symbol of Christ, 90

Piers Plowman, 188, 191; excerpt, 106

Pistis-Sophia, 57, 58

Pleroma, 57 ff.

Pliny, *Natural History*, 120

Plutarch, *Of Isis and Osiris*, 55

Poimandres, 53, 54, 56

Prester John, use of number, 126

Procession of the many from the few, 96

Prognostication, use of astrology for, 22

Psalms interpreted in accordance with their numbers, 76

Pseudo-Clementine Recognitions, 72, 76

Pythagorean number theory, x, 33-49; tetraktys, legendary oath, 42; part in Gnosticism, 51; in Hermetic philosophy, 56; and astrology combined to define cosmic pattern, 89; organization of numerical truths made possible by Pythagoras, 96; philosophy of odd and even numbers, 101

  1: represented as a point, 35; the father of number, 39; God, unity, 42, 44

  2: line, 35; mother of number, 39; the manifold one, 40; image of matter, 47

  3: triangle, surface, 35; first real number, 35, 41; triad as perfect unity, 42; image of a solid body, 47

  3, 4, 5 right triangle, marriage number derived from, 36

  4: first solid number, 35, 36, 42; the square, 35, 42; earth, 35; completes list of archetypal numbers; tetraktys, 42; basic number of cosmos, 46

  5: Plato's theory of the fifth solid, 35; quintessence, 36; marriage number; nature, 43; akin to animals, 49

  6: first perfect number, 36, 43, 47; female marriage number, 43; mortal beings measured by, 48

  7: heptad granted absolute isolation; virgin number, 43; universal number, 44, 46; sanctified in Sabbath; archetypal position, 48

  8: first cube; perfect, 43, 44

  9: first masculine square, perfect form of 3, 43, 44

  10: completeness; total of all things, 34, 44, 45; archetypal numbers produce decad; as a triangular number, 42; perfect circle, 43;

multiplicity returns to unity, 44;
comprehension, 45
27: first odd or masculine cube, 45
28: second perfect number, 36, 45;
sum of first seven numbers, 44;
lunar month, 45
35: harmony, 45
36: agreement, 45
40: a glorified tetraktys, 45

Rabanus, Magnentius, *De numero*, 104
Rachel, 175, 176
Right and left, 169
Right hand in gematria, 63
Rose, *see* Celestial rose

Saint Guthlac, quoted, 112
Sanctity of numbers, 12
Scandinavian races, importance of
triads, 203; significance of *8* and *9*,
205
Science and religion unite as result of
astral character of Eastern religions,
50
Scriptures, numerical interpretation,
113
Sefer Yezireh, 60
Seraphim, 152, 178, 179, 195, 196
Shakespeare, *Macbeth*, excerpt, 123;
Merchant of Venice, 128
Simon Magus, origin of Christian Gnos-
ticism ascribed to, 56
Skelton, John, 66
Solomon's seal, use in magic, 124
Spenser, Edmund, *Faerie Queene*, ex-
cerpt, 121
Spherical numbers, 102
Squaring gives extension, 102
Stars, relation of number and, 12, 14;

ordering of all things patterned in,
91
State and church, 167 ff., 179 ff.
Sun, 196; symbol and type of Divin-
ity, 90
Sun-moon analogy, 167, 168

T, or 300, symbol of the cross, 75, 76
Ten Commandments, division into
tables of 3 and 7, 114
Teutonic mythology, triadic pattern,
203
Theologoumena arithmeticae, 104
Theology of numbers, 104, 105
Third age, Joachim's Theory of, 110
Thomas Aquinas, relation of creature
to Creator, 94; quoted, 96, 99, 107,
160
Thorndike, Lynn, quoted, 116, 118
Thoth, Hermes Trismegistus identified
with, 53
Three ages, *see* Golden ages
Thrones, 195 ff.

Universal harmony, Dante's belief in,
136-201
Universe, pattern revealed by analysis
of properties of first ten numbers,
38; strict order of, expressible in
terms of number, 68

Valentinus, *Pistis-Sophia*, 57
Vaughn, Thomas, quoted, 117
Veltro, 181, 189
Virgil as reason, 171

Wells, Henry W., 188
Welsh, triads, 203; use of *9*, 209
Will, 191, 197

Zohar, 60

```
    1
   72
   58
  ────
  576
 360
 4176
 5550
 ─────
  9726


      310
       18
      ────
     2480
     310
   5550
```